THOMAS HOOD

By the same Author

THE MIND AND ART
OF COVENTRY PATMORE
FRANCIS THOMPSON: MAN AND POET

THOMAS HOOD
by William Hilton, R.A., *c.* 1833

THOMAS HOOD

by

J. C. REID

ROUTLEDGE & KEGAN PAUL

London

First published 1963
by Routledge & Kegan Paul Limited
Broadway House, 68–74 Carter Lane
London, E.C.4

Printed in Great Britain
by Butler & Tanner Limited
Frome and London

Contents

v

Illustrations

Acknowledgements

I HAVE pleasure in acknowledging the kind assistance, while writing this book, of various individuals and institutions, all of whom responded most generously to my requests for advice, information or material dealing with Hood. I am particularly indebted to Mr. J. M. Cohen, who lent me some of his notes on the poet, and who drew my attention to the material in the Bristol University Library; Professor Alvin Whitley, of Harvard University, who allowed me to read his unpublished doctoral thesis on Hood; Professor Leslie Marchand, of Rutgers University, who supplied me with a copy of his edition of some Hood letters; Mr. P. J. Molloy, Senior Thoracic Surgical Registrar at Guy's Hospital, London, who gave me valuable help in interpreting the nature of Hood's illness; Dr. A. Nikoljukin, of the Institute of World Literature, Moscow, who supplied me with information concerning Hood's reputation in Russia and the Soviet Union, and Madeline House and Graham Storey, editors of the Pilgrim Edition of Dickens's letters, for allowing me to use unpublished letters of Dickens to Hood.

I have also received the most helpful co-operation from the authorities and staff of the following libraries: Bodleian Library, Oxford; the British Museum Library and Manuscript Room; the Public Record Office, London; the Bristol University Library; the Bristol Public Library; the National Library of Scotland, Edinburgh; the Edinburgh University Library; the Turnbull Library, Wellington, New Zealand, and the New Zealand National Library Service.

To these, and to all others who have helped me, I offer my best thanks for making a task already pleasant from the nature of its subject doubly enjoyable by their cordiality.

J. C. REID

vii

Introduction

WHEN Thomas Hood was born in 1799, Napoleon was threatening England with invasion, Nelson, having won the Battle of the Nile, was sweeping his country's enemies from the seas, King George III, the loss of the American colonies weighing not at all on his conscience, was sliding rapidly into insanity, and Pitt had just passed his Combination Acts rendering trade unions illegal. Although there were intimations of the far-reaching economic and social changes that were soon to transform the life of the whole nation, most Englishmen still worked on the land or in agricultural trades, and for many of them living conditions were extremely harsh. In literature, the dawn of Romanticism's brightest day was breaking; Wordsworth and Coleridge had lately published their epoch-making *Lyrical Ballads*, William Blake, rapt in a vision of glory and terror, was writing his *Prophetic Books*, Walter Scott was collecting his minstrelsy of the Scottish border, and Byron, Keats and Shelley were children growing up in an age in which the ideals of the French Revolution stirred the hearts and inspired the minds of serious young men.

When Hood died in 1845, Queen Victoria had been eight years on the throne, Napoleon was a distant memory and his empire in ruins, slavery had been abolished, income-tax had been introduced, the Reform Bill of 1832 was in operation, Catholics had been emancipated and the Oxford Movement had split open over the conversion of John Henry Newman, Karl Marx was writing *Das Kapital* under the dome of the British Museum, the small yeoman farmer had virtually disappeared and most Englishmen had become town-dwellers engaged in industry. In literature, Robert Browning, with his *Bells and Pomegranates*, had established himself, at least in the eyes of the discerning, as a highly individual talent, John Ruskin had published the first instalments of *Modern Painters*, Charles Dickens, with six novels, had become the undisputed master entertainer of his age, and, with his *Poems* of 1842, Alfred Tennyson had already won recognition as the foremost poet of the new reign.

The Age of Elegance had given place to the Age of Victoria. During Hood's lifetime, new methods of manufacture and transport changed England from the old to the modern, the industrial revolution got firmly under way, and the loose code of Regency living died with the spread of respectability and piety among the middle classes and upwards from them. Other decorous aspects of eighteenth-century mores triumphed, and, in the fresh, confident age, revealed themselves, slightly transmuted, as Victorianism, with all its paradoxes and in all its bewildering complexity.

The forty-six years of Hood's lifetime spanned the period in which the wave of new political and social concepts from the American and French Revolutions broke upon English life, and in which the nation, with tremendous resilience, absorbed the impact of the French Revolutionary and Napoleonic Wars and of two internal upheavals, the industrial and agrarian revolutions. It was a time of violent adaptation, that brought great prosperity to some and misery to many, as industrialization was accelerated and the liberal spirit struggled against vested interests and soulless exploitation. England had entered upon her greatest period of prosperity, which was also one of vast social unrest, dynamic change and strenuous activity, of increasing wealth and imperial ascendency resting upon ruthless competition, sweated labour and inhuman living conditions, that co-existed with social enlightenment, daring enterprise, the philanthropy of men like Robert Owen and Shaftesbury and the idealism of the Chartists.

Hood grew to manhood in the age of the dandy, of Beau Brummell and fashionable balls at Brighton, of hobby-horses, of new novels by Miss Austen and the author of *Waverley*, of horse-racing and prize-fighting. When he was at his most active as a writer, from 1825 onwards, most of this way of life had gone for ever. His chief work was done during the main period of repression and reform, the years of consolidation after the Napoleonic Wars, when the anti-Jacobin spirit was fading, and cottage manufactures were replaced by the factory system. The world he knew as a young man was one of transition, in which the old economic order lingered uneasily with the new, like an ageing relative taking a long time to die in the house of a younger generation.

It was a transition time in literature as well. When Hood's *Plea of the Midsummer Fairies* was published in 1827, the Romantic day had closed in chilly night. Keats, Shelley and Blake were dead, Coleridge was silent and Wordsworth was issuing his dullest verse. Thomas Hood's poetic contemporaries were James Montgomery, Thomas Lovell Beddoes, George Darley, Leigh Hunt, Samuel Rogers, John Clare, Philip 'Festus' Bailey and a host of women poetasters such as Caroline Bowles, Mary Howett, Felicia Hemans and the voluminous Sarah Flower Adams. Hood stands out from this company, not just because of the flatness of the surrounding country, but by virtue of a strikingly individual talent, a fascinating personality and the variety, durability and seminal quality of so much of his work. He remains interesting, too, for other reasons; his poor health and the nature of his occupations kept him from any direct involvement in the social movements of his time and yet his writing is permeated with its liberal values and shows a keen awareness of its major social concerns. His various kinds of poetry have their own particular merits, but his work has an additional significance in that it allows us to see clear signs of an important shift of attitudes, a transition stage in the development of English poetry, comparable in this respect with the Georgian verse of our own century.

If this seems a bleak Hist. Lit. way of looking at Hood's achievement, or an inflating of its importance, the relationship between his poetry and the mood of his age is close enough to make the generalization difficult to escape and perhaps a little more excusable than it would be with poets of greater stature. Nor need a realization that Hood's poetry is, in a special way, representative of the temper of his generation necessarily impair a recognition of its distinctive quality. There was a certain sickness in the poetry of these transition years. Hood's personal sickness reflected in his writings coincides with that of his time and is both image and incarnation of it.

To understand the nature of the poetry produced during the interregnum of which Hood is part is, I believe, to understand also why Victorian poetry took the direction it did. Most surveys of the literary developments in the early years of the nineteenth century pass directly from the Romantics to the Victorians with barely a glance at the imaginative universe of the intervening generation, who, because of the very early deaths of the second generation of Romantics, had the field almost to themselves for nearly twenty years. It is usually taken for granted that the Victorian poets derive from, and continue in the line of, the Romantics, as in some cases, with a certain loss of urgency, they do. True, in Victorian verse, there is not apparent such a far-reaching change of sensibility as separates the poetry of Coleridge, Wordsworth, Shelley and Keats from that of Pope and Johnson. Yet what can be found, even in the work of Tennyson and Browning, is a progressive failure by the poet to recognize and give form to the symbolic aspects of his material and the substitution of often shaky intellectual systems for that intuitive perception of poetic truth and order in which the poet's deepest sensibilities are in full harmony with his subject and which the Romantics, for all the woolliness of their articulated philosophies, frequently attained.

A partial explanation for the decay of the Romantic impulse may be found in the inability of the philosophic idealism of the early Romantic period to withstand the battering-ram of utilitarianism. It may be, too, that the very intensity of the Romantic pursuit of emotional experience carried in it the seeds of its own destruction, and that the impossibility of shaping a religious substitute or a coherent philosophy from the impact of emotional experiences on highly sensitized spirits accounts for the brief creative life of the later Romantics. The fact is that in just over a generation the challenging insights of the early Wordsworth had given place to the eccentric fantasies of Beddoes and Darley and to a type of verse that seems the product of neurotic tensions and emotional aberrations.

Yet, although it may properly be said that the Romantics prepared the way for the major Victorian poets, and that Tennyson begins in Keats and Browning begins in Shelley, the origin of some of the characteristic features of the poetry of the later age must be sought in the products of the interregnum. In Hood's generation, perhaps more than in the previous one, the basis was laid for Victorian popular poetry. It was Hood and his contemporaries who diluted the spirit of the Roman-

4

tics, blended their manners with elements from a pre-Words-worthian style and by adapting Romantic themes and forms to the taste of lower middle-class readers, established precedents in the poeticizing of the commonplace. More often than not, their verse is minor and has the general feel of second-handness, yet it is not without originality or surprising flashes of insight and of pure poetry. Hood's work, in particular, has an impressive power and energy that are the marks of a strange, vital talent.

Some of the paradoxes of Victorian poetry, for instance, the combination of delicacy in the perception of detail with a vagueness in the presentation of wholes, or the hardening of the fresh language of Wordsworth into poetic clichés, can be best apprehended in the work of Hood's generation. In the 1820's, the Romantic energy peters out in spiritual and imaginative exhaustion, vulgarity creeps in where once refined sensibilities ruled and poetry becomes uneasily betrothed to journalism. Interwoven with all this is the energetic expression of a freakish vision, sometimes merely whimsical or grotesque, yet quite often full of a compulsive horror, a cathartic disgust and a sense of nightmare that are more likely to be appreciated by a generation that has read Kafka and Samuel Beckett than one reared on Arnold Bennett and John Galsworthy.

With the exception of John Clare, Thomas Hood is the most gifted poet of this period and certainly the most influential. As an integral part of his febrile imagination, we can distinguish a highly individual amalgam of the farcical and the sinister, the pathetic and the ghoulish, that has few ancestors but many heirs. His verse epitomizes many of the literary trends of his time; he stands in a curious way between the Romantics and the Victorians, yet belongs strictly to neither; he looks back to the late eighteenth century and he looks forward to Rossetti and Wilde at the end of the Victorian age; as one of the most popular poets of the century he exercised a persistent influence on literature for at least fifty years after his death, especially by his expression of domestic sentiment and by his humanitarian poems, which were models for a whole school of social poets in Britain and Europe; his immense comic legacy was a mine of imitation by middle-class humorists; as a punster he has had no equal, and, despite the low repute to which this form of humour has fallen, Hood's work remains full of delightful surprises even for those who despise the pun and ignore its kinship with more respectable types of literary ambiguity.

The fact that most of his work was ground out under the pressure of economic necessity and composed in bushels to meet the exigencies of deadlines means that much of it is mere ephemera. Few writers of any merit benefit more than does Hood from rigorous selection. At the same time, the pressures of journalism, of not only editing magazines but of writing most of their contents, too, although it undoubtedly resulted in a high proportion of trivial and mechanical work, had at least one beneficial effect; it enlarged Hood's range. One reason for his survival as a poet is the diversity of accomplishment in his best-remembered pieces. There is no other poet of his generation who had so wide a range and who did so many things so well.

For all the harm that journalistic demands may have done to areas of his talent, for all the shallowness of much of his work, I believe that this high-pressure career of Hood gave him both incentives and outlets for his diverse imaginative experiences, while leisure and financial security may well have limited his achievement through indolence. Just as in every fat man there is a thin man screaming to be let out, so in many industrious people there is an idler who clamours for escape. Few writers have been more prolific than Thomas Hood; yet by temperament he was a procrastinator who required the incessant spur of want and of inexorable publishers. His virtuosity, his inventiveness in form and metre, his experiments with words—these, too, would seem to have been forced upon him by the need constantly to provide his readers with something new and different. If these pressures often squeezed out work much below his best—despairing 'fillers', last-minute improvisations, dreadful puns and inferior jests, they had the advantage of also forcing him to explore his resources to the limit and to drag desperately from his inner self fresh ideas, new forms and unusual experiences with which, in more comfortable circumstances, he might never have been confronted. I cannot, with most of Hood's critics, lament what is to them a waste of poetic talent on trumpery journalism. It seems to me more likely that, had he been less driven by necessity, he would have produced only fainter carbons of the Keatsian style that pervades his first serious volume. The circumstances in which Hood wrote, while they were responsible for much that is sub-literary, were equally responsible for a larger measure of good and original work than he would otherwise have produced. He gave of his best, as well as of his worst, under the unremitting application of the screw of want.

The pity of it is that such work was done in conditions of physical and mental strain. It would be callous to say that it was worth it, that a lifetime of suffering is not too great a price to pay for a handful of memorable poems. But, in fact, it seems never to have occurred to Hood himself that he was paying a price for any kind of achievement. He is happily free from the immature attitude that makes a religion of art and measures its martyrdoms at so many drops of bloody sweat to each imperishable line. It is his perpetual ability to jest about his disabilities, to turn them to humorous profit, to console his friends for having to console him, to wring a lyric from a spasm of pain or a comic ballad out of a week of thin gruel that, as much as anything, makes him a man to treasure. It is impossible not to be moved by his smiling heroism, his refusal to yield to despair, no matter how light his purse, how bare the larder, how treacherous the publishers, how grasping the creditors, how gnawing the rats of pain.

This attitude was no mere passive acquiescence in the face of continued adversity; it was the product of a sensibility that had disciplined itself to transform reality into a jest and of an acquired virtue that triumphed over temptations to despair. 'I have to be a lively Hood for a livelihood', is his characteristic utterance, and if, at times, in intimate letters to friends, the cheerful philosophy cracks and terrible strains show briefly through, such rare outbursts serve only to enhance the nobility of Hood's acceptance of the buffets of life and the toughness of spirit with which this man who, with Pope, could speak of 'this long disease, my life', faced up to misfortune. It is for this lack of self-pity, this gallantry and sweetness of disposition, this resourcefulness of laughter, even in the face of death, that Hood wins our special esteem. Some men live in our hearts for the poems with which they touch the common chords of humanity; others for the example they give of moral courage. Not many deserve, like Thomas Hood, to be remembered on both counts.

7

I

Childhood and Youth

THOMAS HOOD's paternal grandparents were diligent Scottish farmers, who lived at Errol, a small village in the Carse of Gowrie, between Perth and Dundee. A little over a century before Hood's father was born there, the great Montrose had led his forces through this little spot on the left bank of the Tay to defeat the Covenanters of Aberdeen. In the traditional Scottish way, the Hoods struggled to give their five sons and one daughter a start in life that would lift them above their own humble level. Thomas, the eldest son, and father of the poet, was apprenticed to a bookseller; Robert, the second son, studied for the ministry and became a tutor in the family of Admiral Duncan; while two others, James and George, became shopkeepers.

If it is true that certain qualities skip a generation, we may find intimations of Thomas Hood's sense of humour in the keen wit and easy laughter recorded of his grandmother. Something of his whimsicality, too, marked the temperament of his uncle George. While James was a 'douce canny' grocer, George, who was both a saddler and a butcher, seems to have been a 'character', an individualist whose nonconformism gained him a reputation for eccentricity. One story told of him might have been a short piece from *Hood's Own*. Finding a dead calf in a field, and thinking to make use of it in his shop, he waited until early evening, then carried the carcase home on his shoulders. Since he knew that the animal would be considered unfit for human consumption, he entered Errol crying, 'Beh! Beh! Beh!', in imitation of the bleat of a calf, hoping to convince

9

anyone who was around that he was taking a live beast home for slaughter. Unhappily, the villagers were out in force and, seeing through his ruse, pursued him through the streets crying 'Beh! Beh! Beh!' For years afterwards, George's public appearances would be greeted by the same sound. Perhaps the same uncle's individuality took a less engaging turn at times, for his wife left him in later years and his children were scattered.

Like his brothers and his sister, Jean, Thomas, who was born in 1759, attended the Errol school before going to Dundee to learn the bookselling trade. When his apprenticeship expired, he followed the path to London that so many young Scots had trodden before him, taking with him a relative, Patrick Gardiner, whose father was the tenant of the farms of Mains of Errol. Hood's first years in the metropolis were spent in establishing himself in the world of the large London publishing houses. From about 1784 he was employed as an assistant by Mr. Vernor, a prominent bookseller. Vernor, formerly of Vernor and Chater, of Ludgate Hill, had set up his own bookseller's shop in Fore Street and a circulating library in St. Michael's Alley, Cornhill; later he combined both enterprises in Birchin Lane, where the young Scot worked. In 1798, by which time the elder Hood had become a partner, the company of Vernor and Hood moved to 31, The Poultry, in the parish of St. Michael's, and here the firm's interests were extended into the field of publishing. It seems that, by then, Vernor was considerably advanced in years, for Hood was the active partner. In January, 1806, presumably just before, or on, Vernor's death, a new partner, Charles Sharpe, joined the business, which became Vernor, Hood and Sharpe, and so remained, until Hood's death in 1811.

Vernor and Hood was an enterprising firm, and much of its initial success can be attributed to the literary taste and business canniness of the elder Hood. He was a member of the Associated Booksellers, which selected important old books for reprinting, and, according to his grandson, Tom Hood, he was 'one of the first, if not *the* first, who opened the book trade with America'. Among the firm's most successful publications were *The Farmer's Boy* and *Rural Tales* by Robert Bloomfield, the peasant poet, whom they encouraged and treated handsomely, *The Pleasures of Nature* by David Carey and *The Beauties of*

England and Wales, a handsome volume in part by John Britton, who was for a time employed by the firm as a typographer.

Vernor and Hood were also well known for their periodicals, among them the *Poetical Magazine*, the *Lady's Monthly Museum*, consisting of 'Amusement and Instruction, being an Assemblage of whatever can tend to please the Fancy, interest the Mind, or exalt the Character of the British Fair', and the *Monthly Mirror*. The latter, their most popular journal, which ran from 1797 to 1810, was owned by the eccentric Thomas Hill and edited by Edward Dubois, who had some reputation as a wit and satirist. With a lively editorial policy which took especial note of current drama, the *Mirror* published the work of writers like James and Horace Smith, and the tragic young Henry Kirke White, and hit the taste of the public to such a degree that several earlier issues went into second editions. Robert Southey praised it in his memoir on Kirke White as the magazine 'which first set the example of typographical neatness in periodical publications'.

On one occasion, the firm of Vernor, Hood and Sharpe contributed an intriguing footnote to legal history. Sir John Carr, a peripatetic and prolific writer of light-weight travel-books, and an occasional contributor to the *Monthly Mirror*, issued a book called *The Stranger in Ireland in 1805*. Dubois wrote a bright little parody of Carr's gossipy, superficial style in *My Pocket Book or Hints for a Ryghte Merrie and Conceited Tour . . . by a Knight Errant*, which pretended to be Carr's jottings for his book. When this appeared in 1807, the indignant Carr sued Vernor and Hood for £2,000 in damages for this 'false, scandalous, malicious and defamatory libel'. The case, which was tried before Lord Ellenborough at the Guildhall in July, 1808, resulted in a verdict for the defendants by a special jury. The summing-up of the learned judge, heavily in favour of the firm, indicated that 'a writer, in exposing the follies and errors of another, may make use of ridicule, however poignant', and drew a distinction between the criticism, even ridicule, of an author as an author, and reflections on his personal character. Both Carr and Hood published reports of the trial; to his own version Hood added footnotes which show that he had a vivacious pen and an ironical turn of phrase.

By the time of the Carr libel suit, Thomas Hood the elder

had become a widely respected figure in the London publishing world, carrying the weight of the firm's business,[1] and not sparing himself or his employees in long days of eleven and twelve hours' work. He was well-liked by his staff, one of whom, John Taylor, who was later to become a publisher himself, and to give employment to Thomas Hood the poet, gratefully remembered his punctiliousness and kindness. From the scanty records of the elder Hood's character, the firm impression emerges of a hard-working, honest, prudent Scot, with an excellent knowledge of his trade, who was good-natured, rather than dour. He appears to have had some urge to write as well as to publish: the poet said, 'There was a dash of ink in my blood. My father wrote two novels.' But no trace of these has been found, and while it is possible that the older Hood produced work under a pseudonym and that he helped Dubois with his parody, the only surviving writings that are undoubtedly his are the notes on the Carr trial. His religious profession is unknown, but he may have belonged to the Glasites, a sect founded by a Dundee minister, John Glad, in 1725, which rejected the idea of a national church and practised a primitive form of Christian worship. It had many adherents in the district of Perth and Dundee, and Hood's partner, Vernor, was one of the sect's elders, which, if Hood did in fact belong to the Glasites, may have formed the original contact between them. Hood's profession cannot have gone very deep, however, since his son seems to have been reared in a vague kind of liberal Protestantism, loosely that of the Established Church.

Not surprisingly, the successful publisher married a woman whose family was closely connected with the book trade. She was Elizabeth Sands, whose father, James, and brother, Robert, were engravers of some reputation. Of their several children, only six survived beyond infancy—two sons, James and Thomas, and four daughters, Elizabeth, Annie, Jessie and Catherine. The poet's medical history and the early deaths of James in 1811 and Catherine in 1828, as well as other premature deaths in the family, suggest that the children inherited frail constitutions.

Thomas Hood the poet, the second son of his parents, was

---

[1] There are several business letters in the Bodleian Library addressed by authors and other publishers to Hood senior.

born on May 23, 1799, in The Poultry. In later life, Hood showed some uncertainty about this when he wrote that he was 'a native of The Poultry, or Birchin Lane, I forget which, and in truth am not particularly anxious to be more certainly acquainted with my parish. It was a metropolitan one, however, which is recorded without the slightest repugnance; firstly, for that, practically, I had no choice in the matter, and secondly, because, theoretically, I had as lief been a native of Stoke Pogis or Little Pedlington. . . . Next to being a citizen of the world, it must be the best thing to be born a citizen of the world's greatest city. . . . A literary man should exult rather than otherwise that he first saw the light—or perhaps the fog—in the same metropolis as Milton, Gray, De Foe, Pope, Byron, Lamb and other town-born authors, whose fame has nevertheless triumphed over the Bills of Mortality. In such goodly company, I cheerfully take up my livery; and especially as Cockneyism, properly so called, appears to be confined to no particular locality or station in life.'

When Hood was eight, his family moved from The Poultry to 5 Lower Street, Islington, later renamed 50 Essex Road, which was to be his home for about twenty years. It was almost certainly from this house, and not The Poultry, that he was to remember 'the little window where the sun came creeping in at morn' and 'the fir trees dark and high' of his well-known poem. Very little is known of his childhood, but J. A. Hessey, who was later to employ him on the *London Magazine,* recalled him as 'a singular child, silent and retired, with much quiet humours and apparently delicate in health'.

For details of his education, we have to depend upon his own 'Literary Reminiscences', scrappy recollections published many years afterwards in *Hood's Own.* He had his first schooling in a private establishment in Tokenhouse Yard from 'two maiden ladies that were called Hogsflesh. The circumstances would scarcely be worth mentioning, but that being a day boarder, and taking my dinner with the family, I became aware of a Baconian brother, who was never mentioned except by his initial, and was probably the prototype of the sensitive "Mr. H." in Lamb's unfortunate farce.'

When the Hoods moved to Islington, Thomas was sent to a seminary. His recollections of this preparatory school were anything but warmly sentimental. 'My memory presents but a very dim image of a pedagogical powdered head amidst a more vivid group of females of a more composite character—part dry-nurse, part house-maid and part governess—with a matronly figure in the background, very like Mrs. S. allegorically representing, as Milton says, "our universal mother". But there is no glimpse of Minerva. Of those pleasant associations with early school days, of which so much has been said and sung, there is little among my retrospections, excepting, perhaps, some sports which, like charity, might have been enjoyed at home, without the drawback of sundry strokes, neither apoplectic nor paralytic, periodical physic, and other unwelcome extras. . . . Nevertheless, I yet recall, with wonder, the occasional visits of grown-up scholars to their old school, all in a flutter of gratitude and sensibility at recognizing the spot where they had been caned, horsed, and flogged and fagged, and brimstone-and-treacled, and blackdosed and stickjawed and kibed and fined—where they had caught measles and the mumps, and had been overtasked and undertaught—and then, by way of climax, sentimentally offering a presentation snuff-box to their revered preceptor, with an inscription, ten to one, in dog Latin on the lid! For my own part, were I to revisit such a haunt of my youth, it would give me the greatest pleasure out of mere regard to the rising generation, to find Prospect House turned into a floor-cloth manufactory, and the playground converted to a bleachfield.'

From this unhallowed seminary, Thomas went as a full boarder to a 'finishing school', Alfred House Academy at Camberwell Green, a fairly costly establishment presided over by Dr. Nicholas Wanostrocht, the founder, and later by his great-nephew, Vincent, who as 'N. Felix', became well known as a cricketer. Hood's memory of this school was even less happy than of his earlier one. Here, he wrote, 'there seemed little chance of my ever becoming what Mrs. Malaprop calls "a progeny of learning"; indeed my education was pursued very much after the plan laid down by that feminine authority. I had nothing to do with Hebrew, or Algebra, or Simony, or Fluxions, or Paradoxes, or with such inflammatory branches; but I obtained a supercilious knowledge of accounts, with enough of geometry to make me acquainted with the contagious countries.

Moreover, I became fluent enough in some unknown tongue to protect me from the French Mark; and I was sufficiently at home (during the vacations) in the quibbles of English grammar to bore all my parents, relatives, friends, and acquaintances, by a pedantical mending of their "cakeology". Such was the sum total of my acquirements.'

It was this same school that Hood celebrated sardonically in his 'Ode on a Distant Prospect of Clapham Academy' ('No connection with any other Ode') which begins:

> Ah me! those old familiar bounds!
> That classic house, those classic grounds
> My pensive thought recalls!
> What tender urchins now confine,
> What little captives now repine
> Within yon irksome walls?

and goes on to recall

> The weary tasks I used to con,
> The hopeless leaves I wept upon!
> Most fruitless leaves to me!

From this unregretted place, Thomas was withdrawn on the death of his father in the autumn of 1811. James, Thomas's elder brother, had been sent for his health to stay with his uncle, Robert Sands, at Sandhurst in Berkshire. After a visit to him, the elder Hood caught a chill in the night air on the return journey and died on August 20 of a 'malignant fever'. James himself followed him soon after, on December 10.

Despite the apparent prosperity of the firm of Vernor, Hood and Sharpe, it seems to have gone downhill in its later years; Charles Sharpe, it is clear, lacked the business acumen of his partners. Soon after Hood's death, he was compelled to declare bankruptcy and dissolve the business. The extent of the firm's operations, however, is shown by the fact that a certified valuation of the property on April 2, 1812, attests assets amounting to £17,320.[1] Left in reduced, if not exactly straitened circumstances, Mrs. Hood withdrew Thomas from 'Learning's woeful tree', and sent him to 'what might have been called a High School, in reference to its distance from the ground'. This was a humble day school kept by 'a decayed Dominie'

[1] This certificate is in the Bristol Public Library.

and located over a grocer's shop. Not only was Hood happier there than he had been at any of his other schools, but, in later years, he felt that he had gained the most from it.

The worthy Dominie 'less resembled, even in externals, the modern worldly trading Schoolmaster, than the good, honest, earnest, olden Pedagogue—a pedant, perchance, but a learned one, with whom teaching was a "labour of love", one who had a proper sense of the dignity and importance of his calling, and was content to find a main portion of his reward in the honourable proficiency of his disciples. Small as was our College, its Principal maintained his state, and walked gowned and covered. His cap was of faded velvet, of black, or blue or purple, or sad green, or as it seemed, of all together, with a *nuance* of brown. His robe, of crimson damask, lined with the national tartan. A quaint, carved, highbacked, elbowed article, looking like an *émigré* from a set that had been at home in an aristocratical drawing-room, under the *ancien régime*, was his Professional Chair, which with his desk was appropriately elevated on a dais, some inches above the common floor. From this moral and material eminence, he cast a vigilant yet kindly eye over some dozen of youngsters; for adversity, sharpened by habits of authority, had not soured him, nor mingled a single tinge of bile with the peculiar red-streak complexion, so common to the healthier natives of the North.'

Under this kindly tutelage, young Thomas took more readily to his studies. He became an avid reader of poetry and even, at times, wrote 'something which was egregiously mistaken for something of the same nature'. 'It was impossible', he said, 'not to take an interest in learning what he seemed so interested in teaching; and in a few months my education progressed infinitely farther than it had done in as many years under the listless superintendence of B.A. and LL.D and assistants.'

With boy pupils only, however, the dominie found it hard to make ends meet, and girls were imported to bolster up the numbers. 'It is amusing', Hood recalls, 'yet humiliating to remember the nuisances the sex endured at the hands of those who were thereafter to honour the shadow of its shoe-tie—to groan, moan, sigh, and sicken for its smiles—to become poetical, prosaical, nonsensical, lack-a-daisical, and perhaps even melodramatical for its sake. Numberless were the desk-quakes, the ink-spouts, the book-bolts, the pea-showers, and other unregistered phenomena, which likened the studies of these four unlucky maidens to the "Pursuit of Knowledge under Difficulties"—so that it glads me to reflect that I was in a very small minority against the persecution. . . . The final result of the struggle in the academic nest—whether hen cuckoos succeeded in ousting the cock-sparrows, or *vice-versa*—is beyond my record.'

Hood's formal education was scanty enough, but the influence of the dominie lingered with him, and he remained grateful to the man who had encouraged him in his reading. Some recollections of his days in the little school undoubtedly underlie his poem 'The Irish Schoolmaster', where he also shows, as he did on other occasions, a chip-on-the-shoulder attitude towards University-educated men:

> Now all is hushed, and, with a look profound,
> The Dominie lays ope the learned page;
> (So be it called) although he doth expound
> Without a book, both Greek and Latin sage;
> Now telleth he of Rome's rude infant age,
> How Romulus was bred in savage wood,
> By wet-nurse wolf, devoid of wolfish rage;
> And laid foundation stone of walls of mud,
> But watered it, alas! with warm fraternal blood. . .
>
> And so he wisely spends the fruitful hours,
> Link'd each to each by labour, like a bee;
> Or rules in Learning's hall, or trims her bow'rs—
> Would there were many more such wights as he,
> To sway each capital academie
> Of Cam and Isis; for, alack! at each
> There dwells, I wot, some dronish Dominie,
> That does no garden work, nor yet doth teach,
> But wears a floury head, and talks in flow'ry speech!

Shortly after the invasion of the girls, Thomas was removed from the scene of contest, in 1813 or 1814, to be initiated into 'profitable mercantile mysteries'. His mother had not been left destitute at her husband's death, since, although Thomas had been withdrawn from Dr. Wanostrocht's academy, he continued to go to school and the family kept up its house by

Islington Green. But the Hood girls were growing up, and in his fourteenth or fifteenth year, the boy was ripe to contribute to their support. Through the offices of a family friend, he found himself planted on a counting-house stool, 'which nevertheless served occasionally for a Pegasus on three legs, every foot, of course, being a dactyl or spondee'.

The firm, 'Bell and Co.', were importers engaged in the Russian trade; that his career there was brief was not, he assures us, through his habit of composing verses at his desk. 'The principal of *our* firm . . . had a turn for Belles Lettres, and would have winked with both eyes at verses which did not intrude into an invoice or confuse their figures with those of the Ledger.' It was failing health that cut short his period in the counting-house. Advised by his doctors to give up his commercial stool for some occupation that would allow him more exercise, he left the office without regret; his chief memory of his time there was of an odd mixture of commerce and poetry that he commemorated in a sonnet:

> Time was, I sat upon a lofty stool,
> At lofty desk, and with a clerkly pen
> Began each morning, at the stroke of ten
> To write in Bell and Co's commercial school:
> In Warnford Court, a shady nook and cool,
> The favourite retreat of merchant men;
> Yet would my quill turn vagrant even then,
> And take strong dips in the Castalian pool.
> Now double entry,—now a flowery trope—
> Mingling poetic honey with trade wax—
> Blogg Brothers—Milton—Grote and Prescott—Pope—
> Bristles—and Hogg—Glyn Mills and Halifax—
> Rogers—and Towgood—Hemp—the Bard of Hope—
> Barilla—Byron—Tallow—Burns—and Flax!

Much of the information about the early stages of Hood's career comes from his 'Literary Reminiscences'. These were written in middle age when imperfect recollection spattered their pages with inaccuracies; they were also exaggerated and imaginatively heightened for a popular audience. It is impossible to tell how long he spent with the firm, or even what its name was, for 'Bell and Co.' seems to have been a fictitious one. We do know, however, that after leaving the office life as unsuitable for one of his fragile constitution, he began to study engraving, the craft of his mother's father and brother. From his uncle, Robert Sands, he learned the fundamentals, and he received further instruction from John and Henry Le Keux, prominent craftsmen of the time. The youngster proved an apt pupil, for within a year he was doing saleable work. In 1815, he wrote to his uncle from Scotland: 'I did some things for Mr. Harris before I went to Scotland with which he was very well pleased, but have had no proofs, as I did them when H. was busy on the Battle of Waterloo, and could not prove for me. I desired him to send you a proof I did in Spring, which I suppose you have had.'

In fact, Hood had only exchanged one sedentary occupation for another. The long hours spent at the desk engraving were quite as bad for his health as his former job; soon doctors were called in again, and found, on examining him, that 'by so much sitting, I was hatching a whole brood of complaints'. His principal illness was to come later, with a bout of rheumatic fever, but even before this, he proved himself easily subject to a succession of disorders. Some years later, he was to tell his friend, Lieutenant de Franck, in 1837, 'When I was a boy I was so knocked about by illness, and in particular by a scarlet fever so violent that it ended in a dropsy, that as I grew up I only got over by living rather well.' The scarlet fever, his first really severe trouble, was but the forerunner to a long line of such crises, which were to rack his feeble body to the hour of his death. At this time, in his sixteenth year, he was so run down that his mother decided that he was in immediate need of a change of climate, and a temporary respite, at least, from the dust and germ-laden air of London. She wrote to her relatives in Dundee, who agreed to give him hospitality, and some time in the summer of 1815, the young lad was shipped off in search of health to his father's native soil.

When he sailed for the North, Napoleon had not long been defeated, and Britain was still rejoicing in its long-deferred release from the menace of 'Boney'. The seas were free. Hood tells us himself that he was 'shipped, as per advice, in a Scotch Smack, which "*smacked* through the breeze" as Dibdin sings, so merrily that on the fourth morning we were within sight of the prominent old Steeple of "Bonny Dundee" '. The ship was the trading smack, *Union*, and its skipper, Captain Lyon, became one of Hood's most steadfast friends.

Despite the fact that the Dundee in which Thomas landed was a large shipping centre, it was still a reposeful place, not yet disturbed by industrial developments, with an attractive countryside close at hand, and with homely and conservative inhabitants. The 'bracing breezes of the North' which Hood felt on his face as the ship raced into the harbour, would, he hoped, bring the glow of health to his cheeks again. On landing, he went to stay with his aunt, Jean Keay, the wife of Captain Keay, owner and master of the trading brig, *Hope*, who lived in a tenement in the Nethergate. A quarter of a century afterwards Hood, following his journalist's instinct for comic exploitation, described his reception like this: 'Like other shipments, I had been regularly addressed to the care of a consignee; but the latter, not anxious, probably, to take charge of a hobbledehoy, yet at the same time unwilling to incur the reproach of having a relative in the same town and not under the same roof, peremptorily declined the office. Nay, more, she pronounced against me a capital sentence, so far as returning to the place from whence I came, and even proceeded to bespeak my passage and reship my luggage.'

The informants of Alexander Elliot, when he was compiling *Hood in Scotland* in the 1880's, told quite another story.[1] According to them, the young man was greeted warmly by his aunt, and kindly treated, in the early months at least, although some disagreement developed later. When the Captain went on a voyage to Riga, Thomas accompanied his aunt and her children, including the youngest daughter, Jessie, with whom he had become especially friendly, to summer lodgings in Newport, a pretty town on the Fifeshire side of the Tay. He kept up an affectionate correspondence with his aunt all his life; in fact, his very last letter was written to her. Yet in his reminiscences the 'crabbed auld Scotchwoman' is treated far from generously. It is common experience that relatives and acquaintances are often able to maintain more friendly rela-

[1] Thanks to Elliot's labours, we have more information about the poet's Scottish sojourn than about any other part of his early life. *Hood in Scotland* (1885), based in great part on interviews with people who remembered the poet and his relatives, and printing several youthful letters, corrects at several points Hood's own highly coloured narrative.

tions by correspondence than when in close and often irritating contact. It is possible, too, that the high-spirited Hood, who had a fondness for practical jokes, brought out an understandable testiness in his otherwise hospitable aunt. Writing some years afterwards for a popular periodical memoirs he had no reason to believe would be more than ephemera, he exaggerated the situation and dramatically foreshortened events.

Still, the memory of a certain incompatibility of temper between Mrs. Keay and himself lingered with Hood, for his son and daughter report what they must have heard from him at first hand that his aunt was a rigid Sabbatarian and one of the 'unco guid'. They tell, too, the story of her placing Hood at her parlour window one Sabbath when she was ill and unable to go to the kirk, so that he might report on the stream of worshippers, and of Hood, with solemn face, inventing scandalous tit-bits about them:

'That's Bailie So-and-So's daughter, aunt, and isn't she making desperate love to young Somebody, who's walking by her side!'

'The graceless hizzie! I'd wauk her, gin *I* were her mammie! Keek oot again, Tam.'

The lad undoubtedly needed a chance to recuperate; his appearance shocked many who saw him. When the wife of his father's old friend, Patrick Gardiner, who was now a grocer in Dundee, introduced Thomas to her sister-in-law at Stobhall in Perthshire, the good lady remarked as she saw his emaciated form, 'Losh, woman! What are ye daein' bringin' that laddie up here to dee!' He took full advantage of the clean Scottish air, spending much time playing in the green meadows with Jessie, or cantering on his uncle's pony through the lanes of Murraygate. It was not long, however, before the disharmony between the lively youth and his aunt burst out in a serious quarrel that sent Thomas from Mrs. Keay's roof to lodge in a boarding-house in the Overgate, kept by a Mrs. Butterworth, a friend of his aunt.

Hood described his landlady as 'a sort of widow with a seafaring husband, "as good as dead", and in her appearance not unlike a personification of *rouge et noir*, with her red eyes, her red face, her yellow teeth and her black velvet cap'. Very likely this description is a composite one, with the florid complexion and the seafaring husband borrowed from Mrs. Keay for the purpose of caricature. Among Mrs. Butterworth's lodgers were several young men working in offices and shops or studying for the ministry. Hood found several of them congenial companions, with whom he kept in touch for years afterwards, in particular, Robert Miln, who became a prominent Dundee lawyer, J. G. M'Vicar, who became a minister, Samuel Messieux, a Swiss scholar later to have a notable academic career in Madras, Andrew Wyllie and George Rollo.

After his move to the lodging-house, Hood continued to spend as much time as he could in the open air, walking and riding in the countryside, and fishing. He acquired a taste for the company of the sailors, lumbermen and fishermen of the Tay, who took kindly to this thin but animated young fellow from London, and told him embellished stories of life at sea, shared gossip with him, and transmitted to him their love of the ocean. At the Craig Pier, where he spent day after eager day, he learned from these old mariners the arts of sailing, rowing and fishing. Although his later health and circumstances made it seldom possible for him to enjoy these open-air sports, he retained a love for them all his life. We do not know how he supported himself in Dundee; it was unlikely that his mother could afford much. Perhaps he worked for a time in an office; perhaps his mother's relatives sent him occasional sums. What is most probable is that he continued to gain some sustenance from engraving work, since he was able to resume this craft at once when he returned to London.

There was much joy for Hood in Scotland, through the leisure he had to enjoy the Scottish countryside, which he was to remember in several of his poems, and in the steady improvement of his health. But if the prospects pleased him, the inhabitants as a whole did not. This is how he recalled his relatives at Errol in his reminiscences: 'I seemed to have come amongst a generation that scarcely belonged to my era; mature spinsters, waning bachelors, very motherly aunts, and experienced fathers, that I should set down as uncles and aunts, called themselves my cousins; reverend personages, apparently grandfathers and grandmothers, were simply great uncles and aunts; and finally I enjoyed an interview with a relative oftener heard of traditionally, than encountered in the body—a great-great-grandmother, still a tall woman and a tolerable pedestrian, going indeed downhill but with the wheel well locked. It was like coming among the Struldbrugs.'

He found especially distasteful that Scottish characteristic that friends call 'thrift' and enemies 'meanness', for over twenty years later, he wrote to Dilke from Germany about the German servants: 'They *are* a heartless race set on the bawbees, from high to low. Indeed in a thousand things, language and all, I could fancy myself, as when a boy, in Dundee. They have *some* of the virtues, all the vices and most of the peculiarities of the Scotch.' And the religious narrowness of his Calvinistic relatives was the basis of his antipathy to Sabbatarians and Pharisees and inspired poems like his 'Ode to Rae Wilson, Esq.', with such lines as

> The Saints! the Bigots that in public spout,
> Spread phosphorous of zeal on scraps of fustian,
> And go like walking 'Lucifers' about,
> Mere living bundles of combustion.

From Mrs. Butterworth's, Hood wrote the two earliest letters that survive from his hand. The first, dated September, 1815, addressed to his aunts at home, shows him already fascinated by human oddities. 'I am principally diverted here', he writes, 'with the singular characters that come to lodge here in succession. When I first came we had a kind of itinerant minister, who loved his bottle,

> And oft would rehearse
> In defence of his custom this scriptural verse—
> "Take a little wine for thy stomach's sake"—
> But in practice the little, but jolly divine
> Would oft substitute whisky instead of the wine!

Since then we have been enlivened by a French captain, who possessed in an eminent degree the gaiety and politeness peculiar to that nation; and I have been particularly amused with a pedantic Perth schoolmaster who went up to London during the vacation, and resided a fortnight at *Wapping*—in order to improve himself in English! and said he was "vary sure he wadna be takken for a Scotsman"!'

He continues with a description of a lottery at a shilling a ticket, run by a company of tumblers, and of the struggle in the hearts of the canny Scots before venturing their bawbees, 'but when the drawing began, it was ludicrous to observe the whimsical effects of disappointment in the faces of some of the multitude. It was a scene indeed worthy of the pencil of Hogarth!' The letter ends with a postscript which leaves little doubt of his tepid regard for his father's fellow-countrymen. 'As I am to remain and take my Christmas in the Land of Cakes, you will perhaps expect me to return a complete Scot—but to tell you the truth, I approach it as yet in but a small degree. I sicken with disgust at the sight of a singed sheep's head, and notwithstanding the arguments of Lismahago and the preference of the mouse, which I admit is some support of them, I cannot bring myself to endure oatmeal, which I think harsh, dry, and insipid. The only time I ever took it with any kind of relish was one day on a trouting party, when I was hungry enough to eat anything. As to their dialect, I have acquired rather more than I could wish, through the broad brogue of our landlady, whose blunders would do credit to an Hibernian.'

Gauche and naïve though such observations are, they show Hood already developing his observant eye, which was to be one of his greatest assets later as an author and illustrator. He was also reading omnivorously, if indiscriminately: 'Whatever books,' he wrote in his memoirs, 'good, bad, or indifferent, happened to come within my reach, were perused with the greatest avidity, and however indiscriminate the course, the balance of the impressions thence derived was undoubtedly in favour of the allegorical lady, so wisely preferred by Hercules when he had to make his selection between Virtue and Vice.' With his mind excited by such reading and his health improving, there came a new urge to write seriously. We have his word for it that his first acquaintance with the press began while he was in Scotland, when he sent a 'quizzing letter' on Dundee Town Council affairs to a Dundee newspaper, which the editor prominently featured, and followed this up with a contribution to the *Dundee Magazine*. Neither of these youthful pieces has been identified; they can hardly have been of any consequence, anyhow. But for Thomas they marked the beginning of his true career. 'Here was success sufficient to turn a young author at once into "a scribbling miller" and make him sell himself, body and soul, after the German fashion, to that minor Mephistopheles, the Printer's Devil.'

Two other productions of the Scottish period exist, in part only. In another letter to his aunts, in December, 1815, he tells them that he has tried to describe Dundee after the manner of Anstey's famed *New Bath Guide*, in the form of verse-letters from a Mr. Blunderhead's family to their friends in London. The epistles were written in a manuscript volume which Hood called 'The Dundee Guide'; in 1820 he asked his friend, Rollo, in whose possession it was, to pass it to another friend, Robert Miln, who was to try to arrange for its publication. But, by then, the manuscript had been lost, and the only surviving portions of it are the 116 lines young Thomas quoted in the letter back home. These couplets, immature and frequently clumsy, have still a genuine vivacity and fluency, with enough verbal assurance and touches of lively fancy to promise better things to come. For example:

> Superstition as yet, though it's dying away,
> On the minds of the vulgar holds powerful sway,
> And on doors and on masts, you may frequently view,
> As defence against witchcraft, some horse's old shoe.
> And the mariner's wife sees her child with alarm
> Comb her hair in the glass, and predicts him some harm.
> Tales of goblins and ghosts that alarmed such a one,
> By tradition are handed from father to son,
> And they oft will describe o'er their twopenny ale
> Some poor ghost with no head, or grey mare without tail,
> Or lean corpse in night-cap, all bloody and pale! . . .
>
> Some large markets for cattle, or fairs, are held here,
> On a moor near the town, about thrice in a year,
> So I went to the last, found it full, to my thinking,
> Of whisky and porter, of smoking and drinking.
> But to picture the scene there presented, indeed,
> The bold pencil and touches of Hogarth would need.
> Here you'd perhaps see a man upon quarrelling bent,
> In short serpentine curves wheeling out of a tent,
> (For at least so they call blankets raised upon poles,
> Well enlightened and aired by the numerous holes)
> Or some hobbling old wife, just as drunk as a sow,
> Having spent all the money she got for her cow.
> Perhaps some yet unsold, when the market has ceased,
> You may then see a novelty, beast leading beast.

The only other adolescent literary production of Hood's that survives is 'The Bandit', a narrative poem of something over 800 lines. Hood gave the manuscript of this to George Rollo, whose nephew, David, allowed Alexander Elliot to print it for the first time in *Hood in Scotland*. This humourless piece of juvenilia tells a story strongly reminiscent of Scott's *The Bride of Lammermoor* in a manner redolent of Byron. The bouncing couplets relate how the noble Glenallan, exiled, becomes leader of a band of robbers. At the marriage feast of his beloved, Adelaide, to one of his friends, he bursts in, determined on revenge, but remains to utter these words:

> Oh Adelaide! a joyless wretch I came,
> With frenzied purpose and infernal aim,
> To 'venge the falsehood that had caused my woe,
> And make thy blood as now thy tear-drops flow;
> But lo! my heart forgets not that it knew
> The time, alas, it only throbbed for you,
> And loving yet, rebels against my will,
> And prompts my faltering tongue to bless you still.
> Be blessed! Forget my love! The solemn vow
> That with my wretched heart is broken now.
> But, ah, to you may ne'er its sorrows reach,
> And I alone feel wretched in the breach;
> Forget all these! with that unhappy man
> Who bids you still be happy—if you can!

Unhappily, the altruistic bandit chief is betrayed by his lieutenant, Wolf, and after a fight and a fire, he is sentenced to death, and kills himself, just as 'Pardon! Pardon!' echoes to the castle walls.

This drab melodramatic fustion has energy but no poetic merit, and, although it would be rash to draw any firm conclusion from a comparison of these two boyish effusions, the superior originality of 'The Dundee Guide' seems to indicate the main direction in which Hood's talents were to develop. Certainly, Mrs. Butterworth's young men recognized that young Thomas had an unusual facility with words. His bookishness, he says, 'acquired for me a sort of reputation for scholarship amongst my comrades, and in consequence my pen was sometimes called into requisition in divers and sometimes delicate cases. Thus, for one party, whom the gods had not made poetical, I composed a love-letter in verse; for another,

whose education had been neglected, I carried on a correspondence with reference to a tobacco manufactory in which he
was a sleeping partner.'

In Scotland, then, uncongenial though he found most of the
people, Hood fell under the spell of literature and became
aware of his own power over words. 'Like the literary performances of Mr. Weller Senior,' he writes, 'my lucubrations
were generally committed to paper, not in what is commonly
called written hand, but an imitation of print. Such a course
hints suspiciously of type and antetype, and a longing eye to
the Row, whereas, it was adopted simply to make the reading
more easy, and thus enable me the more readily to form a
judgment of the effect of my little efforts. It is more difficult
than may be supposed to decide on the value of a work in
MS., and especially when the handwriting presents only a
swell mob of bad characters, that must be severally examined
and re-examined to arrive at the merits or demerits of the case.
Print settles it, as Coleridge used to say; and to be candid, I
have more than once reversed, or greatly modified, a previous
verdict, on seeing a rough proof from the press. . . . Wherefore,
O ye Poets and Prosers, who aspire to write in Miscellanies,
and above all, O ye palpitating Untried, who meditate the
offer of your maiden essays to established periodicals, take
care, pray ye take care, to cultivate a good, plain, bold, round
text. Set up Tomkins as well as Pope or Dryden for a model,
and have an eye to your pothooks.' This advice is typical of the
man, reflecting qualities that helped him to success as a journalist—his meticulous care for detail, his finicky craftsmanship,
his regard for order and neatness.

It was in 1817, probably in the autumn, that Thomas left
Scotland for England. The climate of 'stout and original
Scotland' had fulfilled its promise, in his own words, 'to act
kindly to the constitution committed to its care'. He wrote to his
uncle, Robert Sands, soon after he had rejoined his mother in
Lower Street, Islington: 'I have the pleasure of informing you
that my voyage to Scotland has done wonders for me, as, since
my return, my neck has altogether healed, and my leg has
gained so much strength that I have been enabled to walk
several times to the West End and back without any injury,
and I certainly feel and look better than I have done for years.

I now hope to be able to look after business a little, and to do well, both in that and in health.' The Scottish years were behind him, and with them almost the last extended period of real tranquillity of body and spirit that he was to have in his life.

II

Friends of 'London Magazine' Days

BACK in London, Hood resumed the occupation of engraving. It seems that he took up an apprenticeship with Robert Sands or the Le Keuxes for two more years, since he told George Rollo in 1821: 'I have been successful in the plate that has cost me so much anxiety; and the result of four years' learning and experience in the art will appear in a work along with those of my former master, and of others who have generally served apprenticeships of seven years. I was but two years old in engraving when I set up for myself, and have been two more on my own fingers; and, as some of my friends seemed doubtful as to the success of such an experiment, I am very happy and somewhat proud of this result, in which I have obtained one object of my ambition.' The plate to which he refers was a view of the mansion of St. Clerons, Galway, dated April, 1821, which appeared in the sixth volume of J. P. Neale's *Views of Seats of Noblemen and Gentlemen*, together with work by two of Hood's 'former masters', Robert Sands and John Le Keux.

Other letters from the same period show Hood's industry and his determination to work his way to the top of his craft. The only man in the house, he was contributing to the support of his mother and his four sisters, and the chronic need for money drove him then, as later, to enter into transactions in which he obtained immediate advances, but which meant much work for little return. 'I am obliged', he told Rollo in 1820, 'to turn the amusing, if I can, into the *profitable*, not that

I am ambitious, or of a very money-loving disposition, but I am obliged to be so. Otherwise, I believe, if left to myself, I should be content with a very moderate station for, like you, I believe I am of a "domestic indolent turn". . . . I find that I am not yet quite *sharp* enough to cope with veteran men of business, but suppose every rub they give me will make my wit much keener. I am now tolerably content with what I pay for my experience, considering that I have just concluded my first year's apprenticeship to the world.'

The much belated registration of Hood's birth on November 27, 1817, suggests that he needed a birth certificate in connection with an apprenticeship,[1] and from the reference above in the letter to Rollo, we may conclude that, after a couple of years as an apprentice, he set up for himself as a master engraver. He soon had quite as much work as he could possibly cope with, for although when he was twenty-one he told Rollo that 'the little crosses and vexations, and the chicaneries of business in general, are now less new to me, and I can meet them with comparative calmness', he was unable to take a single day's holiday. He visited few people, and was seldom visited. While he occasionally went to painting exhibitions with a Scottish friend, Andrew Wyllie, his recreations were almost wholly sedentary—reading, playing chess and practising on the flute. The latter accomplishment, which he had picked up in his teens, remained an occasional consolation to him throughout his life, although he was forced to ration it for his health's sake. He also tried his hand at little mechanical inventions, designed to help engravers in copying drawings. One of these he submitted in 1819 to the Society of Arts, whose Committee of Mechanics found that the device resembled the convenient triangular compasses (which Hood had not seen), and that his indicator was 'not suitable to other instruments now in use for similar purposes'. After this rebuff, Hood seems to have abandoned any hope of becoming an inventor.

His literary interest continued unabated. His first modest contact with the world of letters came when he joined a 'private select Literary Society that "waited on Ladies and Gentlemen in their own houses" '. In his reminiscences, he gives an entertaining account of the transactions of this genteel body:

[1] Hood's birth certificate is in the Bodleian Library.

'Our Minerva, allegorically speaking, was a motley personage, in blue stockings, a flounced gown, Quaker cap, and kerchief, French flowers and a man's hat. She held a fan in one hand, and a blow-pipe in the other. Her votaries were of both sexes, old and young, married and single, assenters, dissenters, High Church, Low Church, No Church; Doctors in Physics and Apothecaries in Metaphysics, dabblers in Logic, Chemistry, Casuistry, Sophistry, Natural and Unnatural History, Phrenology, Geology, Conchology, Demonology; in short, all kinds of Colledgy-Knowledgy-Ology, including "Cakeology" and tea and coffee. Like other Societies, we had one President—a sort of Speaker who never spoke, at least within my experience he never unbosomed himself of anything but a portentous shirt frill. According to the usual order of the entertainment, there was—first, Tea and Small Talk; secondly, an original Essay, which should have been followed, thirdly, by a discussion, or Great Talk; but nine times in ten, it chanced, or rather mumchanced, that between those who did not know what to think, and others, who did not know how to deliver what they thought, there ensued a dead silence, so "very dead indeed" as Apollo Belvi says, that it seemed buried into the bargain. To make this awkward pause more awkward, some misgiving voice, between a whisper and a croak, would stammer out some allusion to a Quakers' Meeting, answered from left to right by a running titter, the speaker having innocently, or perhaps wilfully, forgotten, that one or two friends in the drab coats, and as many in slate-coloured gowns, were sitting, thumb-twiddling, in the circle.'

'Dove grey Quakers', in fact, seem to have been fairly numerous in the Society; one meeting night, 'in escorting a female Fellow towards her home, she suddenly stopped me, taking advantage perhaps of the awful locality and its associations, just in front of our chief criminal prison, and looking directly in my face, by the light of a Newgate lamp, enquired somewhat abruptly, "Mr. Hood! are you not an infidel?" ' Infidel or not, Hood took the Islington group considerably less seriously than did most of his fellow-members; at the same time he enjoyed his association with this odd circle, and found that writing pieces for their evenings gave him valuable literary experience. He told Rollo in a letter of early 1821, 'I continue to receive much pleasure from our literary society, and from my own pursuits in that way. . . . My last is a mock heroic love tale of 600 lines, with notes critical and explanatory, which I lately finished after many intervals, independent of two poetical addresses to the society on closing and opening a fresh session, with various pieces, chiefly amatory. The society only costs me a page or two once in three months or so, but I join in their discussions every fortnight if able.'

The poetical addresses Hood mentions were given to his son when preparing the *Memorials* by Mrs. Hannah Lawrance, a member of the circle, who later gained some repute as the author of *Historical Memoirs of the Queens of England* (1838–40). The first was reworked by Hood into 'The Departure of Summer' and published in the *London Magazine*. Both are facile doggerel efforts, but already Hood's talent for punning animates lines like these:

> Now Winter joins a graver set,
> Just met—perchance as we are met
> In close divan—but not their parts,
> So gravely ask if trumps be hearts?
> Or hearts be trumps? spades, diamonds, clubs,
> Or mourning fickle Fortune's rubs,
> Sitting so wistfully and mute,
> To trump, revoke or follow suit.
> 'Tis theirs to speak of better things
> Than e'en Court Honours, Knaves, and Kings—
> Which, with the odd trick and the stake,
> And all the rest, the Deuce may take.

Two portions of the second poem, 'Address to the Social Literary Society, July 1820', are of special interest. The first, which leads out of Hood's discussion of the Englishman abroad, reveals the prejudice he shared with most Englishmen of the time against the Catholic Church, an element that recurs throughout his writings. In France, he says,

> Here Folly has its day, and Fashion rules,
> The potent sovereign—the Pope of Fools,
> That can its many votaries control,
> Like Pius' great self from head to sole,
> Can place them Purgatory's pains within,
> And grant indulgences—and sanction sin!

The lines that follow these look forward directly to such poems of social protest as 'The Song of the Shirt', written many years later, and often said to have been prompted by his mature experience. At twenty-one, however, in a largely frivolous address to his little literary circle, he is already expressing an awareness of social misery that, despite the debt to Goldsmith, clearly has roots in his native sensibility:

> Yet, oh! that these would ne'er forget the lot,
> The want and woe in many a British cot,
> Where manly hearts distil the big, round, tear,
> And bleed, in silence, like the stricken deer.
> Shall gay, ungallèd hearts go bounding by,
> And heedless Wealth its patronage deny?
> Sweep on, sweep on, ye citizens, nor look
> On overflowing hearts, that swell the brook.
> Seek other homes, on other pastures range,
> And say, that Tyranny provoked the change,
> Go, make your coward infamy your boast,
> And fly, when Patriots are wanted most!

The literary circle seems to have continued during 1822 and 1823, before fading quietly away, as such groups have a habit of doing; but by the time of its demise Hood was fully engaged in journalism and attended meetings only occasionally, perhaps dropping out completely before the body died. The addresses, essays and poems written for the Society were not his only literary efforts at the time. We have already seen that he had composed a lengthy 'mock heroic love tale', and in the same letter announcing this to Rollo (January–February, 1821), he says, 'I find that I shall not be able to send my poems to you for some time, as they are in the hands of an intelligent bookseller, a friend of mine, who wishes to look them over. He says they are worth publishing, but I doubt very much if he would give me any proof of his opinion, or I should indulge in the hope of sending them to you in a more durable shape.'

A few months later, on June 17, 1821, he told Rollo, 'I begin to have hopes that what I have scribbled in verse will make its appearance in a little volume, and, should that be decided on, I shall necessarily have a great addition to my occupation in arranging, correcting, &c, &c, but I expect that they will, in that case, be out by Christmas.' However, the projected volume never appeared, and we can only guess at the nature of its contents. It may be that some of the material was to make its appearance later in his first serious volume, for Hood was economical of his own work; it seems likely, too, that the poems were serious rather than light ones, since, despite his liking for practical jokes and his high spirits, the young Hood was a sober-minded man, very serious indeed about literature, and silent and solemn in company.

In July of the same year, Elizabeth Hood died, a severe blow to Thomas, who had always been close to his mother, and had become even more deeply attached to her since his father died. He now assumed full charge of his four sisters, and became their sole support. He confided to Rollo in October: 'I have sustained a very severe and irreparable loss in the death of my dear mother, about three months since, by which event a serious charge has devolved upon me; and I have all the concern of a household and family of four sisters—a charge which can never be a light one. I have suffered an inexpressible anguish of mind in parting with my only parent, and but for the consolations which I have had I should have sunk under it.'

His well-known poem 'The Deathbed' may have been prompted by his mother's death:

> We watch'd her breathing through the night,
> Her breathing soft and low,
> As in her breast the wave of life
> Kept heaving to and fro.

> So silently we seem'd to speak,
> So slowly moved about,
> As we had lent her half our powers
> To eke her living out!

> Our very hopes belied our fears,
> Our fears our hopes belied—
> We thought her dying when she slept,
> And sleeping when she died!

> For when the morn came dim and sad—
> And chill with early showers,
> Her quiet eyelids closed—she had
> Another morn than ours!

It is commonly believed, on the assertion of Tom Hood in the

Memorials, that this poem was composed on the death of Hood's sister, Ann, allegedly a month or two later, but there is evidence that Ann was living some years afterwards.[1]

Among the 'consolations' Hood mentioned to Rollo, one of the strongest, undoubtedly, was his obtaining a position on the staff of the *London Magazine* a month or two before his mother's death. He announced to Rollo, 'Perhaps you will ask what I am doing. Why, truly, I am T. Hood, *scripsit et sculpsit.* . . . I am engraving and writing prose and poetry by turns. I have some papers coming forth in next month's *London Magazine*, signed incog. and in the meantime I am busy extending and correcting my long poem and other pieces—perhaps for publication. I have a good deal to do now—more than ever.' This was the turning point of Hood's life. At twenty-two he found himself plunged into the world of letters and in contact with some of the leading writers of his day. He was, as the letters already quoted show, mad to publish. The association with the *London Magazine* marked the virtual abandonment of his first craft, engraving, as a means of livelihood, for journalism and literature. 'It would be affectation to say that engraving was resigned with regret. There is always something mechanical about the art—moreover it is as unwholesome as wearisome to sit copper-fastened to a board, with a cantle scooped out to accommodate your stomach, if you have one, painfully ruling, ruling and still ruling lines straight or crooked, by the long hundred to the square inch, at the doubly hazardous risk which Wordsworth so deprecates of "growing double".' When he was offered a job, humble though it was, on the *London*, he jumped at it 'à la Grimaldi, head foremost', he recalled, 'and was speedily behind the scenes'. In the new environment, his literary gifts flowered under the stimulus of the talented men the magazine numbered among its contributors. It was an exciting apprenticeship.

The *London Magazine* Hood knew was one of the three finest periodicals of its time, in a period when competition among such publications was stern. Its tone and its high standard of material had been set by the original editor, John Scott, who, beginning his task towards the end of 1819, had, in just over

---

[1] J. M. Cohen: 'Thomas Hood: The Language of Poetry', *Times Literary Supplement*, Sept. 19, 1952, pp. 605–6.

a year, made it a formidable rival to *Blackwood's* and the *Edinburgh*. Scott's previous experience as editor of *The Champion* had brought him into touch with many of the best writers of the time, and he was able not only to draw upon these for the *London*, but also to encourage the talents of such men as William Hazlitt, whom he secured as dramatic critic and later as contributor of *Table Talk*, and Charles Lamb in his role as 'Elia'. Other noted contributors to the *London* under Scott were Horace Smith, Peter George Patmore, Allan Cunningham, John Hamilton Reynolds, and T. G. Wainewright. Scott's own features, notably the 'Living Authors' assessments, with their acute considerations of Keats, Clare, Shelley and others, did as much as anything else to establish the prestige of the journal.

Unfortunately, Scott's scorn for *Blackwood's*, and especially for John Gibson Lockhart's vituperations, tempted him into attacks upon the paper and its editor which resulted in the scandalous duel in February, 1821, between Scott, assisted by P. G. Patmore as second, and J. H. Christie, a friend of Lockhart. Scott was wounded, and died on February 27, at the height of his esteem as an editor and a critic. The proprietors of the *London*, Messrs. Baldwin, Cradock and Joy, were in a fix. They asked Hazlitt to take over the editorship, but he declined, so they carried on the paper listlessly themselves for some months and then sold it to John Taylor and James Augustus Hessey in July, 1821.

Taylor, who came originally from Retford, had worked early in his career for the firm of Vernor and Hood, and, in 1806, had joined with James Hessey in a publishing and bookselling business at 93 Fleet Street. When the partners took over the *London Magazine*, they were well established as successful publishers of high-quality literature. The dark, handsome Taylor was in many ways a difficult customer, who was unusually sensitive to criticism and quarrelled with more than one of his authors—Hazlitt, Lamb and De Quincey among them. Yet he was an affable enough editor, and he had exceptionally keen taste and sound judgment as a publisher, issuing, for instance, the poems of Keats and Clare in defiance of warnings from others in the trade. Hessey, a less dynamic person, easily amiable, always wearing a black coat, and equally fond of the ladies and of music, earned from Keats the nickname of 'Mistessy' for his rather colourless personality.

Taylor, who, whatever his faults, had no fear of hard work, decided to edit the *London* himself, in addition to running the firm's bookshop in Fleet Street and the branches in Waterloo Place and at Bath. While looking around for an assistant to help with the chores of proof-reading and correspondence, he thought of the son of his former employer, whom he remembered with affection. In fact, a year earlier, in August, 1820, the idea had crossed his mind of taking Thomas Hood into the firm, for, after having the young man to dinner, he wrote to the elder Mr. Taylor in Retford, 'His talents are very good and he has written some clever things in prose and verse. It occurred to me that his help would relieve me of a good deal of the drudgery of revising MS. etc., and when Hessey returns I will have some talk about it.' This particular suggestion was not followed up, but with the new burden of the *London* on his back, Taylor returned to his original idea and offered a job on the journal to Hood, who eagerly accepted it. The position was no exalted one; Hood himself called it 'a sort of sub-Editor'. Taylor's description was rather less dignified: 'Mr. Hood was engaged to assist the editor in correcting the press, and in looking over papers sent for insertion.' In short his function seems to have been something between that of a proof-reader and assistant sub-editor. But, in addition, he became one of the *London's* most regular contributors, and acquired a taste for seeing his work in print.

John Scott had begun a feature called 'The Lion's Head', which consisted of humorous notes on contributions submitted and replies to correspondents. Hood took this over with relish and poured out brief comments on real and imaginary contributions, which look forward to his future role as punster and professional funny-man. Here are a few of his replies:

We suspect H. B.'s 'Sonnet to the Rising Sun' was written for a lark.

'Lines to Boreas' go rather 'too near the wind'.

The 'Essay on Agricultural Distress' would only increase it.

'The Echo', we fear, will not answer.

M.'s Ode on the Martyrs who were burnt in the *rain* of Queen Mary is original, but wants fire.

Colin has sent us a Summer Pastoral, and says he can supply us with one every month. Has he always got sheep in his *pen*?

We look for very light articles from anonymous contributors who forget to pay the postage.

T. says his tale is out of his own head. Is he a tadpole?

Between July, 1821, and June, 1823, Hood published some thirty pieces in verse and prose in the *London*. Nearly all of these show a considerable advance on the limp couplets of his adolescence; many have a delicacy of tone, others a verbal agility that promise even better work to come. Among his serious contributions were 'Lycus the Centaur', 'The Two Peacocks of Bedfont', 'Fair Ines' (January, 1823), perhaps his most charming lyric, 'Ode: Autumn', echoing Keats, and 'Hymn to the Sun', while his 'Ode to Dr. Kitchener' (November, 1821) was the first of those comic poems which were to launch him into the world of 'bound authors' and 'Faithless Sally Brown' (March, 1822) is a comic ballad in his own individual style, which he himself never bettered.

I intend to discuss these poems later; at the moment, it is interesting to reflect that Hood, in his early twenties, and, on his first series of appearances in print, had already evolved the several styles and hit upon the main types of subject he was later to employ regularly. As the years go by, there is an enhancement of his facility and continually fresh invention; but in a sense Hood developed comparatively little as a poet, and even the melancholy and macabre notes which mark his later work so strongly sound clearly in early poems like 'Lycus the Centaur' and 'Fair Ines'. This remarkable outpouring of mature work from a young man of twenty-three was undoubtedly prompted by the opportunities Hood now had of seeing himself in print and by the stimulating contacts he had with the gifted personalities of the *London Magazine*.

He was in his element. 'Not content with taking articles, like candidates for holy orders—with rejecting articles like the Belgians—I dreamt articles, thought articles, wrote articles, which were all inserted by the editor, of course, with the concurrence of his deputy. The more irksome parts of authorship, such as the correction of the press, were to me labours of love.'

When penning his reminiscences, he remembered with special affection the *London's* monthly dinners at Fleet Street, at which he mingled on terms of intimacy with the magazine's contributors. His description of one such dinner, almost certainly a composite one, contains vivacious word-pictures of some of them: 'On the right hand of the editor sits Elia, of the pleasant smile, and the quick eyes—Procter said of them that "they looked as if they could pick up pins and needles"—and a wit as quick as his eyes, and sure, as Hazlitt described, to stammer out the best pun and the best remark in the course of the evening. Next to him, shining verdantly out from the grave-coloured suits of the literati, like a patch of turnips amidst stubble and fallow, behold our Jack i' the Green—John Clare! In his bright, grass-coloured coat, and yellow waistcoat (there are greenish stalks, too, under the table), he looks a very cowslip, and blooms amongst us as Goldsmith must have done in his peach-blossom. . . . Little wonder, either, that in wending homewards on the same occasion through the Strand, the Peasant and Elia, *Sylvanus et Urban*, linked comfortably together; there arose the frequent cry of "Look at Tom and Jerry!" for truly, Clare in his square-cut green coat, and Lamb in his black, were not a little suggestive of Hawthorn and Logic in the plates to "Life in London". . . .

'The Brobdingnagian next to Clare, overtopping him by the whole head and shoulders—a physical "Colossus of Literature" the grenadier of our corps—is Allan, not Allan Ramsay "no, nor Barbara Allan neither", but Allan Cunningham. . . . He is often called "honest Allan", to distinguish him, perhaps, from one Allan-a-Dale, who was apt to mistake his neighbour's goods for his own—sometimes, between ourselves, yclept the "C. of Solway", in allusion to that favourite "Allan Water", the Solway Sea. There is something of the true, moody poetical weather observable in the barometer of his face, alternating from Variable to Showery, from Showery to Set Fair. At times he looks gloomy and earnest and traditional—a little like a Covenanter—but he suddenly clears up and laughs a hearty laugh that lifts him an inch or two from his chair, for he rises at a joke when he sees one like a trout at a fly, and finishes with a smart rubbing of his ample palms. . . .

'The Reverend personage on the Editor's right, with the

studious brow, deep-set eyes, and bald crown, is the mild and modest Cary—the same who turned Dante into Miltonic English blank verse. . . . Pity, shame and pity, such a Translator found no better translation in the Church! Is it possible that, in some no-popery panic, it was thought that by merely being Dragoman to Purgatory, he had *Romed* from the true faith?

'. . . Procter—alias Barry Cornwall . . . —the kindly Procter, one of the foremost to welcome me into the Brotherhood, with a too-flattering Dedication . . . is my own left-hand file. But what he says shall be kept as strictly confidential; for he is whispering it into my Martineau ear. On my other side, when I turn that way, I see a profile the shadow of which ever confronts me on opening my writing-desk, a sketch taken from memory, the day after seeing the original.'

This was Thomas De Quincey, whom Hood describes as 'almost boyish', partly from 'a peculiar delicacy of complexion and smallness of features'. 'There is speculation in the eyes,' he goes on, 'a curl of the lip, and a general character in the outline, that reminds one of some portraits of Voltaire. And a Philosopher he is every inch. He looks, thinks, talks and walks, eats and drinks, and no doubt sleeps philosophically—*i.e.* deliberately. There is nothing abrupt about his motions—he goes and comes calmly and quietly—like the phantom in Hazlitt, he is here—he is there—he is gone! He speaks slowly, clearly, and with very marked emphasis— . . . the tide of talk flows like Denham's river, "strong without rage, without over-flowing, full".'

At this dinner, and at many others, there was also a young man who was to become Hood's collaborator and close friend, John Hamilton Reynolds. 'That smart, active person opposite with a game-cock-looking head, and the hair combed smooth, fighter fashion over his forehead—with one finger hooked round a glass of champagne, not that he requires it to inspirit him, for his wit bubbles up of itself—is our Edward Herbert. . . . He is "good with both hands", like that nonpareil Randall, at a comic verse or a serious stanza—smart at a repartee—sharp at a retort—and not averse to a bit of mischief. 'Twas he who gave the runaway ring at Wordsworth's Peter Bell. Generally, his jests, set off by a happy manner, are only ticklesome, but now and then they are sharp-flavoured—like the sharpness of the pineapple. Would I could give you a sample. Alas! What a pity it is that so many good things uttered by Poets, and Wits, and Humorists, at chance times—and they are always the best and brightest, like sparks struck out by Pegasus' own hoof, in a curvet amongst the flints—should be daily and hourly lost for want of a recorder!'

Such is Hood's recollection of the happy days of the *London* and of his initiation into the company of the illustrious. But, in point of fact, the magazine never really recovered from Scott's death. After a brief, brilliant period in which it outdid all its contemporaries, Taylor's inadequacy as a successor to Scott became plain. He lacked his predecessor's flair, he devoted only part of his time to the journal, and his tactless, not to say high-handed, treatment of several of the contributors, led to increasing dissatisfaction. John Clare, among others, complained of manuscripts altered and other irritations. In 1823, Lamb murmured, 'The *London*, I fear, falls off,' and, more loudly, in February, 1825, 'The second number is all trash. What are Taylor and Hessey at? Why did poor Scott die?' By that time, he had transferred his allegiance to the *New Monthly*, which was rising to usurp the *London's* place. Hazlitt also withdrew, as did Procter, and other writers who had helped the *London* gain its ascendency.

Early in 1825, Taylor, seeing the writing on the wall, passed the editorship over to Henry Southern, and in May sold him the firm's interest in the paper. Southern struggled on as editor, but the *London* was now 'whip syllabub, thin sown with aught of profit or delight'. It went into a steady decline that ended with its absorption into the *New Monthly Magazine* in 1829. 'Arrah, honey, why did you die?' lamented Hood. 'Had you not an editor, and elegant prose writers, and beautiful poets, and broths of boys for criticism and classics, and wits and humorists? . . . Hadn't you Lion's Heads with Traditional Tales? Hadn't you an Opium-Eater, and a Dwarf, and a Giant, and a Learned Lamb, and a Green Man? . . . Arrah, why did you die?'

Certainly, Taylor and Hessey were not conscious of their being in any way to blame for the *London's* falling off. In fact, Taylor felt that he had been let down by his contributors.

Writing to Hessey in 1826, after their partnership had been dissolved, he complained, 'The Loss of the London Magazine cut the String that tied us together, then I found that what was called Friendship was nothing but Self-Interest. Darley and Cunningham and Lamb are almost all I see now.' Nevertheless many of the *London* circle, like Hood, looked back on the days of Scott and Taylor with nostalgic affection. J. H. Reynolds, writing to Taylor in October, 1837, said, 'What days—*were* the days of the London!—I "try back" as the Huntsman says—over the hours of Early—Hood—Earnest—Hessey—bleak Dr. Darling—twinkling Clare—"tipsy-joy and jollity"—Lamb—Drear—Carey—Long-*taled* Cunningham—and beautiful Mrs. Jones!—Where are all?—or most of them?' Hessey writing to Taylor in 1858, when both had outlived most of their contributors, said, 'I was very sorry that both Hood and Reynolds left us so entirely, especially Reynolds, after the great intimacy that had so long existed between us. I don't think either you or I intentionally gave any cause for it, and I am sure they both were under great obligation to us.'

Be that as it may, Hood began to drift away from the journal in the early days of its decline. His last contribution as an employee appeared in June, 1823, but he may well have continued in his sub-editorial capacity after this. The appearance in January, 1825, of 'Ode to George Colman the Younger' in a vein similar to that of his first published book, *Odes and Addresses to Great People*, suggests that he remained an occasional contributor after he had ceased to be in Taylor and Hessey's employ.

Relations can hardly have been cordial between Hood and the firm at the time of the break, however, for in 1825, he wrote to his sisters-in-law from Hastings, 'In coming home I killed a viper in our serpentine path and Mrs. Fermor says I am by that token to overcome an enemy. Is Taylor or Hessey dead? The reptile was dark and dull, his blood being yet sluggish from the cold; howbeit, he tried to bite, till I cut him in two with a stone. I thought of Hessey's long backbone as I did it.' Even allowing for the kind of heightening to which Hood was prone, this comment is unexpectedly bitter, for the break does not seem to have been acrimonious. Hood was in the main a placid man, good-natured and unmalicious, but there were occasions—and this appears to have been one—on which he reacted with an unpredictable sharpness to some setback, although he never allowed such a happening to rankle over the years. We can only suspect that, at this time, he had reason to feel that Taylor and Hessey had let him down. Certainly, in later years, Hessey could write to Taylor, in 1860, thanking him for a copy of the first volume of the *Memorials* of Hood by his children, 'I did rather hope to receive one from the Editors, as one of his earliest friends, and I should have valued it exceedingly as the memorial of a man whom I sincerely regarded.' Although the lapse of thirty-five years may have softened the memory of differences, this remark hardly suggests that anything of great moment led to Hood's resignation from the *London*. But it is Hessey, not Taylor, who is speaking.

One contributor to the *London* in its heyday, who was to achieve an unenviable reputation in fields other than literary ones, was T. G. Wainewright ('Janus Weathercock'), artist, and art-critic for the magazine from 1820 to 1823, who was later transported to Australia for his poisonings and forgeries. Wainewright, for all his crimes, was a shrewd critic, and he quite early recognized Hood's gifts. In one of the several rallying addresses which 'Janus Weathercock' contributed to the *London*, there is an interesting, if partly facetious, estimate of Hood's powers. The article, dated January, 1823, is called 'Janus Weatherbound, or the Weathercock steadfast for lack of oil', and is a mock farewell to the journal. In the course of it, Hood is apostrophized as 'Theodore', a nickname that stuck to him throughout his life, and whose origin is obscure, although it may have arisen from the frequent confusion of the initials 'T. H.' with those of Theodore Hook, the contemporary wag, punster, entertainer, and practical joker.

'Young Theodore!' writes Wainewright. 'Young in years, not in power! Our new Ovid!—only more imaginative!—Painter to the visible eye—and the inward;—commixture of, what the superficial deem, incongruous elements!—Instructive living proof, how close lie the founts of laughter and tears! Thou fermenting brain—oppressed, as yet, by its own riches! . . . Though melancholy would seem to have touched thy heart with her painful (salutary) hand, yet is thy fancy mercurial—undepressed;—and sparkles and crackles more from the contact—as the northern lights when they near the frozen pole. Still is "Lycus" without mate?—Who can mate him but thyself? Let not the shallow induce thee to conceal thy depth ... leave "*Old Seamen*"—the strain thou held'st was of a higher mood; there are others for your "Sketches *from* Nature" (as they truly call 'em)—*******—and such small deer! As for thy word-gambols, thy humour, thy fantasies, thy curiously conceited perception of similarity in dissimilarity, of coherents in incoherents, they are brilliantly suave, most innocuously exhilarating:—but not a step further, if thou lovest thy proper peace!'

Despite Wainewright's warning, it was the word-gambols that did, in fact, become Hood's chief concern, largely from sheer necessity. But even allowing for the jesting extravagance of Wainewright's comments, it is a measure of the mark Hood had made in distinguished company that, without publishing a single book, he should have been recognized as having already accomplished work of value in more than one vein, and of having in him the capacity for development in more than one direction.

Hood gained useful experience on the *London Magazine*: he made first-hand acquaintance with the hurly-burly of the capital's journalism; he learnt many of the tricks of successful periodical writing; he acquired the editorial skills and sensitivity to public taste that later made him a more than competent editor. But the chief personal gain the *London* provided was the friendship of two of its contributors—Charles Lamb and John Hamilton Reynolds.

That between Hood and Lamb was based upon an attraction between likenesses. Both men were alike in their literary gifts and in their personalities. Lamb was the more urbane and sophisticated and the better educated, while Hood, who had a nervous energy in place of Lamb's charm, owned a less refined sensibility. Yet they had much in common. Both were fundamentally serious and charitable men, who at the same time were conspicuous for their joy in life and sense of fun; both were men of sentiment and of a playful fancy; both were punsters of unflagging inventiveness; both, too, faced lives shot through with pain and tragedy with tireless optimism and high spirits—Lamb, under the heavy burden of his insane sister, Mary, Hood weighed down by his endless ills and nagging poverty. It is no wonder that each was drawn to the other, and that a warm friendship should have developed between them.

When they first met, Lamb, twenty-four years older than Hood, had a firm reputation among the discerning as a zealous advocate of the merits of Elizabethan and Jacobean drama, and was becoming more widely known for his 'Elia' essays in the *London*. The younger man had learned to admire Lamb's work, and in his first full-length essay for the *London*, 'Sentimental Journey from Islington to Waterloo Bridge', he had mixed with the overt parody of Sterne more than a little of the manner of 'Elia'.

In his reminiscences, Hood describes the initial encounter of the two, which took place probably in the summer of 1821, in the offices of the *London*: 'I was sitting one morning beside our Editor, busily correcting proofs, when a visitor was announced. . . . The door opened, and in came a stranger—a figure remarkable at a glance, with a fine head, on a small, spare body, supported by two almost immaterial legs. He was clothed in sables, of a bygone fashion, but there was something wanting, or something present about him, that certified he was neither a divine, nor a physician, nor a schoolmaster: from a certain neatness and sobriety in his dress, coupled with his sedate bearing, he might have been taken, but that such a costume would be anomalous, for a *Quaker* in black. He looked still more like (what he really was) a literary Modern Antique, a New-Old Author, a living Anachronism, contemporary at once with Burton the Elder, and Colman the Younger. Meanwhile he advanced with rather a peculiar gait, his walk was plantigrade, and with a cheerful "How d'ye", and one of the blandest, sweetest smiles that ever brightened a manly countenance, held out two fingers to the Editor.'

While Lamb and Taylor talked, young Hood carefully scrutinized the face of the visitor. 'It was a striking intellectual face, full of wry lines, physiognomical quips and cranks, that gave it great character. There was such earnestness about the brows, and a deal of speculation in the eyes, which were brown and bright, and "quick in turning"; the nose, a decided one, though of no established order; and there was a handsome smartness about the mouth. . . . In short, his face was as original as his figure; his figure as his character, his character as his writings; his writings the most original of the age.'

Lamb's natural shyness set some barriers in the way of Hood's attempts to improve the acquaintance. As Hood himself said, 'despite a desperate attempt on my part to attract his notice' at the *London* dinners, the contact remained for a time superficial. But the young man saw another chance to win Lamb's friendship when the latter's 'Complaint of the Decay of Beggars' appeared in the *London* for June, 1822. He wrote a letter of thanks to Lamb 'on coarse paper and in ragged English as if from one of his mendicant clients'. But, despite the inspiration of the joke, Lamb made no response.

'I had given up all hope', wrote Hood, referring to some time later, possibly in the summer of 1823, after both men had severed their connection with the *London*, 'when one night sitting sick and sad, in my bedroom, racked with the rheumatism, the door was suddenly opened, the well-known quaint figure in black walked in without any formality, and with a cheerful "Well, boy, how are you?" and the bland sweet smile, extended the two fingers. They were eagerly clutched, of course, and from that hour we were firm friends.'

Hood learned from his visitor that the Lambs had become his near neighbours, having moved a few weeks before to Colebrooke Cottage, in Colebrooke Row, Islington, which was only a few minutes' walk from Hood's own home in 5 Lower Street. The propinquity, and Lamb's new confidence as a householder, prompted the visit. A few days later, Lamb called again on his young friend, and asked him to come to take tea and meet Wordsworth. Hood was delighted to accept, and so began the first of many visits to Colebrooke Cottage, 'A House of Call for All Denominations', with a door that opened as frankly as its master's heart.

The first visit was a little disappointing, perhaps, not because of Lamb but because of his guest. 'Beside the fire,' Hood remembered, 'sate Wordsworth, and his sister, the hospitable Elia, and the excellent Bridget. As for the bard of Rydal, his outward man did not, perhaps, disappoint one; but the *palaver*, as the Indians say, fell short of my tanticipaions. Perhaps my memory is at fault; 'twas many years ago, and, unlike the biographer of Johnson, I have never made Bozziness my business. However, excepting a discussion on the value of the promissory notes issued by our younger poets, wherein Wordsworth named Shelley and Lamb took John Keats for choice, there was nothing of literary interest brought upon the carpet. But a book man cannot always be bookish. . . . It is a "Vulgar Error" to suppose that an author must always be authoring, even with his feet on the fender.'

For the nearly four years during which the two men were neighbours, Hood had the freedom of the Lambs' home, where he met many important writers, among whom Coleridge stood out most brightly in his memory: 'What a contrast to Lamb was the full-bodied Poet, with his waving white hair, and his face round, ruddy and unfurrowed as a holy Friar's! Apropos to which face he gave us a humorous description of an unfinished portrait, that served him for a sort of barometer, to indicate the state of his popularity. So sure as his name made any temporary stir, out came the canvas on the easel, and a request from the artist for another sitting; down sank the Original in the public notice, and back went the copy into a corner, till some fresh publication or accident brought forward the Poet; and then forth came the picture for a few more touches. I sincerely hope it has been finished! What a benign, smiling face it was! What a model, methought, as I watched and admired the "Old Man eloquent", for a Christian bishop! But he was, perhaps, scarely orthodox enough to be trusted with a mitre! At least some of his voluntaries would have frightened a common everyday congregation from their propriety. . . .

'After dinner he got up, and began pacing to and fro, with his hand behind his back, talking and walking, as Lamb laughingly hinted, as if qualifying for an itinerant preacher. . . . With his fine, flowing voice, it was glorious music of the "never-ending, still-beginning" kind, and you did not wish it to end. It was rare flying, as in the Nassau Balloon; you knew not whither, nor did you care. Like his own bright-eyed Marinere, he had a spell in his voice that would not let you go. To attempt to describe my own feeling afterward, I had been carried, spiralling, up to heaven by a whirlwind intertwisted with sunbeams, giddy and dazzled, but not displeased, and had then been rained down again in a shower of mundane sticks and stones that battered out of me all recollection of what I had heard, and what I had seen!'

Lamb enjoyed Hood's company as much as Hood did that of his 'literary father'; and his respect for Hood's talents grew with the years. To Bernard Barton, the Quaker poet, he wrote: 'What a fertile genius (and a quiet good soul withal) is Hood. . . . You'll like him much,' and to C. K. Ollier: 'My head is very queerish and indisposed for much company; but we will get Hood, that half Hogarth, to meet you.' The description, 'that half Hogarth' was inspired by one of Hood's etchings, 'The Progress of Cant', published at the end of 1825, and highly praised by Lamb in the *New Monthly Magazine* for February, 1826. He may also have written the description of the etching for the previous month's *London*, which contains the words: 'We can fearlessly say, that we know of no production so nearly approaching to the admirable works of Hogarth, in their forcible delineations of nature, and their comic and pungent satire, as this etching of "The Progress of Cant".' When Lamb gave his friendship, he gave it in generous measure.

III

Marriage and Literary Beginnings

WHILE Hood's acquaintance with Lamb was ripening, his friendship with the mercurial John Hamilton Reynolds was developing even more rapidly. Reynolds, who began writing for the *London Magazine* in 1821 as 'Edward Herbert', met Hood through the journal, and the two men quickly became intimates. It was Reynolds who, seemingly, inspired Hood's first attempts at comic verse. In a *London* article, Hood tells how, hearing Reynolds set the table vibrating with mirth at some humorous verses while dining with him at a friend's house, he tried himself at home that evening to imitate Reynolds's style. But his own verses, read later at the same table, provoked only meek and melancholy smiles. 'I learned,' says Hood, 'what I should have known before—that we have more chance of our own than of another man's originality.'

There can, therefore, be little truth in the suggestion that Hood modelled his comic poetry on that of Reynolds, at least after this initial failure. In any case, Reynolds's subsequent career and accomplishments lend no support to this notion. But it is clear that Hood's friendship with Reynolds did affect him in several important ways—it inspired him with a love for the poetry of Keats, who formed the most potent influence on his own serious poems, it encouraged him to branch out into a form of light verse that he practised for the rest of his life, and it introduced him to his beloved wife, Jane, John Hamilton's sister.

The Reynoldses, who played so important a part in the life of Keats, lived in Little Britain, near Christ's Hospital, where the father, George H. Reynolds, was head writing-master. John

Hamilton and his four sisters, Jane, Marianne, Eliza (later Mrs. Longmore) and Charlotte were all close friends of Keats, who found congenial companionship and early recognition of his genius at their home. In 1817, Reynolds wrote a sonnet to the young poet, beginning

> Thy thoughts, dear Keats, are like fresh-gathered leaves,
> Or white flowers plucked from some sweet lily bed,

and ending prophetically

> So shall thy music be ever in her May.
> And thy luxuriant spirit ever young.

References to the Reynolds family run in and out of Keats's letters and poetry. In a letter of October 31, 1817, he presented Jane, the eldest of the family, with the song, 'O Sorrow' from *Endymion*, then in process of composition, and he signed one of his letters to her and Marianne, 'Your affectionate Brother'. To John he addressed several poems, including the sonnet, 'O that a week could be an age', 'What the Thrush said', and his spirited 'Epistle—John Hamilton Reynolds'. The two men had, in fact, planned works in collaboration, among them a volume of metrical versions of Boccaccio, but Reynolds gave over that project after reading 'The Pot of Basil' which he urged Keats to publish, saying 'You ought to be alone'. He came vigorously to Keats's defence after the attacks in *Blackwood's* and the *Quarterly*, with a letter in *The Alfred, West of England Journal* for October, 1818, which attracted much attention when reprinted in the *Examiner*. Keats owed much to Reynolds and more than once acknowledged in his letters his debt to him as friend and adviser and his realization that the sage counsel of Reynolds had saved him from several errors of judgment.

A coolness developed later between Keats and the Reynolds sisters, chiefly over their attitude to Fanny Brawne. Perhaps Jane was a little in love with Keats herself, although his letters to her are those of a friend only, with touches of affectionate brotherly raillery. Certainly she and, to a lesser degree, Marianne, set themselves very strongly against Fanny. Jane wrote to Mrs. C. W. Dilke just before Keats set off for Rome. 'I sincerely hope it will benefit his health, poor fellow. His mind and spirits must be bettered by it; and absence may probably

weaken, if not break off, a connexion that has been a most unhappy one for him.' John Hamilton himself, affected perhaps
by the opinion of his sisters, asserted to Taylor on the same
occasion, 'Absence from the poor idle Thing of woman-kind, to
whom he has so unaccountably attached himself, will not be
an ill thing.' Keats reacted quickly and angrily to such evi-
dences of dislike on the part of the Reynoldses, whom he described to Fanny as 'these Laughers, who envy you for your
Beauty, who would have God-bless'd me from you for ever;
who were plying me with discouragements eternally'.

The death of Keats in 1821 prevented what would probably
have been a complete estrangement from the Reynolds sisters.
But the mutual dislike of Fanny and the family outlasted the
poet's death; the story is told of Fanny encountering John
Hamilton at a ball in 1827, while she was wearing a dress
decorated with bugles. 'It's good to wear bugles,' said Reynolds, 'and be heard wherever one goes.' 'And it's good to be a
brother-in-law of Tom Hood's,' replied Fanny, 'and get jokes
for nothing.'

Partisans of Fanny, such as Joanna Richardson and Marie
Adami, have placed much of the blame for the common critical
opinion of Fanny's character and intelligence on the freely
expressed disapproval of the Reynoldses. But it still has to be
proved that they were wholly wrong or that their distrust of the
young girl was inspired by anything other than a genuine
concern for the poet's welfare. However, Keats thought otherwise, and his feelings for the Reynolds girls cooled off. He wrote
to his sister-in-law, Georgiana, in January, 1820, about a
'pianoforte hop' at the Dilkes: 'The Miss Reynolds and some of
their friends made a not very enticing row opposite us,' and
later in the same letter, 'The Miss Reynolds I am affraid [*sic*]
to speak to for fear of some sickly reiteration of Phrase or Sentiment. When they were at the dance the other night I tried
manfully to sit near and talk to them, but to no purpose, and if
I had't would have been to no purpose still. My question or
observation must have been an old one, and their rejoinder
very antique indeed.' At the same time, his relations with John
Hamilton remained cordial; for his last letter to him in the
following month, when Reynolds was leaving for the Continent,
is extremely friendly, 'If I had been well enough,' he writes, 'I

should have liked to cross the water with you.' Reynolds, who by that time had become a lawyer and entered into partnership, in 1817, with James Rice, the kindly, witty, glib-tongued friend of Keats, remained the Keats family solicitor.

Thus, when Thomas Hood came to know the Reynoldses, he entered a circle saturated with the memory of Keats, and one in which the poet and his work were held in the highest esteem. He was already an admirer of Keats before meeting John Hamilton, and had essayed some poems in Keats's manner, but the contact with the family which brought the poet alive for him, deepened his love and appreciation. It is extremely unlikely that Hood met Keats in the flesh. As there is no record or hint of such a meeting, Keats had probably gone abroad before Thomas and John Hamilton became acquainted.

When the latter met, Reynolds was twenty-seven, five years Hood's senior. He had been a clerk in the Amicable Insurance Company before taking up law, but, in his young days, his whole heart, like that of Keats, was devoted to poetry. He possessed an agile, witty mind, a quick tongue and an eager sensibility, and had already given earnest of burgeoning talent in his publications—*Safie,* an Eastern tale in imitation of Byron, published before he was twenty, *The Eden of the Imagination,* on which the evident influence of Wordsworth is not strong enough to hide a personal vision, *The Naiad,* published in 1816 by Taylor and Hessey and thus starting his connection with that firm, the famous 'ante-natal *Peter Bell*', that clever parody which came out before Wordsworth's own poem saw print, *The Fancy* (1820) and his most considerable volume, *The Garden of Florence* (1821). His large and creditable body of youthful work led Leigh Hunt in an article in the *Examiner* for December 1, 1816, to couple him with Keats and Shelley as one of the most promising younger poets of the time.

Reynolds had also attracted notice by his critical articles on literature and drama in *The Champion* and as the author of *One, Two, Three, Four, Five,* a one-act musical entertainment in which the principal character appears in five different guises, and which John Reeve played with great success for some fifty performances at the English Opera in 1819. When he entered into his legal apprenticeship, Reynolds announced his abandonment of literature in a sonnet, 'Farewell to the Muses'; this he

wrote on the fly-leaf of the volume of Shakespeare he gave to
Keats, the same volume in which Keats inscribed his 'Bright
Star' sonnet. 'Sweet Farewell', wrote Reynolds, 'Be to the
Nymphs that on the old Hill dwell'; but this resolve had not
been kept by 1821, when he was a regular contributor to the
London, and was still turning out poems and theatrical enter-
tainments.

Hood, the shy, silentish young man, attracted by Reynolds's
wit and gaiety, and by his intimacy with Keats, was just a
little over-awed by the accomplishment and promise of the
older man, for whom the law remained a kind of elegant
pastime. Within a few weeks of meeting Reynolds, Hood had
become a regular visitor at Little Britain, and was quickly
accepted as a family friend. His own sister, Betsy, was keeping
house for him at Lower Street; his other sisters, Jessie, Kate and
Anne, were at some house or establishment at Brompton, and
visited him occasionally. Missing the warm atmosphere of a
true home, he speedily adopted the Reynoldses as his own
family. Here he found the sympathy and enfolding domesticity
a man of his temperament needed, together with a not too
demanding literary milieu that accorded with his own tastes.

Before long he had fallen deeply in love with Jane Reynolds,
who was seven years older than he, and became engaged to her,
with the blessing of her family. Hood's children, in the
Memorials, suggest that the marriage was opposed by the
Reynoldses, but this goes counter to the impression given by the
letters exchanged between Hood and his future mother-in-law
and sisters-in-law. Perhaps the Reynoldses did have some
slight reservations, which would be hardly surprising in view of
the indifferent health of Jane and the poor health of Thomas
himself and his seeming lack of solid prospects, but there is no
sign that these, at any time, hardened into opposition to the
match.

To Charlotte, then at Upwell visiting Eliza, her married
sister, he wrote soon afterwards, in October, 1822, an affectionate description of the household at Little Britain as it was in
her absence. It is characteristic of Hood's style at this time—a
little Lambish, but in its animation, unabashed cosiness and
sense of domestic fun, very much his own: 'I will draw you a
little picture—as I saw it on Monday evening in that Blue

Beard room of Little Britain, and so "tease you out of thought" about us and ours. You know the place—the folding doors—the tables, the two windows—the fire-place—the antique china tea-pots which if they were hearts, would break themselves for your absence—the sofa—and on it with her eyes like compressed stars, and her eloquent brows—but your father will tell you about those—and her mouth like somebody's you have never seen, and with her easy grace of manner which Jane will tell you of—and her smile which herself will show you—sits the unimaginable reality—the tantalizing mystery—the still-undiscovered Mrs. Reynolds—Mrs. John—John's wife—with a great thick misty veil between her and Upwell—which Jane is trying to fan away with a very circumstantial sheet of paper—but it won't do—you must still wish to see her, and then see her to your wish—as I have done——. Only look at John—what a talk he makes! With the horns of his mouth upwards like a fair moon—laughing like a fugleman to let off our laughters—and lo! that farce brown with the steel but—and then that—like a footman with—did you ever see such a—it is impossible to describe it. There—between me and the teapot—her cheek the very colour of content, and her eyes how earnest, sits Jane, the kindly Jane—hugging her own hands for very happiness—she one side of me—I beside myself—and on the other hand gentle maid Marianne, making good tea as if for Robin Hood and smiling as if her heart drank cream and sugar. How the tea dimples in the cup and the urn sings for joy! Now if you look through the urn you will see your father smiling towards the sofa, and there is Rice smiling towards nine o'clock. How slily the under half of his visage sneers at the upper gravity, as if his nose were Garrick between Tragedy and Comedy, and how his jests come stealing seriously out as if from his sleeve. There is Mrs. Buller with a face that Good Nature might borrow for a year's wear—and there are John Lincoln and William—"my friend" as it hath been said—— And there in the distance, looking blue as is usual with such objects, is Lotty in the background of Upwell;—peeping perhaps thro' a little opera glass that diminishes us to nothing. This is the picture that I saw on Monday at Little Britain—with all the drawing-room for its frame.'

'John's wife' mentioned in this letter is Eliza Drewe whom

John Hamilton Reynolds had married on August 31, 1822, while Mrs. Reynolds and Charlotte were in Norfolk. Hessey told John Clare: 'Reynolds is gone off to Exeter to be married, to-morrow is the happy day to witness the union of as interesting a couple as I ever met—a fine sensible high-spirited generous warm-hearted young fellow in the prime of youth and health and a pretty, intelligent, modest, interesting young girl as warmly attached to him as he is to her.' Hood wrote a mock programme of the wedding in the form of a State procession, beginning:

> People of Exeter with Banners.
> Glovers.
> Honourable Company of Match Makers.
> Banner.
> Beadle with his Banner.
> Hymen and Amen with their Banners.
> 1st, 2nd and 3rd Times of Asking with their Axes.
> Page bearing the Matrimonial Yoke with the Milk of Human Kindness.
> The Happy Pair.

After this are listed several characters, some allegorical and some real, including members of the *London* circle and of the Reynolds family.

From 1821 to 1825, then, Thomas Hood was a familiar of the Reynolds household; several long, chatty letters exist that he wrote to Charlotte (Lottie) in Upwell, to Marianne and to his future mother-in-law. They are full of a brotherly friendliness and an ebullient gaiety, with just a touch of flirting; they reveal an attitude of mind that values domesticity and the homely pleasures above literature, of which there is scarcely a mention in the entire correspondence. At this time, Hood was, in fact, writing some of his best serious verse; but poetry was never for him the devouring experience it had been for the Romantics. Unlike Keats, he can pen lengthy epistles—he was always a voluminous letter-writer—in which there is barely the slightest hint that the correspondent is in the least concerned with any form of artistic expression.

Although we may be inclined to see this as indicating that Hood was not properly serious as a poet, there is, in all his letters, a human warmth and a spontaneous love for people that

55

is the source of most of what is fine in his poetry. His love for, and understanding of, children, for instance, comes out not only in the letters he wrote in later years to the children of Dr. Elliot and which have much of the intuitive sympathy with the fantasy world of the child shown in Lewis Carroll's letters, but also in such incidental comments as this, written in a letter to Charlotte towards the end of 1823, in reference to Eliza's baby: 'I feel much pleasure in sending her a little present, whilst she is so unconscious as she must be of the giver to show that my love is quite disinterested and looks for no return. Pray teach her to carry it in a genteel and ladylike manner—like her mother—or it may not be amiss to remind her of the carriage of her aunt in London—Miss Marianne Reynolds, mind and call her Miss Marianne, as it will give the little dear a feeling of her own importance, and say that she—her Aunt Marianne—never soils the pretty pink lining by thrusting into it mutton bones or whatever else she may happen to hold in her ivory fingers. . . . Pray also give her a kiss for me—but wipe her mouth first—though her mother will call me over nice for it—and then give her the muff—calling it pitty-pitty, or puss-puss, or some other such words adapted to her comprehension, or tickling her little nose with it or bopeeping her eyes—or a creep-mouse, creeping it as your own judgment shall think most expedient.—But I am growing Nurselike!—besides instructing you in your own business.'

For the Reynolds womenfolk he made verses as a gifted brother might. One of them, a sonnet to Marianne, who was in indifferent health, ends with a typical pun:

> The patient paleness of thy cheek so steals
> With more than chill of winter to my veins;
> And conscious sympathy of blood reveals
> The tender Brother-hood that now obtains.

Another, in much lighter vein, he put into the mouth of the elder Mrs. Reynolds, portraying her in the midst of domestic management. The character it reveals is of a hospitable, bustling woman, but one inclined to domineer and with a touch of the dragon about her:

> Mary, I believ'd you quick
> But you're as deaf as any beadle:
> See where you have left the plates,

You've an eye and so's a needle.
Why an't Anne behind the door,
Standing ready with her dishes?
No one ever had such maids,
Always thwarting all my wishes.
Marianne, set up that child,
And where's her pinafore—call Mary—
The frock I made her will be spoiled—
Now, Lizzie, don't be so contrary.
Hand round the bread—'Thank God for what?'
It's done to rags! How wrong of Ann now,—
The dumplings too are hard as lead,
And plates stone-cold—but that's her plan now—
Mary, a knock—now, Hood, take that
Or go without—Why, George, you're wanted,
Where is that Lottie? Call her down,
She knows there's no white wine decanted.
Put to the door, we always dine
In public.
Jane, take that cover off the greens;
Our earthenware they play the deuce to;
There's Mr. Green without a fork—
And I've no plate—but that I'm used to.

The somewhat fulsome tone of Hood's letters to Mrs. Reynolds, with their heavily guarded caution against saying the
wrong thing, suggest that he was a little in fear of her. In fact,
for all his cosy response to his adopted family, he seems at times
to have found the heavily matriarchal Reynolds household
rather stifling. This feeling just peeps through in his description
of the entry of the child of Eliza, who had married a Dr. Longmore of Upwell, into Little Britain, where, says Hood playfully,
she is likely to set at naught 'the awful brow of Marianne, the
muscular powers of Lottie, the serious remonstrances of Aunt
Jane, the maternal and grandmaternal authorities'. He was not
unaware, either, of the atmosphere of gossip and character-
mauling that seems to have been a feature of the Reynolds
household—the kind of thing that had alienated Keats; for he
writes in a letter to Charlotte while she was staying at Upwell:
'I really wonder what you do (when the Child is asleep) for by
this time you must have dissected us all, your friends here, into
atoms.'

Still, whatever may have been Mrs. Reynolds's reservations about having Thomas Hood as a son-in-law, and whatever may have been his own occasional sense of being smothered in a feather-bed of femininity, there can be no doubt of the real affection each party had for the other and of the real joy Hood derived from his intimacy with the society of Little Britain. Writing to Mrs. Reynolds in 1824 to congratulate her on the birth of a son to Eliza Longmore, he ends: 'Pray accept my love, which is large enough for a longer letter if time allowed me, and believe me how truly, my dear Mother, I am yours, and dear Lizzy's and dear Lotty's, affectionate Son and Brother —Theodore.'

His courtship of Jane proceeded apace, with occasional vacuous verses and a few letters written to her during their infrequent periods apart. On at least one occasion, in August, 1823, he accompanied her on a visit to the Longmores in Norfolk, to 'pick up a month's health in a fortnight' as he told his sister, Betsy. While there he visited Norwich with Dr. Longmore, who was summoned to the assizes, and in addition to attending a 'grand Charity Musical Festival' at the Cathedral, he spent some time sketching churches, houses and rectories. The trip did him some good—'Indeed I could pass a month of my life in my present way very willingly, and I think it would make my life a month longer, I eat, drink and sleep so well.'

But in the winter of 1823–4, he had a bad attack of fever, almost certainly the first bout of that recurrent rheumatic fever which was to ruin his health and cause his early death. This kept him in bed for several months, during which the Reynoldses were kind to him and his own sisters also rallied round. By the spring of 1824, he had recovered sufficiently to tell Jane: 'My Doctor has just gone and as usual we have had a long literary chat. He says I must expect to feel such days as this—and not to gain much strength till I get out of this room—and he has given me leave to go down the first fine day—I have hopes, after so much rain, that it will happen tomorrow— . . . Think of me, dear, cheerfully, and let us dream away the interval of each other. I know when that blessed hour comes, with the delight of clasping you again to my heart, I shall think that the pain of separation is all atoned for, and that you will try to make all possible amends for an increased affection if greater can be.'

To convalesce, Hood spent some of the summer of 1824 at Hastings, which he had learned to love and frequently visited in later years also. Probably it was Lamb's recommendation that first sent him to the coastal resort, for his friend wrote to him there in August a letter full of sight-seeing hints, advising him of the choice things to hunt out: 'You do not tell me of those romantic land bays that be as thou goest to Lovers' Seat; neither of that little churchling in the midst of a wood (in the opposite direction, nine furlongs from the town) that seems dropped by the Angel that was tired of carrying two packages; marry, with the other he made shift to pick his flight to Loretto. Inquire out and see my little Protestant Loretto. It stands apart from trace of human habitation; yet hath it pulpit, reading-desk, and trim front of massiest marble, as if Robinson Crusoe had reared it to soothe himself with old church-going images. I forget its Christian name—and what she-saint was its gossip.

'You should go also to No. 13 Stangate Street—a baker, who has the finest collection of marine monsters in ten sea counties— sea dragons, polypi, mer-people, most fantastic. You have only to name the old gentleman in black (not the Devil) that lodged with him a week (he'll remember) last July, and he will show courtesy. He is by far the foremost of the Savans. His wife is the funniest thwarting little animal. They are decidedly the Lions of green Hastings.'

Whether or not Hood managed to meet the 'Lions' on this occasion, we do not know. He came back to London about the end of August, and soon afterwards entered into close collaboration with John Hamilton Reynolds on what was to be his first book of verse, *Odes and Addresses to Great People*. Since he had ceased to be directly concerned with the editing of the *London Magazine*, he had been engaged in some engraving and drawing and in miscellaneous writing for one or two periodicals like the *New Monthly Magazine*. In the latter appeared his Spenserian poem, 'The Two Swans' in February 1824, and his delightful parody of Grey, 'Ode on a Distant Prospect of Clapham Academy' in April of the same year. He had also been writing other serious poems, as well as *Lamia: A Romance*, a dramatization of Keats's poem, of which more later. But the *Odes* comprise his most substantial achievement up to this date.

The volume seems to have been his first collaboration with

59

John Hamilton Reynolds, although the *Memorials* claim that he had a hand in Reynolds's five-act farce, *Gil Blas! At 17, 25, 52*, first presented at the English Opera House in August, 1822. Dr. Alvin Whitley has effectively disposed of this claim,[1] chiefly by showing that Richard Brinsley Peake, who had a share in the farce, did not meet Hood until 1824. Peake's letter to the comedian, Charles Mathews, in which he records this meeting, is especially interesting as giving a dispassionate impression of Hood as he was at twenty-five, and showing how his boyish shyness persisted. 'I have met,' writes Peake, 'at the house of the father of my worthy colleague, John Hamilton Reynolds, an odd, quaint being, by name Thomas Hood. He appears to be too modest to *let* a pun; but when it is effected, it is capital. On better acquaintance (though he is the most shy cock I ever encountered) I think I perceive under his disguise one of the shrewdest wags of the age. I predict that before your present authors are worn threadbare, he will be your man.'

Of course, Hood may have given Reynolds one or two hints for the play and suggested some jokes to him, but there is no evidence of active collaboration on any major scale between the two until the publication of *Odes and Addresses* in February, 1825. The book met with tremendous success, and this reception had two immediate effects: it confirmed Hood, if he really needed confirmation, in his determination to live by his pen, and it encouraged him to take the plunge into matrimony.

The volume seems to have been Hood's idea. He had already printed the 'Ode to Dr. Kitchener' in the *London Magazine* in 1821, and it was this that gave him the notion for a book of similar whimsical pieces addressed to 'great people'. He wrote to Reynolds in 1824:

My dear Reynolds—I send you the Ode on Martin which, with those on Graham and Kitchener, makes three completed.

These are the names I have thought of to choose from— Elliston you would make a rich one—and then there's Pierce Egan or Tom Cribb—ditto—Mr. Bodkin—Mr. McAdam—Mrs. Fry—Hy. Hunt—Sir R. Birnie—Joseph Grimaldi, sen.—The Great Unknown—Mr. Malthus—Mr. Irving—Mr. Wilber-

---

[1] Alvin Whitley: 'Thomas Hood as a Dramatist', *University of Texas Studies in English*, Vol. XXX, 1951, pp. 184–201.

force—Prince Hohenhoe—Capt. Parry—Dr. Combe—Mr. Accum—The Washing Company—Sir W. Congreve—Bish—Cubitt on the Treadmill—Tattersall—Owen of Lanark—Bridgman, on the Iron Coffins—W. Savage Landor, on the use of cork armour and bows and arrows—Fitzgerald on Literature—Dymoke. I think the thing is likely to be a hit—but if *you* do some, I shall expect it to run like wildfire. Let's keep it snug—Pray, remembrances to Rice—and in the kindliest at Home.

—I am, dear Reynolds, yours very truly,

T. Hood.

Reynolds was delighted to co-operate, and, of the fifteen poems in the book, all save three were on subjects selected from Hood's list. There has been some doubt as to the contribution each man made to the volume. In a copy formerly in the possession of Buxton Forman, Hood marked five poems as being entirely Reynolds's, those to M'Adam, Dymoke, Sylvanus Urban, Elliston of Drury Lane Theatre, and the Dean and Chapter of Westminster, and indicated that he and Reynolds together wrote the Address to Maria Darlington. But in another copy which Reynolds gave to Richard Monckton Milnes, he claimed not only the poems mentioned by Hood, but also a share in those to Graham, Joseph Grimaldi, The Steam Washing Company, Captain Parry and Dr. Kitchener. It is most likely that Reynolds, who in later life became a disappointed and frustrated man, may either have genuinely forgotten the circumstances or have been tempted to lay claim to more than was his due. It is also possible that, in the give and take of collaboration, an idea or two, or a line here and there, was contributed by each to works for which the other was mainly responsible.

Undoubtedly the lion's share in this delightful work was Hood's; in it he established what was to be one of his most typical forms of expression. Much of the whimsicality of *Odes and Addresses* is now faded, its topicalities render whole poems obscure and blunt the edges of many of the jokes, and there are times when the authors seem to be stretching fragile jokes to breaking point. But its vivacity is unmistakable, and its verbal facility often dazzling; it abounds in puns, epigrams, witticisms and freakishly comic analogies. Particularly typical of Hood in their blending of fun and puns with a dash of melancholy are the verses to the great clown, Joseph Grimaldi, on his retirement:

> Ah, where thy legs—that witty pair!
> For 'great wits jump'—and so did they!
> Lord! how they leap'd in lamplight air!
> Caper'd—and bounc'd—and strode away!
> That years should tame the legs—alack!
> I've seen spring thro' an Almanack!
>
> But bounds will have their bound—the shocks
> Or Time will cramp the nimblest toes;
> And those that frisk'd in silken clocks
> May look to limp in fleecy hose—
> One only—(Champion of the ring)
> Could ever make his Winter—Spring!
>
> And gout, that owns no odds between
> The toe of Czar and toe of Clown,
> Will visit—but I did not mean
> To moralize, though I am grown
> Thus sad—Thy going seemed to beat
> A muffled drum for Fun's retreat!

It is in the general kindliness of the humour and the gentleness of what satire there is in *Odes and Addresses* that the pieces differ most markedly from the frequently malicious light verse of the previous century. The work of Hood and Reynolds is in the tradition of amiable humour, of wit tempered with pathos, of the twinkle in the eye rather than the curl of the lip, that Lamb too so agreeably cultivated, that takes its rise perhaps from Sterne and Goldsmith, and that Hood was to carry over into the Victorian age, and help by his example to make the norm of benevolent middle-class humour as opposed to the savage thrusts of the tougher age of Pope. When Coleridge said of Voltaire's wit that it is 'without that pathos which gives the magic charm to genuine humour', and when Keats, after dining with Horace Smith, Thomas Hill, Edward Dubois and some other wits, wrote to his brothers, 'They only served to convince me, how superior humour is to wit in respect to enjoyment', they were both thinking of this amiable humour, more domestic than of the salon, less intellectual than everyday, a form of humour that was a romantic form of the comic, a humour touched as De Quincey said of Lamb's essays, 'by cross-lights of pathos'. Here are jokes that all can enjoy, and a humour that is no less clever or amusing for being just a couple of removes from the homely.

Hood and Reynolds added something in this way to a developing tradition of light verse; they did not invent the form or the mood. Many influences helped to shape *Odes and Addresses*—the parodies of John Philips and John Hookham Frere, the *Rejected Addresses* of the Smiths, Southey's *Abel Shufflebottom Sonnets*, and, apart from parodies, the light verse of Coleridge, Keats, Leigh Hunt and Thomas Moore. This was a happy time for burlesque, parody and comic poetry; most of the Romantic poets of Hood's youth had pointed the way he was to follow. But it is in the Smiths' *Rejected Addresses* of 1812 and in Hood's and Reynolds's *Odes and Addresses* that we see the first distinct signs of the modern type of light verse that leads through Barham, J. K. Stephens, Calverley and W. S. Gilbert up to J. C. Squire, E. V. Knox, Belloc, A. P. Herbert, Chesterton and the generally kindly rhymsters of *Punch*. Gone is the personal animosity of much eighteenth-century verse, parody is incidental, verbal high-jinks are preferred to epigrams, and throughout there is a tone of good-tempered raillery and even of humorous self-criticism. This is a vein Hood was to explore most rewardingly in the future. But already here in his earliest humorous poems are his typical verbal somersaults, joy in practical jokes and friendly nudge in the ribs.

Since he was to become best known for his humanitarian poems written in later years, it is worth while to note here the tone of his '*Friendly* Epistle to Mrs. Fry, *in* Newgate', which is one of humorous sympathy, and the point of view, which, while praising the Quaker prison-reformer for her work in teaching children in prison, suggests that prevention is better than cure and that her schools are even more needed outside prison than within:

> I like you, Mrs. Fry! I like your name!
>   It speaks the very warmth you feel in pressing
> In daily act round Charity's great flame—
>   I like the crisp Browne way you have of dressing,
> Good Mrs. Fry! I like the placid claim
>   You make to Christianity—professing

Love, and good *works*—of course you buy of Barton,
Beside the young *fry's* bookseller—Friend Darton. . . .

Come out of Newgate, Mrs. Fry! Repair
    Abroad, and find your pupils in the streets.
O, come abroad into the wholesome air,
    And take your moral place, before Sin seats
Her wicked self in the Professor's chair.
    Suppose some mortals raw! the true receipt's
To dress them in the pan, but do not try
To cook them in the fire, good Mrs. Fry!

In the *Odes*, the pun is already a highly developed and characteristic device—both the superficial kind in which the play on words dominates, and the more subtle, highly meaningful type, wherein the pun becomes the vehicle of a genuinely poetic ambiguity or of a penetratingly witty insight, as in the final line of

    I like your carriage, and your silken grey,
      Your dove-like habits, and your silent preaching;
    But I don't like your Newgatory teaching.

or in these agile lines from the delightful 'Ode to the Great Unknown':

    Thou Scottish Barmecide, feeding the hunger
    Of curiosity with airy gammon!
        Thou mystery-monger
    Dealing it out like middle cut of salmon,
    That people buy and can't make head or tail of it;
    (Howbeit that puzzle never hurts the sale of it;)
    Thou chief of authors mystic and abstractical,
    That lay their proper bodies on the shelf—
    Keeping thyself so truly to thyself,
        Thou Zimmerman made practical!
    Thou secret fountain of a Scottish style,
        That, like the Nile,
    Hideth the source wherever it is bred,
        But still keeps disemboguing
        (Not disembrouging)
    Thro' such broad sandy mouths without a head!
    Thou disembodied author—not yet dead—
    The whole world's literary Absentee!

With the *Odes and Addresses* Hood first came before the general public as an author, when his part in the work leaked out; it was an open secret, anyhow. Few writers could have hoped for a more auspicious debut. The first edition was soon exhausted; a second followed a few months later and a third in 1827. Coleridge was sure that Lamb was the author. 'Charles, it is *you*', he wrote. 'I have read them over again, and I understand why you have *anon'd* the book. The puns are nine in ten good—many excellent—the *Newgatory* transcendent. And then the *exemplum sine exemplo* of a volume of personalities and contemporaneities, without a single line that could inflict the infinitesimal of an unpleasance on any man in his senses; saving and except perhaps in the envy-addled brain of a despiser of your *Lays*. If not a triumph over him, it is at least an *ovation*. Then, moreover, and besides, to speak with becoming modesty, excepting my own self, who is there but you who could write the musical lines and stanzas that are intermixed? . . . You are found in the *manner*, as the lawyers say! so, Mr. Charles, hang yourself up, and send me a line, by way of token and acknowledgment.'

Lamb replied on July 2, in a letter which has something of the same polite reserve about the merits of the book which he had expressed in a brief review of it for the *New Times* in April: 'The Odes are 4/5ths done by Hood, a silentish young man you met at Islington one day, an invalid. The rest are Reynolds's, whose sister H. has recently married. I have not a broken finger in them.

'They are hearty good-natured things, and I would put my name to 'em cheerfully, if I could as honestly. I complimented them in a Newspaper, with an abatement for the puns you laud so. They are generally an excess. A Pun is a thing of too much consequence to be thrown in as a make-weight. You shall read one of the addresses over, and miss the puns, and it shall be quite as good and better than when you discover 'em. A Pun is a Noble Thing per se; O never lug it in as an accessory. A Pun is a sole object for reflection (vide *my* aids to that recessment from a savage state)—it is entire, it fills the mind: it is perfect as a sonnet, better. It limps asham'd in the train and retinue of Humour; it knows it should have an establishment of its own. The one, for instance, I made the other day; I forget what it was.

'Hood will be gratify'd as much as I am by your mistake. I liked "Grimaldi" the best: it is true painting of abstract Clownery, and that precious concrete of a Clown; and the rich succession of images and words almost such, in the first half of the Mag. Ignotum.'

In his 'Literary Reminiscences', Hood records an amusing sequel to Coleridge's mistake. He met Coleridge again at the Lambs', this time with one of the poet's sons present. 'The Poet, talking and walking as usual, chanced to pursue some argument, which drew from the son, who had not been introduced to me, the remark, "Ah, that's just like your crying up those foolish Odes and Addresses!" Coleridge was highly amused at this *mal-àpropos*, and, without explaining, looked airily round at me, with the sort of suppressed laugh one may suppose to belong to the Bey of *Tittery*. The truth was, he felt naturally partial to a book he had attributed in the first instance to the dearest of his friends.'

Most of Hood's friends reacted as favourably as Coleridge; some had reservations; Allan Cunningham wrote to him: 'I was an early admirer of your verses. I admired them for other and higher qualities than you have displayed in your odes; but I believe a smile carries a higher market price than a sigh, and that a laugh brings more money than deeper emotion. Even on your own terms I am glad to see you publicly.' Sir Walter Scott, 'the Great Unknown', whom Hood was to meet shortly before the novelist's death, received the *Odes and Addresses* very kindly: 'He wishes the unknown author good health, good fortune and whatever good things can best support and encourage his lively vein of inoffensive and humorous satire.' 'Barry Cornwall', the kindly Procter, sounded a note similar to that of Cunningham when he described the volume to a friend as 'a joint publication by that united Beaumont and Fletcher brotherhood —Reynolds and Hood. What a pity it is that Hood should have given up serious poetry for the sake of cracking the shells of jokes which have not always a kernel!' Like Wainewright a couple of years before, other acquaintances of Hood, while genuinely pleased at the success of the *Odes*, felt that this very success might lead to the extinction of the serious poet they were certain he could become.

Hood himself had few such qualms. His first book, albeit a

collaboration, was out, he had made money from it, his name was before the public and the critics, who wanted more work from him; a promising literary future stretched ahead. He felt secure enough now to establish a home of his own. On Thursday, May 5, 1825, he and Jane Reynolds were married at St. Botolph's, Aldersgate, by the Rev. Edward Rice, with Jane's father, George Reynolds, John Hamilton Reynolds, Charlotte Reynolds and James Rice, Jnr., as witnesses. The newly wed pair went for a honeymoon of some weeks at Hastings; it was the unshadowed beginning of a partnership marked by poverty, sickness and sorrow, but lighted always by perfect love, trust and fidelity. Keats's view of the Reynolds sisters as hard-hearted critics of his Fanny and as irresponsible gossips may have some substance, but Jane, at least, must be exempted from any charge of malice or chuckleheadedness. She married for love a man who had a kindly and tender nature, but who was also an invalid and, for all his optimism and talent, of very uncertain prospects, in the full knowledge that with him she faced a precarious future, that she could never hope for real comfort, much less luxury, and that, while being far from robust herself, much of her time would be devoted to caring for a sick husband.

Jane proved to be an ideal wife; marrying her was one of the best things Thomas Hood ever did; it was a match founded securely on true love and genuine compatibility, and so far as mutual respect, devotion and depth of understanding are concerned, it is hard to think of a happier example among literary people. On the honeymoon, Jane wrote to her sister-in-law, Betsy, 'The love I bear for one you all love, and the happiness I experience in being his wife, will always make me look upon you with affection; and I think I should be very ungrateful if I did not add that your kindness to me will be another motive that I shall love you all. I am getting serious; but you will forgive me, I hope, for my heart is very full, and if I touch it the happiness will overflow. You will laugh at me, perhaps, and talk about the honeymoon; but your brother and I have had many seasons of trouble and vexations that have made our present enjoyment greater. I must say to you all, get married as fast as you can; but don't marry unless you love the man, for then a married state *must* be miserable.'

At Hastings, the Hoods tried in vain to track down Lamb's

'very lions of green Hastings', but they did discover his little church in the wood, which Thomas described to Marianne and Charlotte in words that reflect the happy mood of his honeymoon, and that also show one of his typical prose styles, a half-serious, half-comic imitation of the Romantic manner: 'It is such a church! It ought to have been our St. Botolph's,' he says. . . . 'Such a verdant covert wood Stothard might paint for the haunting of Dioneus, Pamphillus, and Fiammetta as they walk in the novel of Boccacce. The ground shadowed with bluebells, even to the formation of a plumb-like bloom upon its little knolls and ridges; and ever through the dell windeth a little path chequered with the shades of aspens and ashes and the most verdant and lively of all the family of trees. Here a broad, rude stone steppeth over a lazy spring, oozing its way into grass and weeds; anon a fresh pathway divergeth, you know not whither. Meanwhile the wild blackbird startles across the way and singeth anew in some other shade. To have seen Fiammetta there, stepping in silken attire, like a flower, and the sunlight looking upon her betwixt the branches! I had not walked (in the body) with Romance before.'

Back in London, the Hoods entered upon a brief period of relatively untroubled domestic life. They were both home-loving people, and, although Hood's income from miscellaneous journalism and occasional engraving was small, and the health of both was indifferent, to say the least, they had a small circle of friends who cheered their lives with the cordiality of visits, with pleasant evenings together, with amiable gossip, and with the cosiness of shared jokes and homely solicitude such as the lower middle class of the early nineteenth century enjoyed. It was, perhaps, a somewhat stuffy and airless world, whose inhabitants were enamoured of trivialities, but it was one, also, that included a generous, spontaneous humanity, a strong sense of loyalty and an affectionate awareness of the enduring qualities of family life.

Thomas continued his friendship with his brother-in-law, John Hamilton, the Lambs and others and developed increasingly cordial relations with such people as Charles Wentworth Dilke, who had been a contributor to the *London*. He joined with Lamb in gentle leg-pulls and jests at the expense of common friends. For instance, in the summer of 1827, the two spent an uproarious evening framing a picture to send to Bernard Barton. This, a coloured print of a little boy learning to read at his mother's knee, was placed in a frame much too large for it, and clumsily made to fit, and sent with a copy of jointly composed verses. When the amateur framers had finished, Hood said, in reference to Barton's Quaker habit, 'Barton will be sure to like it, because it is *broad-brimmed*.' Hood gave Dash, his pet, 'a large and very handsome dog, of a rather curious and singularly sagacious breed', although very unruly, to the Lambs, from whom it later passed to P. G. Patmore, who kept and trained it.

The pleasant intercourse with the Lambs was interrupted when, in 1827, the Hoods left the Hood home in Lower Street, where they had begun married life, to set up their own home at 2 Robert Street, in the Adelphi, and, in the autumn of the same year, Charles and Mary went to live in Enfield. But just before the move, there was a merry party at Robert Street that has been captured for us by Mrs. Mary Balmanno, the wife of a journalist-friend of Hood and Lamb who was also Secretary of the Artists' Benevolent Fund. In *Pen and Pencil* (1858), Mrs. Balmanno described this occasion, at which were present Charles Lamb and Miss Kelly, 'that most natural and un-rivalled of English comic actresses', of whom Hood wrote in an 'ode':

> with your art
> So much in love, like others, I have grown,
> I really mean myself to take a part
> In 'Free and Easy'—at my own bespeak—
> And shall three times a week
> Drop in and make your pretty house my own!

Mrs. Balmanno's spirited account gives a valuable sketch of Hood as he was at twenty-eight. 'In outward appearance,' she writes, 'Hood conveyed the ideal of a clergyman. His figure slight, and invariably dressed in black; his face pallid; the complexion delicate, and features regular; his countenance bespeaking sympathy by its sweet expression of melancholy and suffering.

'Lamb was of a different mould and aspect. Of middle height, with brown and rather ruddy complexion, grey eyes expressive of sense and shrewdness, but neither large nor brilliant; his head and features well shaped, and the general expression of his countenance quiet, kind, and observant, undergoing rapid changes in conversation, as did his manner, variable as an April day, particularly to his sister, whose saint-like good-humour and patience were as remarkable as his strange and whimsical ways of trying them. . . .

'Miss Kelly . . . with quiet good humour listened and laughed at the witty sallies of her host and his gifted friend, seeming as little an actress as it is possible to conceive.

'Once, however, when some allusion was made to a comic scene in a new play, then just brought out, wherein she had performed to the life the character of a low-bred maid, passing herself off as her mistress, Miss Kelly arose, and with a kind of resistless ardour repeated a few sentences so inimitably, that everybody laughed as much as if the real lady's maid, and not the actress had been before them; while she who had personated the part, quietly resumed her seat without the least sign of merriment, as grave as possible.

'This little scene for a few moments charmed everybody out of themselves, and gave a new impetus to conversation. Mrs. Hood's eyes sparkled with joy, as she saw the effect it had produced upon her husband, whose pale face, like an illuminated comic mask, shone with fun and good humour. Never was happier couple than "The Hoods"; "mutual reliance and fond faith" seemed to be their motto.

'Mrs. Hood was a most amiable woman—of excellent manners and full of sincerity and goodness. She perfectly adored her husband, tending him like a child, whilst he, with unbounded affection, seemed to delight to yield himself to her guidance. Nevertheless, true to his humorous nature, he loved to tease her with jokes and whimsical accusations which were only responded to by "Hood, Hood, how can you run on so?". "Perhaps you don't know," said he, "that Jane's besetting weakness is a desire to appear in print and be thought a Blue."

'Mrs. Hood coloured and gave her usual reply; then observed laughingly: "Hood does not know one kind of material from another, he thinks this dress is blue print." On looking at it I saw it was only a very pretty blue *silk*.'

After supper, one of Jane Hood's exquisitely arranged 'picture suppers', 'Mr. Hood with inexpressible gravity in the upper part of his face, and his mouth twitching with smiles, sang his own comic song of "If you go to France, be sure you learn the lingo"; his pensive manner and feeble voice making it doubly ludicrous.

'Mr. Lamb, on being pressed to sing, excused himself in his own peculiar manner, but offered to pronounce a Latin eulogium instead. This was accepted, and he accordingly stammered forth a long string of Latin words: among which, as the name of Mrs. Hood frequently occurred, we ladies thought it in praise of her. The delivery of this speech occupied about five minutes. On enquiring of a gentleman who sat next to me whether Mr. Lamb was praising Mrs. Hood, he informed me that was by no means the case, the eulogium being on the lobster salad!'

In such simple ways, the Hoods passed many evenings with their small group of friends. They visited the Lambs at Enfield Chase in 1827 and 1828, where, on his first call, Hood found his friend, 'in a bald-looking yellowish house, with a bit of a garden, and a wasp's nest most convanient, as the Irish say'. On these occasions, the two men took long walks together, with Lamb apparently doing most of the talking and pouring out bits of freakish information from his curious store of learning into the receptive ears of Thomas. There can be no doubt that Lamb was a powerful personal influence on the younger man, both by example of character and by his sense of fun and jest and his highly developed taste for oddities. 'In courtesy to a friend,' Hood recalled, 'he would select a green lane for a ramble, but left to himself, he took the turnpike road, as often as otherwise. "Scott", says Cunningham, "was a stout walker." Lamb was a *porter* one. He calculated Distances, not by Long Measure, but by Ale and Beer Measure. "Now I have walked a pint." Many a time have I accompanied him in these matches against Meux, not without sharing in the stake, and then, what fearful and profitable talk! For instance, he once delivered to me orally the substance of the Essay on the Defect of the Imagination in Modern Artists, subsequently printed in the *Athenaeum*. But besides the criticism, there were snatches of old poems, golden lines and sentences culled from rare books, and anecdotes of men of note. Marry, it was like going on a ramble with gentle Izaak Walton, minus the fishing.' The world looked golden and friendly then to Thomas and Jane.

IV

The Comic and the Serious

DURING this period of tranquillity, Hood was pursuing his literary endeavours with tireless application; he now had a wife to support as well as sisters. He did some engraving, too, including the large 'The Progress of Cant'. But the success of *Odes and Addresses* encouraged him to attempt something else in a not dissimilar vein, this time independently of Reynolds. He collected several of the pieces he had written earlier for the *London* and other magazines, added some new ones, and, towards the end of 1826, saw them published by Lupton Relfe of Cornhill as his first 'entire book', *Whims and Oddities*, which appeared under the author's name. Among the poems included were 'The Last Man', 'The Irish Schoolmaster' and two of his most celebrated comic ballads, 'Faithless Nelly Gray' and 'The Ballad of Sally Brown and Ben the Carpenter'. At least the first verse of the former:

> Ben Battle was a soldier bold
> And used to war's alarms:
> But a cannon-ball took off his legs
> So he laid down his arms!

and the last verses of the latter:

> And then he tried to sing 'All's Well',
> But could not though he tried;
> His head was turned and so he chewed
> His pigtail till he died.

> His death, which happened in his berth,
> At forty-odd befell:

72

THOMAS HOOD

by G. R. Lewis, 1838

JANE HOOD

by William Hilton, R.A., *c.* 1833

> They went and told the sexton, and
> The sexton toll'd the bell.

are among the best-known lines in the language.

It is certain that J. H. Reynolds had a hand in 'Sally Brown', although it is impossible to say how much, for it was an early effort of Hood's, appearing in the *London* in March, 1822, when he first knew Reynolds. In the note prefacing the poem in *Whims and Oddities*, Hood wrote: 'I have never been vainer of any verses than of my part in the following Ballad . . . "Sally Brown" has been favoured, perhaps, with as wide a patronage as the "Moral Songs", though its circle may not have been of so select a class as the friends of "Hohenlinden". But I do not desire to see it amongst what are called Elegant Extracts. The lamented Emery, drest as Tom Tug, sang it at his last mortal Benefit at Covent Garden—and, ever since, it has been a great favourite with the watermen of Thames, who time their oars to it, as the wherry-men of Venice time theirs to the lines of Tasso. With the watermen, it went naturally to Vauxhall:—and, over-land, to Sadler's Wells. The Guards, not the mail coach, but the Life Guards,—picked it out from a fluttering hundred of others —all going to one air—against the dead wall at Knightsbridge. Cheap Printers of Shoe Lane, and Cow-cross (all pirates!) disputed about the Copyright, and published their own editions,— and in the meantime, the Authors, to have made bread of their song (it was poor old Homer's hard ancient case!) must have sung it about the streets. Such is the lot of Literature! The profits of "Sally Brown" were divided by the Ballad Mongers: —it has cost, but never brought me, a half-penny.'

Hood's references to 'my part' and 'the Authors' implicitly acknowledge Reynolds's share in the poem, but whether John Hamilton contributed more than an idea or a line or two we shall never know. We may safely leave Hood the best lines and the famous verses, for they are typical of his work thereafter, and there is little in Reynolds's own verse to match the aptness of the wit and puns here. In the *Whims and Oddities*, indeed, are present quite clearly the distinctive qualities of Hood's writing —the exuberant punning, the tremendous, but dangerous facility with rhymes, the concern with low life, the bouncing joy in slapstick comedy, the fondness for eighteenth-century descriptive and landscape verse (showing up, for instance, in 'The

Irish Schoolmaster', with its echoes of Shenstone) and the pervasively good-humoured atmosphere throughout.

In much of Hood's early comic verse, there is the tone of the English music-hall in its palmy days—sunny-tempered vulgarity, jokes about food and drunkenness and physical disabilities, and mothers-in-law and marriage, a dislike of pretension and pomposity and a 'looking on the bright side—thumbs up' philosophy. But these pieces also have something special to Hood, not just the vein of sentimental humanitarianism already evident in both some of the 'whims' and in the prose sketches in the 'Elia' manner which are included in the volume, but that individual blend of the grotesque, the comic and the horrible which was to give strength to his later performances in this lighter style.

'The Last Man', for instance, is a remarkable poem that unites the vision of apocalyptic science-fiction with the charnel-house mood of Poe. After a great plague, the hangman-narrator believes himself to be the sole human survivor in the world. But he meets an old beggar, who cheerfully makes the best of things:

> Now a curse (I thought) be on his love,
> And a curse upon his mirth—
> An' it were not for that beggar man
> I'd be the King of the earth,—
> But I promis'd myself an hour should come
> To make him rue his birth.

They walk together through the desolation of a world struck down in the midst of its everyday activities; the horror of the devastation is brought home with sharp economy in lines like these:

> For the porters all were stiff and cold
> And could not lift their heads;
> And when we came where their masters lay,
> The rats leapt out of the beds.

But the hangman is angry to see the beggar capering in the king's crown and cloak, and hangs him. As he watches hounds come and rend the body, the thought comes to him:

> I know the Devil, when I am dead,
> Will send his hounds for me.

And so he is left alone with his conscience.

74

'The Last Man' is a strangely moving and haunting poem, a horror story that is also a parable. I have no difficulty myself in accepting it exactly as it is—that is, until the last verse where Hood seems to let his readers down from the Gothic terror with an anti-climax, as he does in 'The Demon Ship' and other poems:

> For hanging looks sweet—but, alas! in vain
> My desperate fancy begs—
> I must turn my cup of sorrows quite up,
> And drink it to the dregs,—
> For there's not another man alive,
> In the world, to pull my legs!

And yet I wonder if he does, whether the grisly pun of the final line is not, in fact, congruous with what has gone before, and does not make quite good sense on two levels, in which the different moods are complementary rather than conflicting. When Hood is at his best, this, indeed, is the effect of his puns, to create an oddly ambivalent atmosphere in which the horror is never quite swallowed up by the farce.

The reviewer in *Blackwood's* for June, 1827, who devoted a long article to a eulogy of *Whims and Oddities* and who found Hood to have 'taste, feeling and genius', quoted the whole of 'The Last Man', but saw in it only a clever parody of Thomas Campbell's poem of the same name, and found the very idea of a Last Man more of an absurdity than an atomic age can afford to. Even Hood's wood-cut with which the poem, like several others in the volume, is illustrated, and which the *Blackwood's* reviewer described like this: 'The Last Man is a sort of absurd sailor-like insolent ruffian, sitting with arms a-kimbo, cross-legged and smoking his pipe on the cross-tree of a gallows', has today a disturbing element of 'sick humour' about it that is beyond the reach of the merely farcical. To call it 'Cruik-shankish', as *Blackwood's* does, is to imply a good deal more to those who nowadays look at the grotesque, thin-lined, cruelly comic and vaguely sinister illustrations to Dickens than it did to Hood's contemporaries. In a sense, in such poems as 'The Last Man', Hood is one of the primary ancestors of 'comédie noire' and, to some degree, of that 'sick humour' with which the Americans have recently made us familiar. Death, disease, mutilation, physical ills, mental strains, cannibalism are all subjects for his jesting verses, and while the tone, the 'disposition amiable and facetious' of Hood prevents the humour from being either pathological or neurotically unpleasant, the constant preoccupation with illness which his own condition induced, combined with his particular talent for freakish analogies, makes him the innovator of a strain that runs right through Victorian humour, often in forms cruder and in considerably less good taste than his.

Although the success of *Whims and Oddities*, which went into several editions at once, greatly pleased Hood, he felt that those of his friends who believed him to be basically a serious poet may have had the right of it. With a typically humorous inversion of the facts, he announced in the preface to *Whims and Oddities* that 'At a future time, the Press may be troubled with some things of a more serious tone, and purpose—which the Author has resolved upon publishing, in despite of the advice of certain critical friends. His forte, they are pleased to say, is decidedly humorous; but a gentleman cannot be always breathing his comic vein.' The first fruit of such a promise came with the publication in February, 1827, by W. H. Ainsworth of two volumes of stories called *National Tales*. These imitations of the Italian *novella* form, inspired no doubt by Hood's extensive reading, at this time, of Elizabethan literature, were at best tepidly received by the critics, sold only modestly, and were not reprinted. There are no concealed gems or neglected masterpieces here. In the main they are poor stuff, inflated anecdotes set in Arabia, Venice, Persia and England, dull in their formal style, imitative in plot, shallow in characterization and often marked by the anti-Catholic prejudices of Hood whose notions of the Catholic religion were almost wholly derived from Gothic novels and Little England Protestant stereotypes. Some of the stories, it is true, such as 'The Fair Maid of Ludgate', a tale of the Great Plague, have considerable fluency and a certain thin charm. But in general the *National Tales* lack substance and originality and anything of the distinctiveness of *Whims and Oddities*.

Before Hood could undertake another book, calamity overtook his little household. His first child, a girl, was born in April, 1827, but Jane's poor health made the delivery a most difficult one, and the child died immediately after birth. This tragedy deeply affected Thomas and Jane who loved children and longed for infants of their own. After Hood's death, a little lock of golden hair was found wrapped in a piece of paper bearing these touching lines, written in his sorrow:

> Little eyes that scarce did see,
>   Little lips that never smiled;
>   Alas! my little dear dead child,
> Death is thy father, and not me,
> I but embraced thee, soon as he.

When Thomas wrote to tell Charles Lamb the sad news, his friend replied, 'Your letter elicited a flood of tears from Mary. . . . God bless you and the mother (or should be mother) of your sweet girl that should have been.' A few weeks later he sent to Jane Hood the poem, 'On an Infant Dying as soon as Born', which E. V. Lucas considered in many ways Lamb's most remarkable poem. Lamb identified himself with Hood's sorrow; the lost child became one of the dream children he had never had, and out of this empathy came the gently sincere metaphysical verses that end

> Why should kings and nobles have
> Pictured trophies to their grave;
> And we, churls, to thee deny
> Thy pretty toys with thee to lie,
> A more harmless vanity?

The Hoods treasured this mark of friendship, and later, when Hood was editing *The Gem*, he printed the poem in full in its pages.

The death of their first child was not the only trouble that 1827 brought to the Hoods. During the winter, Thomas suffered a severe recurrence of rheumatic fever, that laid him low for some months. He continued to write furiously during his convalescence, and as soon as he was out of bed, he went to Brighton to seek the strength that seemed always just around the corner. It was virtually the end of his period of reasonable health; from then onwards, he was rarely to be free from physical ills. The immediate cause of his relapse was debilitation brought on by excessive work, since, early in 1827, he had produced, in addition to two volumes of *Whims and Oddities* and the two volumes of *National Tales*, and many contributions to periodicals, his most ambitious collection of serious poems, *The Plea of the Midsummer Fairies and Other Poems*. No matter what the cost in nervous and bodily energy, Thomas Hood was determined to establish himself firmly as a writer, above all as a serious one.

Some of the poems contained in *The Plea of the Midsummer Fairies* had been written in 1821, and even earlier, and belong to the period when Hood was first thinking of issuing a serious volume; he had published thirteen in the *London Magazine* of the 1820's; fifteen only of the thirty-seven poems were new. But the book represented a carefully organized attempt to win a name as a poet of substance. And this despite the fact that when the volume appeared in July, 1827, under the imprint of Messrs. Longmans, Rees, Orme, Brown and Green, the author was described as 'Thomas Hood, Author of "Whims and Oddities", etc., etc.' The longest poems in it were the title-piece, 'Hero and Leander', and 'Lycus the Centaur', all very much in the current Romantic manner, and showing Hood as a sensitive young writer susceptible to the influences of Coleridge, Wordsworth, Keats, and, behind them, of the Elizabethans.

'The Plea of the Midsummer Fairies' itself was dedicated to Lamb in a prefatory letter, which acknowledges what Hood had learnt from him in love for Shakespeare's plays, and especially for his comedies: 'I desire to record a respect and admiration for you as a writer, which no one acquainted with our literature, save Elia himself, will think disproportionate or misplaced. If I had not these better reasons to govern me, I should be guided to the same selection by your intensive yet critical relish for the works of our great Dramatist, and for that favourite play in particular which has furnished the subject of my verses. It is my design, in the following Poem, to celebrate, by an allegory, that immortality which Shakespeare has conferred on the Fairy mythology by his Midsummer Night's Dream.'

Hood's poem is in many ways an enchanting work, which retains much of its charm for a modern reader. The form is that of the Spenserian stanza with the final alexandrine replaced by a pentameter. In his fancy, the poet views a 'shady and sequester'd scene' in the midst of which is 'Titania and her pretty crew'. The fairy queen is melancholy, for she has dreamt of the passing away of the fairies, whose 'lives are leased upon the fickle faith of men', and of the monstrous figure of Saturn who, representing Time and Change, has come in her dream to destroy the fairy world. No sooner has she described this to her retinue than Saturn himself appears and menaces the little people. Titania pleads with him, and, following her, Puck, Ariel, and other fairies, in long, jewelled speeches, urge their claims to be spared, pointing out that they are the custodians of music, the flowers, love and kindness, the trees, insects, bees and small forest creatures, springs and fountains and nature's sweet sounds, and that they are friends to men and especially to children. Saturn rejects their pleas and has just raised his destroying scythe when

> a timely Apparition
> Steps in between, to bear the awful brunt.

It is Shakespeare himself, to whom Titania makes an eloquent appeal for help. The kind Shade rebukes Saturn, praising the 'kindly ministers of nature', and Mutability, defeated, vanishes, leaving the fairies to pay homage to their preserver.

In this lengthy conceit most of the virtues and defects of Hood's serious verse appear plainly. The poem is far too long—126 stanzas of it—for the slender theme; the detail, often rich and exquisite in a faintly precious way, is excessive; and there is considerable repetition as the stanzas carry the thought along, rather than the thought the stanzas. Yet there is a truly refined sensibility at work here, which, in several places, manages to recapture the atmosphere of Shakespeare's own fairy world, as, for instance, in Puck's words:

> Sometimes we cast our shapes, and in sleek skins
> Delve with the timid mole, that aptly delves
> From our example; so the spider spins,
> And eke the silk-worm, pattern'd by ourselves:
> Sometimes we travail on the summer shelves
> Of early bees, and busy toils commence,
> Watch'd of wise men, that know not we are elves,
> But gaze and marvel at our stretch of sense,
> And praise our human-like intelligence.
>
> Wherefore, by thy delight in that old tale,
> And plaintive dirges the late robins sing,

79

> What time the leaves are scattered by the gale,
> Mindful of that old forest burying;—
> As thou dost love to watch each tiny thing,
> For whom our craft most curiously contrives,
> If thou hast caught a bee upon the wing,
> To take his honey-bag,—spare us our lives,
> And we will pay the ransom in full hives.

There is also a genuinely Shakespearian ring to stanzas like these:

> Then Saturn with a frown:—'Go forth, and fell
> Oak for your coffins, and thenceforth lay by
> Your axes for the rust and bid farewell
> To all sweet birds, and the blue peeps of sky
> Through tangled branches, for ye shall not spy
> The next green generation of the tree,
> But hence with the dead leaves, whene'er they fly,—
> Which in the bleak air I would rather see
> Than flights of the most tuneful birds that be.'

The weaknesses, which fight against the poem's charm, are its seemingly too calculated slips into deliberate quaintness, and a playfulness that, as in much of the work of the Cockney School, often falls into something close to poetic vulgarity, such as:

> But Puck was seated on a spider's thread,
> That hung between two branches of a briar,
> And 'gan to swing and gambol, heels o'er head,
> Like any Southwark tumbler on a wire,
> For him no present grief could long inspire.

Echoes of earlier writers, even in passages of decided originality, give the reader a feeling of *déjà vu*. Spenser is one obvious model in descriptive stanzas like the ones beginning

> And there were crystal pools, peopled with fish,
> Argent and gold; and some of Tyrian skin,
> Some crimson-barr'd.

Drayton's *Nymphidia*, too, has suggested some of the details of fairy life. But it is above all Keats whose tone is here, especially when Hood delights in the fantastic and sensuous and in the soft golden glow of the scenes:

> 'Twas in that mellow season of the year
> When the hot Sun singes the yellow leaves
> Till they be gold;

in such images as

> others from tall trees
> Dropp'd, like shed blossoms, silent to the grass,
> Spirits and elfins small, of every class;

and in the use of typically Keatsian epithets:

> and deftly strips
> That ruddy skin from a sweet rose's cheek

and

> some bloomy rain
> That, circling the bright Moon, had wash'd her car

and

> . . . in ancient might and hoary majesty.[1]

Several lines unashamedly draw upon particular poems by Keats, e.g. 'like foolish heifers in the holy rite' and 'to some un-wasted regions of my brain'. Hood's whole poetic personality vibrated to that of Keats; his poetic instincts were given direction by Keats's example, and during his twenties he felt himself called to carry on the type of imaginative exploration Keats had begun. It was hardly his fault that he lacked the high vision and dedication and the keen critical intelligence of his predecessor.

From the Elizabethans as well, especially Marlowe, Spenser, and Chapman, back to whom he followed Keats, and from Lamb, Hood learned the poetic value of classical myth. This shows most clearly in 'Hero and Leander', which may have found its first inspiration in Reynolds's *The Naiad*, but which echoes Marlowe's poem, Shakespeare's 'Venus and Adonis', and 'The Rape of Lucrece' also. Of all the poems in the volume, this is the one that gives most earnest of Hood's poetic power in a traditional vein. Douglas Bush calls it 'probably the most remarkable example in modern verse of almost complete reproduction of the narrative manner of the Elizabethan Ovidians. One cannot quite dismiss as pastiche what is written with the youthful

---

[1] For other examples of Keats's influence on Hood, see Federico Olivero: 'Hood and Keats', *Modern Language Notes*, December, 1913, pp. 233-5.

freshness and spontaneity of a contemporary of Shakespeare and Marlowe.' [1] High praise, indeed, but not, I feel, undeserved, for the many felicities of 'Hero and Leander', its firm narrative line, its decorative richness and the beauty of its imagery make it an astonishing poem to have come from the pen of a writer usually regarded as primarily a funster and a punster.

Perhaps to avoid comparison with Marlowe, Hood reshaped the classical story. He opens with Leander leaving Hero in the morning to swim back to Abydos; while

> The drowsy mist before him chill and dank,
> Like a dull lethargy o'erleans the sea.

The description of Leander struggling through the waves contains one of the many intimations of illness that are sown through Hood's poems; here it is a more direct self-revelation than usual, one that expresses both his persistent awareness of physical frailty and a poignant sense of the duality of his own poetic personality:

> His face was pallid, but the hectic morn
> Had hung a lying crimson on his cheeks,
> And slanderous sparkles in his eyes forlorn;
> So death lies ambush'd in consumptive streaks;
> But inward grief was writhing o'er its task,
> As heart-sick jesters weep behind the mask.

In the middle of the journey, Leander encounters a seanymph, who falls in love with him:

> She's all too bright, too argent, and too pale,
> To be a woman;—but a woman's double,
> Reflected on the wave so faint and frail,
> She tops the billows like an air-borne bubble;
> Or dim creation of a morning dream,
> Fair as the wave-bleach'd lily of the stream.

The nymph drags the exhausted Leander down to her home below the waves, unknowing that this means his death:

> She read his mortal stillness for content,
> Feeling no fear where only love was meant.

She sings to the corpse, whom she thinks is sleeping, a song of

---

[1] *Mythology and the Romantic Tradition in English Poetry*, New York: Pageant Book Co., 1957.

love, full of the verbal exuberance of Elizabethan lyrics, both directly felt and as filtered through Keats:

> Look how the sunbeam burns upon their scales,
> And shows rich glimpses of their Tyrian skins;
> They flash small lightnings from their vigorous tails,
> And winking stars are kindled at their fins;
> These shall divert thee in thy weariest mood,
> And seek thy hand for gamesomeness and food.

At last the nymph realizes that Leander is dead. In an attempt to restore him to life, she brings his body to the surface and lays it on 'the glowing sand'. A group of fishermen bear the corpse away while she is seeking for weeds to make a bed for it. When, in a storm in the night, Hero wanders grief-stricken by the shore, she hears the sea-nymph echo Leander's voice calling 'Hero! Hero!' and, thinking it is her lover, she leaps into the sea; her body is enshrined in a crystal cave by the weeping nymph.

'Hero and Leander' suffers from being loaded with more detail than the story can bear. It is almost as if Hood, city-bred but loving the country, felt obliged to expend his wonder at nature over-generously. Many of the 130 stanzas, in Shakespeare's six-line 'Venus and Adonis' measure, are self-indulgent in their catalogues. Yet this was an Elizabethan fault, too, and it is a measure of Hood's skill in this often enchanting poem that, far from its being merely a clever exercise in pseudo-Elizabethan poetic rhetoric, it has an individual blend of poignancy and colour. The tone of melancholy, especially in the nymph's lament, shades the poem in an attractive way. Echoes there are in abundance, from 'Venus and Adonis' and Marlowe's poem on the same subject. Keats is here, too, in such adjectives as 'hoary' and 'gusty' and phrases like 'golden crevices of morn' and Shelley as well in

> Lo! how the lark soars upward and is gone;
> Turning a spirit as he nears the sky.
> His voice is heard, though body there is none,
> And rain-like music scatters from on high;
> But Love would follow with a falcon spite,
> To pluck the minstrel from his dewy height.

Occasionally Cockney faults of poetic tact mar particular

effects, as in the description of Leander's first sight of the nymph:

> Like murder's witness swooning in the court,
> His sight falls senseless by its own report.

And yet everywhere there is abundance of true talent, especially of a gift for the ringing phrase and a capacity for gnomic lines. The nymph's black hair lies behind her white shoulders

> Making her doubly fair, thus darkly set,
> As marble lies advantaged upon jet;

when Leander's body is stolen, the nymph goes to her deep home

> and there
> Weeps in a midnight made of her own hair;

and throughout the poem, the most skilful use of light and colour reflects Hood's training in the pictorial arts:

> Poor gilded Grief! the subtle light by this
> With mazy gold creeps through her watery mine,
> And, diving downward through the green abyss,
> Lights up her palace with an amber shine;
> There, falling on her arms,—the crystal skin
> Reveals the ruby tide that fares within.

However, the most remarkable of the long poems in this volume, although in some ways the most imperfect technically, is 'Lycus the Centaur', dedicated to John Hamilton Reynolds, as 'written in the pleasant springtime of our friendship', that is, in 1822, and described as 'from an unrolled manuscript of Appolonius Curius'. Hood's prefatory note outlines the occasion of the poem, which was suggested to him by the episode of Glaucus, Scylla and Circe in Book III of *Endymion*: 'Lycus, detained by Circe in her magical kingdom, is beloved by a Water Nymph, who, desiring to render him immortal, has recourse to the Sorceress. Circe gives her an incantation to pronounce, which should turn Lycus into a horse; but the horrible effect of the charm causing her to break off in the midst, he becomes a Centaur.' The poem itself is a monologue by Lycus, who tells of his love for the nymph, Aegele, his incurring the jealousy of Circe, the Sorceress's revenge, his greater misery as a centaur than as a man, his rejection by men, and even by children, and his final journey to Thessaly where he meets others of his kind.

'Lycus the Centaur' is more characteristically Hood's than is either of the other two long poems. Despite the charm and delicate fancy of 'The Plea of the Midsummer Fairies', despite the poignancy and rich detail of 'Hero and Leander' and despite the radiant poetic promise they both display, they are 'literary' pieces; they derive from other men's work in subject and, in part, in treatment; they stand apart from life; for all their delightful natural detail, they smell of books. There is not quite enough personal pressure behind the verses; one never feels that Hood would be capable of high emotional intensity or of the large awe that charges great poetry; in his poems, the tragic becomes the melancholic, and regretfulness, rather than agony, suffuses the lines; gentle pity is more evident here than burning compassion.

'Lycus the Centaur' is 'literary', too, in its origins and in its occasional echoes of Keats:

> till one day in the sun,
> In its very noon-blaze, I could fancy a thing
> Of beauty, but faint as the cloud-mirrors fling
> On the gaze of the shepherd that watches the sky;

and in its far from happy echoes of the Cockney poets:

> There were women! there men! but to me a third sex.
> I saw them all dots—yet I loved them as specks.

and

> Where witchery works with her will like a god,
> Works more than the wonders of time at a nod.

The alliterative insistence of the last couplet, typical of the poem as a whole, as well as the bouncing anapaests of the metre, have been praised as fitted to the hysteria of Lycus as he relives the horror of his transformation and the pangs of his rejection. For me, they hamper the poem, and the jolting lines, with their pat rhymes, dilute the seriousness of the theme. Nevertheless, throughout 'Lycus', we feel something quite special to Hood— a sense of the horrible, of grotesque terror, of thin wires plucked hard, which, if it often assumes a freakish form in his poetry, and in his later work is to be crossed with extravagant humour, was to persist in him as a nightmare vision of life and reality.

In a perceptive discussion of this poem in *The Darkling Plain*, Mr. John Heath-Stubbs writes: 'The poem is a vision of the world as it must have appeared to Hood's imagination, tormented by disease, exposed to the cruel pressure of a hostile world. A sense of pitiful frustration pervades the story'—which seems to me to be a comment more appropriate to the work of Hood's later years rather than to that of a young man still with his disasters before him. Mr. Heath-Stubbs sees in the poem parallels with Dante, as Lycus gazes upon the human form distorted in Circe's victims; and, when Lycus's gesture of affection for a child is rejected by the infant, clearly Hercules, the future destroyer of the race of centaurs, he remarks: 'The Hero, intended as a Saviour-figure for mankind, can only appear as the stern Destroyer for the soul rendered monstrous by sin.' This surely puts more weight on the poem than it can bear, for one of the ways in which Hood's poetry is inferior to that of Keats and of the great Romantics, is in the comparative absence from it of genuine symbolism, innerness and of an interior ethical structure.

At the same time, the mood expressed in 'Lycus the Centaur' may well be taken as an intuitive response by a sick man to the spiritual enervation and malaise of his time. This comes out especially in those several passages wherein horror and pathos are fused, as in

> For once, at my suppering, I pluck'd in the dusk
> An apple, juice-gushing and fragrant of musk;
> But by daylight my fingers were crimson'd with gore,
> And the half-eaten fragment was flesh at the core;
> And once—only once—for the love of its blush,
> I broke a bloom bough, but there came such a gush
> On my hand, that I fainted away in weak fright,
> While the leaf-hidden woodpecker shriek'd at the sight,
> And oh! such an agony thrill'd in that note,
> That my soul, starting up, beat its wings in my throat;

and, as Lycus strokes the sad men made animals

> So they passively bow'd—save the serpent, that leapt
> To my breast like a sister, and pressingly crept
> In embrace of my neck, and with close kisses blister'd

My lips in rash love,—then drew backwards, and glister'd
Her eyes in my face, and loud hissing affright,
Dropt down, and swift started away from my sight!

The Plea of the Midsummer Fairies also contained another
longish piece, 'The Two Peacocks of Bedfont'. This moral poem
about two proud and fashionable ladies transformed into peacocks for their vanity seems better fitted to a comic treatment
than to the solemn one Hood gave it, although it has some
pleasant touches, such as the words of the preacher, who expresses Hood's own blue-domer religious sentiments:

Oh go, and gaze—when the low winds of ev'n
    Breathe hymns, and Nature's many forests nod
Their gold-crown'd heads; and the rich blooms of heav'n
    Sun-ripened give their blushes up to God.

The influence of Keats, felt again in this poem, is everywhere
apparent in the briefer pieces that make up the volume, in subject, in vocabulary and even in the titles: 'Ode: Autumn', 'Ode
to Melancholy', 'Sonnet: To Fancy', and 'Ruth', which is inspired by the famous lines in 'Ode to a Nightingale'. Hood's ode
on Autumn is especially instructive as showing how, in assimi-
lating Keats, he made something less, but his own, out of the
earlier poet. Phrases like 'lustrous eyes' from 'Ode to a Nightingale', 'Where are the blooms of Summer?' after 'Ode to
Autumn', and 'Last leaves for a love-rosary' and 'whose doom
is Beauty's' echoing 'Ode to Melancholy', and several similar
recollections, show how carefully Hood had read poems known
in his day to a comparatively small public. Yet the tones of the
two poems on Autumn are radically different. Hood's quite
lacks the mellow sensuousness of Keats's, and has nothing of the
exuberant fullness of his embrace of the season. Not only has he
modified to something approaching blandness the ripeness of the
original ode, but he has also tempered its sensuous langour to a
dreamy melancholy. Both poems are marked by an underlying
reflectiveness, but Hood's outlook is bleaker than that of Keats,
both more wan and less convinced of life within the season of
fall:

Oh go and sit with her, and be o'ershaded
Under the languid downfall of her hair, . . .
There is enough of sorrowing, and quite

Enough of bitter fruits the earth doth bear—
Enough of chilly droppings for her bowl;
Enough of fear and shadowy despair,
        To frame her cloudy prison for the soul!

Those other poems in this book written wholly or partly under the influence of Keats, Shelley or the Elizabethans show Hood as a very adept imitator. He can weave half-recollections and direct echoes into his poems, write lines similar in feeling and texture to those of his models, and still produce verses that are more than pastiche. The trouble is that his own sensibility and his conception of poetic values are at once less sensitive and less serious than those of Keats, and that he responds to experience in a more ordinary and less intense way. Still, there are times when, on his own level, he manages to express something like Keats's romantic apprehensions of magic and mystery, and his love for the more ambient aspects of the imagination, as in his sonnet, 'To Fancy':

> Most delicate Ariel! submissive thing,
> Won by the mind's high magic to its hest,—
> Invisible embassy, or secret guest,—
> Weighing the light air on a lighter wing;—
> Whether into the midnight moon, to bring
> Illuminate visions to the eye of rest,—
> Or rich romances from the florid West,—
> Or to the sea, for mystic whispering,—
> Still by thy charmed allegiance to the will
> The fruitful wishes prosper in the brain,
> As by the fingering of fairy skill,—
> Moonlight, and waters, and soft music's strain,
> Odours, and blooms, and *my* Miranda's smile,
> Making this dull world an enchanted isle.

Some of Hood's sonnets, in fact, deserve to rank high among those written in the nineteenth century, as much for their assurance as for their markedly personal tone. One of his best, 'Silence', was imitated by Edgar Allan Poe in his own sonnet of the same name, after he had published Hood's poem in *Burton's Gentleman's Magazine* in 1839, oddly enough over the signature, 'P.'. As has often been remarked, Hood's opening lines recall well-known lines from Byron's 'Childe Harold', beginning 'There is a pleasure in the pathless woods'; and there is perhaps, too, a distant memory here of Shelley's 'Ozymandias', but its muted tone and sombre-hued melancholy are unmistakably Hood's:

> There is a silence where hath been no sound,
> There is a silence where no sound may be,
> In the cold grave,—under the deep, deep sea,
> Or in wide desert where no life is found,
> Which hath been mute, and still must sleep profound:
> No voice is hush'd,—no life treads silently,
> But clouds and cloudy shadows wander free,
> That never spoke, over the idle ground:
> But in green ruins, in the desolate walls
> Of antique palaces, where Man hath been,
> Though the dun fox, or wild hyena, calls,
> And owls, that flit continually between,
> Shriek to the echo, and the low winds moan,
> There the true Silence is, self-conscious and alone.

Whatever reservations we may have about the longer poems of Hood, we must acknowledge his success with the short lyric and song, forms that the Romantics cultivated so capably. Hood went back to the seventeenth century, it would seem, for some of his inspiration, since, at his best, he has a touch of Suckling and Herrick, as in

> It was not in the Winter
>   Our loving lot was cast;
> It was the time of Roses,—
>   We plucked them as we pass'd;

or

> Spring, it is cheery,
> Winter is dreary,
> Green leaves hang, but the brown must fly;
>   When he's forsaken,
>   Wither'd and shaken,
> What can an old man do but die?

In these and in poems like 'O lady, leave thy silken thread', 'I love thee', 'The stars are with the voyager', 'Song for music', 'Ruth', one of the best pieces in the 1827 volume, and 'Fair Ines', the lovely poem in which Poe found 'inexpressible charm', Hood establishes his right to be regarded as one of the most gifted writers of the little lyric in English.

The Plea of the Midsummer Fairies introduced this form and, even in later years, when he had largely abandoned wholly serious verse, he continued on occasion to produce such poems. His temperament responded readily to the courtly romanticism of Elizabethan song, and his talent for unpretentious language and languid sentiment, and his taste for the flower and jewel stereotypes of earlier lyrics and for the engaging conceit make his songs successful exercises in an old convention:

> O Lady, leave thy silken thread
>   And flowery tapestrie:
> There's living roses on the bush
>   And blossoms on the tree;
> Stoop where thou wilt, thy careless hand
>   Some random bud will meet;
> Thou canst not tread but thou wilt find
>   The daisy at thy feet.

In the 1827 book, there are, as we have seen, several poems that disclose Hood's preoccupation with death and decay. Further indications of this strain are found in 'I remember, I remember', one of his best-known poems and 'A Retrospective Review', both of which, although written by a quite young man, look back upon childhood with nostalgia and a sense of loss more appropriate to a very old one. Although the terms may be in part literary, the mood is obviously perfectly genuine. In the final stanza of 'I remember', which, as an expression of the loss of the childhood sense of wonder, has few equals on its own level, he effectively uses the near-pun, that exploitation of the double significance of a word that so often gives an extra strength to his verse, as indeed real puns, used seriously, also do:

> I remember, I remember,
> The fir trees dark and high;
> I used to think their slender tops
> Were close against the sky;
> It was a childish ignorance,
> But now 'tis little joy
> To know I'm farther off from Heav'n
> Than when I was a boy.

'A Retrospective Review', as the punning title indicates, is a less serious approach to the same subject, with some light-hearted puns of this order:

> I'd 'kiss the rod' and be resign'd
> Beneath the stroke, and even find
>   Some sugar in the cane!

But already the doomed awareness of his life's work, with its endless writing, in pain and sickness, for a scant living, forces its way out in occasional verses of undiluted seriousness:

> No more in noontide sun I bask;
> My authorship's an endless task,
>   My head's ne'er out of school:
> My heart is pain'd with scorn and slight,
> I have too many foes to fight,
>   And friends grown strangely cool!

Since the shadow of Keats lies so heavily on this volume and on almost all the early serious poems Hood wrote, for instance, 'The Poet's Portion' which ends:

> So that what there is steep'd shall perish never,
> But live and bloom, and be a joy for ever,

this is the appropriate place to mention one work which, although it was not published until many years later, belongs to this period of Keats's influence, and shows his effect on Hood more strongly than anything else the latter wrote. This is 'Lamia', a dramatization of Keats's poem. Presumably written in the 1820's, it remained in manuscript until after Hood's death, when Jane sent it to William Jerdan, editor of the *Literary Gazette*. Jerdan had known her husband, and had highly praised *The Plea of the Midsummer Fairies* as like 'a lovely summer day, sunny, not scorching; placid, enchanting, its airs balmy and refreshing'. He gave 'Lamia' its first publication in his own *Autobiography*.

The theme of the work seems to have fascinated Hood, for he makes more than one reference to it in 'Lycus the Centaur', as in

> And the snake, not with magical orbs to devise
> Strange death, but with woman's attraction of eyes.

His closet drama need not detain us long. Even granted that the subject is an unpromising one for a play, Hood completely lacked the theatrical instinct necessary to make it dramatically exciting. He does attempt to give the story dramatic shape, and introduces new characters, but they are thinly conceived, and the dialogue is stuffed with inflated nineteenth-century pseudo-Shakespearean rhetoric:

> Go! desperate man; away!—and fear thy gods,
> Or else the hot indignation in my eyes
> Will blast thee!

The play has none of the inner significance, however vague it be, of Keats's poem, and, although there is some power and insight in the conception of Lamia herself, Hood's attempt can only be called a failure. Perhaps he recognized this himself, since he never published it—an unusual thing for a man who was forced to turn every scrap of writing to profit—and since the huddled ending indicates that it was neither properly finished nor revised. The most interesting thing about 'Lamia' is that it shows a certain waning of the impact of Keats's style. Despite the many Keatsian touches, of the order of

> And gold and silver chafers bobbed about;
> And when there came a little gust of wind,
> The very flowers took wing and chased the butterflies,

the language is in the main simple and closer to Hood's own in his lyrics.

The 1827 volume, then, was an ambitious assault on the high tors of poetry; it was imitative, yet intelligently and sensitively so; it showed excellent discrimination in its choice of models, most notably Keats, at that time fully appreciated by few; it showed a versatility, a metrical dexterity and a gracious sensibility that gave promise of better things; it contained a number of short poems that succeed completely on their own modest level and others with flashes of pure poetry; all in all, it was one of the most interesting and appealing books of poetry of its decade. Yet the public response was disappointing; the book sold badly, despite the encomiums of friends such as Lamb, who replied to what he described to Hood as 'unworthy to be cared for attacks' with a prose paraphrase of 'The Plea' in Hone's *Table Book*, and Edward Moxon, who wrote a laudatory notice beginning

> Delightful bard! what praises meet are thine,
> More than my verse can sound to thee belong;

Well hast thou pleaded with a tongue divine,
    In this thy sweet and newly breathèd song.

Tom Hood says in the *Memorials*, 'My father afterwards bought up the remainder of the edition, as he said himself, to save it from the butter shops.' In many journals it was ignored completely; the most common opinion was that it was a pity that Hood had turned from comic and satirical verse for which he had so obviously a flair to write trivialities of this serious kind; the *Monthly Review* went so far as to compare him with the comedian hankering to play Hamlet. Hood's disappointment was profound; his attempt to establish himself as a serious poet had, apparently, lamentably failed. But it is typical of the man's unbounded resilience that he did not waste time lamenting but wrote off *The Plea of the Midsummer Fairies* to experience, and turned at once to writing and compiling another volume of *Whims and Oddities*.

This appeared in October, 1827, and contained the mixture as before—prose pieces, lyrics, comic poems, narrative poems, comic ballads. 'The Demon Ship' is perhaps the best of those pieces in which Hood leads the reader up the garden path with a horrific description, in this case of a seemingly demonic crew on a black ship, only to let him down with a bump at the end; the ship here proving to be a coal-freighter. 'Bianca's Dream', a lightly satirical 'Venetian story' in Byron's manner, has its fair share of verbal tricks and puns:

Maidens who cursed her looks forgot their own,
    And beaux were turned to flambeaux where she came . . .

Born only underneath Italian skies,
Where every fiddle has a Bridge of Sighs,

and so on. 'Death's Ramble', an early exercise in the comic-macabre, pours out its grisly puns in stanza-loads:

He met a dustman ringing a bell,
    And he gave him a mortal thrust;
For himself, by law, since Adam's flaw,
    Is contractor for all our dust.

He saw a sailor mixing his grog,
    And he marked him out for slaughter;
For on water he scarcely had cared for Death,
    And never on rum-and-water.

> Death saw two players playing at cards,
> But the game wasn't worth a dump,
> For he quickly laid them flat with a spade,
> To wait for the final trump!

This volume went into a second edition in 1829, and in 1832 the two series of *Whims and Oddities* were combined and continued to be reprinted up to the 1890's. The reviewers who had ignored his serious verse accepted the new *Whims and Oddities* with joy. Hood was never a man to nurse a wrong, but that his disappointment at the reception of *The Plea* went deeper than his mien at the time indicated is seen from scattered references in his later poems, the lines, for instance 'To a Critic', written in a very rough imitation of Chaucer, that begin:

> O cruel one! How littel dost thou knowe
> How manye Poetes with Unhappynesse
> Thou may'st have slaine ere they beganne to blowe
> Like to yonge Buddes in theyre firste sappynesse!

Yet, although he was to write serious verse in the future, never again was he to tempt the critics by issuing a collection of wholly straight verse. The public wanted him to be a funny man; and he would oblige them—for a living.

It has often been claimed that the hostile and indifferent reception given to *The Plea of the Midsummer Fairies* was a disaster for poetry in that it diverted the considerable talents of Hood into second-rate entertainment, and verbal slapstick. It is easy to understand such a point of view when, knowing Hood only as a jester, one comes across the book for the first time. Yet, for all the promise and the real accomplishment of the work, I wonder whether, in fact, Thomas Hood would have been able to do again anything very much better than this had he received support and encouragement. Among his contemporaries of the interregnum, Thomas Moore had written better lyrics, John Clare much more exquisite nature poetry, Thomas Lovell Beddoes was exploring the freakish areas of sensibility with more originality, George Darley, in *Nepenthe* at least, was carrying forward the Keatsian mode, and Alfred Tennyson, whose first volume of poems, written with his two brothers, appeared in the same year as Hood's book, was to develop the post-Keatsian style in directions unglimpsed by Hood.

94

The Comic and the Serious

For all the charm and talent of his early serious poems, I cannot feel that they represent the character of his authentic gifts and individuality, which was for the grotesque, as in 'The Last Man' and 'Miss Kilmansegg and her Precious Leg', the exuberantly comic and pun-crammed piece, the sombre and macabre, as in 'The Dream of Eugene Aram' and 'The Haunted House', the poem of gentle domestic sentiment, as in 'The Death-Bed', and 'Farewell Life', and such human-itarian verses as 'The Song of the Shirt' and 'The Bridge of Sighs'. In these poems is to be found the real Hood the poet, not in the clever, but overly bookish productions that make up the bulk of *The Plea of the Midsummer Fairies*. It was not, however, until Hood had rid himself of his ambition to become another Keats and came to draw his subjects and his emotions more directly from life that he wrote poetry that is remembered. The critics of his first serious book may not have been wholly wrong, then, nor may it have been altogether a bad thing that Hood was diverted into other fields by its failure and so avoided be-coming, as well he might, a poet as unreadable and as sterile as Leigh Hunt.

V

The World of Journalism

WHEN Hood recovered something like normal health after the
Brighton visit, he plunged once more into journalism, where his
pen could most readily earn his daily bread. During previous
years, he had been writing tirelessly for magazines and annuals
—the *New Monthly Magazine*, the *Literary Gazette*, *Blackwood's*,
Friendship's Offering, *Forget-me-Not* and the *Literary Sampler*, and
other miscellanies whose inane titles were usually matched by a
mediocrity of content. Selling by the thousand as Christmas gifts,
these volumes, which included such works as Lady Blessing-
ton's *Book of Beauty* (1834–47) and *The Keepsake* (1841–9), were
a curious manifestation of the literary taste of the 1830's and
1840's. Bound in velvet or watered silk, they contained a
strange mixture of scraps by distinguished writers, a few good
works by conscientious ones, trifles by obscure poetasters, and
vapourings by aspiring noblemen, illustrated with steel engravings showing mourning maidens, drooping nymphs,
saucer-eyed dogs, urns and vapid landscapes, with a ruin or
two tastefully disposed therein.

In these journals and annuals, Hood first published some of
his better poems, such as 'The Water Lady', 'I remember',
'Autumn' and 'Ruth'. In 1826, he had taken on a more regu-
lar and exacting job, that of dramatic critic for a newly estab-
lished journal, *The Atlas*, described by its editor, Robert
Stephen Rintoul, as 'A General Newspaper and Journal of
Literature, on the Longest Sheet Ever Issued from the Press'.
In a letter to Alaric A. Watts, Hood later referred to this weekly

paper on large folio sheets 'nearly double the size of *The Times*'
as 'A large sheet quotha—a patch-work quilt rather! Twice as
big as a daily without being any better, like a spread-eagle to
an eagle *au naturel*! A little intelligence going a long way, like a
puddle overflowing Lincolnshire level. Poor in matter but
prodigious, like Bankruptcy enlarged! A Gog among news-
papers, and as wooden!'

This uncomplimentary letter was written after Hood, following a disagreement with Rintoul, had severed his connection
with the journal. During the four months or so he served on the
paper, he had a pretty free hand with his weekly couple of
thousand words on current drama. He brought to his job no
real knowledge of the professional theatre, nor indeed any
genuine enthusiasm for drama as such, but, as always, an alert
and lively mind, a bouncing wit, much common sense and a
down-to-earth taste that knew what it liked. For instance,
commenting on a dramatization of Scott's *Woodstock* at Covent
Garden, he wrote: 'As soon as the Great Unknown has treated
the public with a novel, the next operation is to hash it up for
the drama; and, in most cases, it does not bear the after process
quite so well as hare. The present is one of those cases—the three
volumes are served up again, in five acts; and the public have
accepted it with a sufficiently hearty relish. The novel did not
seem to us furnished with plot enough for stage adaptation—
and for want of a sufficient story, the play drags on rather
heavily. We would have Mr. Farren to reconsider the character of Sir Henry Lee, against the next representation. There
was too much of face-making, and not enough of the hearty,
hunter-like roughness—it was not, in fact, the Sir Henry Lee
of the novel; he looked too much an innocent to be classed
amongst the Malignants but it would have made a capital
Polonius. Let Mr. Warde, too, sober his transports of anguish
a little at sight of the first Charles's portrait. Old Noll might
perchance feel as tenderly, but he certainly would never have
displayed it—and before a cavalier. . . . We would advise a
great deal of pruning before the piece is played again—or, to
refer to our first comparison, let the gristles and the skin be
taken out.'

On occasion, he would include poems in his weekly articles,
such as vivacious addresses to Miss Kelly and the well-known

comic actor, Mr. Wrench, and a celebration of the pleasures of Vauxhall Gardens:

> Come, come, I am very
> Disposed to be merry—
> So hey! for a wherry
>   I beckon and bawl!
> 'Tis dry, not a damp night,
> And pleasure will tramp light
> To music and lamp light
>   At shining Vauxhall!

It was probably Hood's experience as drama critic on *The Atlas*, which ended in August, 1826, that inspired him to try his hand in the commercial theatre. His efforts in this direction call for little attention, since what has survived, or has been identified as his work, belongs to the sub-literary level of the contemporary popular stage. *York and Lancaster or A School without Scholars*, which he wrote in 1828 for Frederick Henry Yates, actor-manager of the Adelphi, and Charles Mathews, the comedian, and was finally produced after many delays, in October, 1829, is a dismal farce of the burletta type, with disguises, feeble puns and dispirited songs. He also wrote sketches, songs and recitations for the Mathews and Yates' 'At Homes', or one-man revues, some very amusing in their way, but hardly dramatic material. Mathews, who specialized in 'monopolylogues', or sketches in which he played all the characters, called his Adelphi entertainments between 1830 and 1833 'Comic Annuals', advertising them in imitation of Hood's books, 'With comic cuts and other embellishments'. An 1830 review stresses the resemblance to Hood by saying 'The rogue has this year baptized his packet of whims and oddities a "Comic Annual".'

A two-act musical work, *Mr. Sims*, first played at the Surrey during a benefit for C. R. Elliston, the actor, has disappeared. A fragment survives of *Lost and Found*, probably part of a farce accepted for Drury Lane in 1826–7 but never produced.[1] This is straightforward eighteenth-century style farce, some distance after George Colman, without life, wit or originality. There is nothing in these pieces to suggest that Hood had any talent

[1] Whitley: 'Thomas Hood as a Dramatist', op. cit.

for the theatre, or that he expended any serious effort on it, although it is only fair to recall that the poverty-stricken state of drama at the time and the coarse commercialism of the professional stage provided neither encouragement nor opportunity for gifted men of letters, and works of high quality would have had small chance of appearing on the boards.

Hood's spell of recuperation at Brighton in 1828 did something at least for his spirits, as witness his words to Robert Balmanno in March of that year: 'The effect of the sea upon me is almost incredible. I have found some strength and much appetite already, though I have but sniffed the brine a single time. . . . I don't bore myself with writing . . . but amuse myself with watching the waves, or a seagull, or the progress of a fishing boat, matters trifling enough, but they afford speculation seemingly to a score old smocked, glazed hatted, blue-breeched boatmen or fishermen before my windows, and why not to me? There is great pleasure in letting a busy restless mind lie fallow a little, and mine takes to its idleness very complacently.'

Back home at Robert Street, however, Hood's restless mind impelled him once more into the hurly-burly of miscellaneous journalism. 1828 was a year of almost incredible productivity. He undertook to edit a new annual called *The Gem*. These gift-books, in general, were highly profitable Christmas trade items for the publishers, but they involved the poor editor in an immense amount of work, including bullying friends into contributing 'some little thing', and writing innumerable letters of sometimes grovelling solicitation to well-known authors for scraps from their work-bench. Hood was to be forced to do this many times in the future when he issued his own annuals; compiling *The Gem* gave him plenty of experience in the genteel art of editorial begging.

He met with considerable success in this initial venture. From Jane he obtained the manuscript of Keats's unpublished sonnet, 'On a Picture of Leander'; he printed Lamb's piece 'On an Infant Dying as Soon as Born', and he managed to prise contributions from 'Barry Cornwall', John Clare, Reynolds (writing as 'Edward Herbert'), Bernard Barton, Hartley Coleridge, and others. Perhaps his main showpiece was Sir Walter Scott, who readily and cordially supplied his stanzas on

'The Death of Keeldar' for *The Gem*. On March 4, Scott wrote
to Hood from Edinburgh:

My dear Mr. Hood—It was very ungracious in me to leave
you in a day's doubt whether I was gratified or otherwise with
the honour you did me to inscribe your whims and oddities to
me. I received with great pleasure this new mark of your kindness and it was only my leaving your volume and letter in the
country which delayed my answer as I forgot the address.

I was favoured with Mr. Cooper's beautiful sketch of the
heart-piercing incident of the dead greyhound ('The Death of
Keeldar') which is executed with a force and fancy which I
flatter myself that I who was in my younger days and in part
still am a great lover of dogs and horses and an accurate
observer of their habits can appreciate. I intend the instant
our term ends to send a few verses if I can make any at my
years in acknowledgment. I will get a day's leisure for this
purpose next week when I expect to be in the country. Pray
inform Mr. Cooper of my intention, though I fear I will be
unable to do anything deserving of the subject.

I am very truly your obliged humble servant,
    Walter Scott.

Hood had the pleasure of meeting Scott a few months later
when the Great Unknown invited him to pay a visit on May
19 to the Lockharts' house in Sussex Place, where Scott was
staying. Hood records in his reminiscences: 'The number of
the house had escaped my memory; but seeing a fine dog down
an area, I knocked without hesitation on the door. It happened,
however, to be the wrong one. I afterwards mentioned the circumstance to Sir Walter. It was not a bad point, he said, for he
was very fond of dogs; but he did not care to have his own
animals with him in London "for fear he should be taken for
Bill Gibbons". I then told him I had lately been reading the
Fair Maid of Perth, which had reminded me of a very pleasant
day spent many years before, beside the Linn of Campsie, the
scene of Conachar's catastrophe. Perhaps he divined what had
really occurred to me—that the Linn, as a cataract, had greatly
disappointed me; for he smiled, and shook his head archly, and
said he had since seen it himself, and was rather ashamed of it.
"But I fear, Mr. Hood, I have done worse than that before now,

in finding a Monastery where there was none to be found; though there was plenty (here he smiled again) of Carduus Benedictus, or Holy Thistle."

'In the meantime, he was finishing his toilet, in order to dine at the Duchess of Kent's; and before he put on his cravat I had an opportunity of observing the fine massive proportions of his bust. It served to confirm me in my theory that such mighty men are, and must be, physically, as well as intellectually, gifted beyond ordinary mortals; that their strong minds must be backed by strong bodies. Remembering all that Sir Walter Scott had done, and all that he had suffered, methought he had been in more than one sense, "a Giant in the Land". After some more conversation, in the course of which he asked me if I ever came to Scotland, and kindly said that he should be glad to see me at Abbotsford, I took my leave, with flattering dreams in my head that never were, and now, alas! never can be, realized!'

In Hood's reference to Scott's robust frame, we can see again that constant awareness he had of his own physical frailty and of a need for mental stamina beyond the ordinary to meet the claims his work made on him.

The Gem appeared in October, 1828, to snare the Christmas trade, and was a most considerable success, exhausting 5,000 copies in its first printing, and about half that number in a second. Hood's own contributions were 'A May-Day', a prose diversion, four poems—'On a Picture of Hero and Leander', a punning piece of comic verse on the same subject as his long serious poem, 'The Farewell', a lyric, 'Birthday Verses' and 'The Dream of Eugene Aram', as well as a little essay in imitation of Lamb, 'The Widow'. The two latter pieces attracted more attention than anything else in the volume, one favourably, the other not.

Lamb had promised him a prose sketch to accompany an engraving called 'The Widow'. In Hood's own words: 'A prose article, in *The Gem*, was not from his hand, though it bore his name. He had promised a contribution, but being unwell, his sister suggested that I should write something for him, and the result was the "Widow" in imitation of his manner.' This brief piece was a skilful pastiche in the familiar style of 'Elia', and Hood printed it over the signature, 'C. Lamb'. He goes on to say: 'It will be seen that the forgery was taken in good part', and quotes a letter Lamb wrote, as Thomas Hood, to him, as Charles Lamb!:

Dear Lamb—You are an impudent varlet, but I will keep your secret. We dine at Ayrton's on Thursday, and shall try to find Sarah and her two spare beds for that night only. Miss M. and her Tragedy may be d—d, so may *not* you and your rib. Health attend you.——Yours

T. Hood, Esq.

Enfield.

Miss Bridget Hood sends love.

Unhappily for the little jest, 'The Widow', which accompanied a sickly engraving of a woman and child, struck several critics as being in poor taste; and, to be sure, Hood's jocularity is rather heavy-handed here: 'A widow, that hath lived only for her husband, should die with him. She is flesh of his flesh and bone of his bone; and it is surely not seemly for a mere rib to be his survivor.' The critic in the *Eclectic Review* said that the piece profaned C. R. Leslie's picture by its 'heartless ribaldry'. Despite Hood's assertion that the forgery was taken in good part, and Lamb's letter just quoted, it seems that the latter came, on reflection, to take some offence at the tone of the parody.

He wrote to Hood on December 17, 1828, after seeing the piece in print: 'When I got the proof sheet, I was puzzled and stagger'd. I did not at all expect that you would put my name to anything; I only understood that you were going to write something in my way. However, I did accept it, and by that acceptance am bound to incur whatever penalties, &c—with the exception of two words in inverted commas near the beginning, which has raised up all the stir, I see no reason why any objection should have been raised against it'. The two words to which Lamb refers are in the sentence 'Her sables are a perpetual "Black Joke" '. Lamb was very jealous of his reputation as a clean writer, one above the kind of smutty innuendoes common enough in eighteenth-century journalism and even in that of the early nineteenth century, and it must have come as a shock to him to have it pointed out, as he tells Hood in the same letter, that the phrase was taken from 'some very old indelicate song'. Hood, who valued his reputation for not bringing a blush to the cheek of the Young Person as jealously as did Lamb his, was surely ignorant of the reference when he used the phrase. At the end, Lamb says: 'I think you had better let it drop, or say we did it between us and make light of it. . . . Having exhausted all my ill blood in the above, let it be as it had never been, and us old friends to the latest day as ever.' Yet the incident rankled with him all the same, and in a letter to 'Barry Cornwall' in January of the next year, he mentions a sonnet of his own published in *Blackwood's*: ' 'Twas written for the "Gem", but the editors declined it, on the plea that it would *shock all mothers*; so they published "The Widow" instead. I am born out of time. I have no conjecture about what the world calls delicacy.'

The whole episode was unfortunate. We may be sure that there was no crude attempt on Hood's part to associate his friend with an obscene song, but he did so, unthinkingly, in not letting Lamb know that he was going to append his name to the parody. Although Hood was without malice, he was sometimes tactless, as men whose social activities are limited frequently are, and on occasion, through an exuberant sense of fun less inhibited than genteel lower middle-class circles would stand for, glancingly gave offence. His love for Lamb was sincere, and it is likely that he could not make out what all the fuss was about. Be that as it may, the incident, for all Lamb's protestations of undying friendship, lowered the temperature of their relationship quite a bit. E. V. Lucas, in his edition of Lamb's letters, prints only two more letters to Hood written in the remaining six years of Lamb's life. One of these contains generous praise of Hood's novel, *Tylney Hall*, and was written just a couple of months before Lamb died in December, 1834, which suggests that the two were at that time on good, if not intimate terms. But, in April, 1832, just after Hood had purchased Lake House, Wanstead, with some idea of farming the land, Lamb had written, rather waspishly, to Edward Moxon, 'Speaking of this, only think of the new farmer with his 30 acres. There is a portion of land in Lambeth parish named Knaves Acre. I wonder he overlook'd it,' which indicates that the halcyon days of their friendship were over.

Happier results followed the publication in *The Gem* of 'The

Dream of Eugene Aram', which was to become one of Hood's most popular poems. This was by no means the first treatment of the story of the usher-murderer. Shortly after Aram's execution in 1759, a pamphlet appeared giving an account of the trial and the text of his defence, and this was continually reprinted. The case was a gift, too, to the many compilers of sensational chapbooks and criminals' biographies so popular in the first decades of the century. It was probably as well known in Hood's day as the Crippen case is in our own. Bulwer-Lytton's novel based upon the same crime, which appeared in 1832 and whose success helped to spread the story throughout Europe, was undoubtedly inspired by the popularity of Hood's poem, which was issued separately, with illustrations by William Harvey, in 1831. But the poem, with its greater conciseness and force, has outlasted the over-written and hectically sentimental novel.

Much of the power of 'The Dream of Eugene Aram' comes from Hood's dexterous use of his six-line stanza, which has behind it a distant memory of Coleridge's 'Ancient Mariner'. As Hood controls it, the form, by its prolongation to the third rhyme, seems to convey the compulsiveness of Aram's guilt-stricken account of his dream to the bewildered boy. But the peculiar force of the poem arises more from Hood's talent for the macabre, his sense of the sinister and his gift for the fantastic, yet apt, image:

> And peace went with them, one and all,
>   And each calm pillow spread;
> But Guilt was my grim chamberlain
>   That lighted me to bed;
> And drew my midnight curtains round,
>   With fingers bloody red!

This potent image of remorse, and also the whole section in which Aram re-lives his crime on the two levels of nightmare and actuality, show a sensitive insight into the psychology of crime and the mind of a criminal, so that, although some of the touches are melodramatic, the total effect is one of mingled horror and compassion. The well-known final stanza:

> That very night, while gentle sleep
>   The urchin eyelids kiss'd,

> Two stern-faced men set out from Lynn,
> Through the cold and heavy mist;
> And Eugene Aram walk'd between
> With gyves upon his wrist.

achieves a kind of catharsis after the mental agony of the murderer's account. Since Aram at his trial was anything but remorseful—on the contrary, coolly defiant, Hood's treatment is as unexpected as it is convincing.

The language of the poem, with such epithets as 'leaden-eyed', 'horrid', 'ghastly', 'dreadful', 'blood-avenging', 'crimson', 'guilty', 'fever'd' is in perfect harmony with the disordered mind of the speaker, and, at times, when the emotion is at its most intense, it can touch heights of stripped and pared statement:

> Then down I cast me on my face,
> And first began to weep.
> For I knew my secret then was one
> That earth refused to keep;
> Or land or sea, though he should be
> Ten thousand fathoms deep.

This harmony between subject and expression makes Hood's poem a work of art in its own somewhat morbidly compelling way. His personal experience of pain, doubtless, too, his own sleepless and worried nights, free from guilt though they were, made him sensitive to the unresting spirit of Aram; but it was his special talent for the horrible that lifts the poem above the average and impressed Poe so much. If it is compared with the broadsheet ballads, which it superficially resembles, it will be seen that here again, as with 'Faithless Nelly Gray' and his comic ballads, Hood had managed to give dignity, freshness and individuality to a popular form.

Hood edited *The Gem* for only one issue, although it appeared for three more years. He seems to have quarrelled with the publisher, Marshall, over terms, to judge from references in a letter by Hartley Coleridge to his mother in 1829:[1] '—item, that I have received a letter from Mr. Hood's Brother [J. H. Reynolds] informing me that Mr. Hood has declined the

[1] See also a letter from Hood to A. Cooper about Marshall's terms. (British Museum.)

Editorship of that work—and referring me for payment to Mr. Marshall—No.—1 Holborn Bars, the person in whose name I was applied to for contributions to the *Gem*, with the somewhat unacceptable information that said Mr. Marshall is a very mean, impracticable, disagreeable sort of personage. . . . Hood is going to publish a comic Annual. I wish his speculation may not prove a tragedy to himself and a farce to the rest of the world. He is a man of real genius, and I wish him well.'

Hood was unfortunate in his relations with many editors and publishers. The fault was unquestionably sometimes on his side; his friends and acquaintances agree that he was of a sanguine temperament and that he was kind and gentle in his personal relations. But his constant invalidism must have made him not always easy to deal with, and his desperate necessity to produce a regular income by his pen meant constant labour. In the circumstances of contemporary journalism, with publishing booksellers anxious to get as much as possible for as little as possible, it is not surprising that Hood must often have felt the remuneration to be inadequate, and that he should have clashed with them over terms. There is no evidence, either, that he was a good business-man—on the contrary—and he may often have engaged in work that called for a monetary return far below the worth of the time and the talent expended.

In 1828 and 1829 he was involved, as we have seen, in the unsatisfactory theatrical ventures with Yates. In the latter year, he became associated with others in a project that might have meant security for him had he not made an error of judgment at a critical point. The venture was the *Athenaeum*, which was founded by James Silk Buckingham, and which, taking the place of the dying *London Magazine*, was to become one of the most characteristic and successful of Victorian periodicals. The paper passed from Buckingham's hands into those of John Sterling, and then in 1829, when its affairs were in some confusion, into those of a small company of joint proprietors consisting of Charles Wentworth Dilke, Allan Cunningham, James Holmes, the printer, John Hamilton Reynolds and Thomas Hood. Dilke was the dynamic member of the group, who was later to stamp his personality firmly on the *Athenaeum*. When he joined the others in controlling the journal, he had behind him eight years of successful journalism, including much-praised articles in *Colburn's New Monthly*, *Fraser's Magazine*, the *London Magazine* and the *Retrospective Review*. The financial arrangements involved in the partnership are obscure, but by the end of 1830, Dilke had gained complete editorial control of the *Athenaeum*.

In the following year, his decision to lower its price from 8d. to 4d. a copy caused consternation among his fellow-proprietors. Reynolds was particularly agitated: 'You astound me with your fall. It is more decided than Milton's "Noon to Dewy Eve" one!' he wrote to Dilke on February 15. 'From 8d. to 4d. is but a step, but then it is also from the sublime to the ridiculous. Remember what an increase must take place to get it all home. A sale of 6,000! Mercy on us!' So distressed was he, in fact, that he wrote a second letter on the same day: 'Hood and I have been calculating this afternoon, and the result is appalling. To lower below 6d. would, in my opinion, be an inadvisable course, and such a fall would show that our previous state was hopeless. The difference between 6d. and 4d. would be 8£. 6s. 8d. a week in a thousand copies. The loss per annum on 5,000 copies would be 2,165£. . . . We are quite against the total change in our paper-constitution which you threaten.'

Dilke was adamant, however, and in a sufficiently strong position to carry his point, whereupon Reynolds withdrew, in June, 1831, and Hood went with him, partly because he felt that Dilke's move might involve him in financial loss, and partly as a gesture of solidarity with his brother-in-law. It was a most unhappy decision, since the lowering of the price meant the turning-point in the fortunes of the *Athenaeum*. Soon after the change, Dilke was able to inform his wife that sales were now six times their former number. By 1832, Dilke and Holmes were the sole owners of the journal, the former owning three-quarters of the shares. Under Dilke's shrewd editorship, the *Athenaeum* went on to become a financial success and a powerful literary influence.

Hood's break with the paper did not affect his relations with Dilke, with whom he remained on the closest terms of friendship and with whom he corresponded for over a decade afterwards. He continued, too, to write regularly for the paper, particularly lively and witty book-reviews which were able to extract fun even from such unpromising subjects as *Vegetable Cookery and The Maid-Servant's Friend* 'by a Lady brought up at the Foundling Hospital'. This solemn work proved irresistible to him: 'The housekeeper', he wrote, 'who peruses the above title, and then reads the work itself will meet with a delightful surprise. Every master and mistress in the United Kingdom knows what a maid-servant's friend is—sometimes he is a brother, sometimes a cousin (often a cousin) and sometimes a father, who really wears well and carries his age amazingly. He comes down the area—or at a window—or through a door left ajar. Sometimes a maid-servant, like a hare, has many friends —the master of the house, after washing his hands in the back kitchen, feels behind the door for a jack-towel, and lays hold of a friend's nose—friends are shy; sometimes the footman breaks a friend's shin while plunging into the coal-cellar for a shovel of nubblys.'

He reviewed *Master Humphrey's Clock* in 1840 and *Barnaby Rudge* in 1842; he frequently contributed verse, both comic and serious. Among his most notable pieces for the *Athenaeum* were his articles on 'Copyright and Copywrong' in 1837, of which more later. And he frequently enlivened the pages of the journal with humorous letters; the following missive in execrable French is typical. It is a reply to a Frenchman's attempt at a letter in English:

Gentilhommes—Comme je ne vis pas dans la cité mais dans la contrée, six milles depuis Londres, je n'ai pas une mode de vous envoyer la Comique Annual, mais je vous envoy un ordre sur mon publisheur, que je vous prie accepte, Son nom est Alfred Tête Baily, vivant à 83, Montagne à Blé, près le Changement Royale. Allez gauchement dans la rue … Mon livre peut être 'amusant' comme vous êtes si bon à dire, mais il n'a pas attempté être *'spirituel'*. Je ne suis pas un clergé-homme qui écrit les serments. Dieu vous blesse. Je suis,
Gentilhommes,
Votre très humble domestique,
Thomas Hood.

In the journal, too, Hood's own works, notably his *Comic Annuals*, received generous treatment, the books being reviewed

at length, with copious quotations, by either Reynolds or
Dilke himself.

In the same year in which he made his ill-advised withdrawal
from the *Athenaeum*, Hood engaged in countless activities with
the industry of a beaver. He had moved with Jane some time
in 1829 from the Adelphi to Rose Cottage, an attractive house
in the rural district of Winchmore Hill, handy to Enfield and
the Lambs; there was done most of his work for the next
three years. His health at this time, while far from robust,
seemed even enough, he was much in demand by editors and
his income was sufficient for him to keep up a moderate standard of living. He contributed to several gift books and annuals,
such as the *Bijou*, the *Amulet*, and *Forget-Me-Not* and others with
titles surprisingly like those of modern shop-girls' magazines,
he did engravings and drawings, and he scored a particular
success with *The Epping Hunt*, published in September, 1829, as a
small volume with six engravings by George Cruikshank.

This rollicking extension of his comic ballad style, which
contains 122 stanzas, begins as a parody of 'John Gilpin's
Ride', and resolves itself into a pun-crammed narrative of the
misadventures of John Huggins, food-warehouseman, at the
Epping Hunt, at least as it was in former times, for Hood wrote
to the publisher, Charles Tilt, 'the sport does not improve, but
appears an ebbing as well as Epping custom'. The poem is a
good-hearted satire on the aspiring sportsman, but its most
extraordinary feature is the torrent of puns it unleashes—some
brilliant, some ingenious, some strained, but in the mass
breeding astonishment at the unique verbal command that
enables Hood to keep it up for so long and with such unflagging
invention:

> Towler and Jowler—howlers all,
>   No single tongue was mute;
> The stag had led a hart, and lo!
>   The whole pack followed suit . . .
>
> Away! away! he scudded like
>   A ship before the gale;
> Now flew to 'hills we know not of',
>   Now, nun-like, took the vale.

Now and then, Hood's rage for a pun betrays him into what

most Christians today would regard as monstrously poor taste, although it probably did not seem so to Protestants of his own time:

> In merriest key I trow was he,
> So many guests to boast;
> So certain congregations meet,
> And elevate the host.

Throughout *The Epping Hunt* are scattered, as in almost all Hood's comic poems, little touches of pure fancy or poetic graces that lift his lighter works above those of, say, his rival punster, Theodore Hook:

> And, lo! the dim and distant hunt
> Diminished in a trice:
> The steeds, like Cinderella's team,
> Seem'd dwindled into mice;
>
> And, far remote, each scarlet coat
> Soon flitted like a spark—
> Tho' still the forest murmur'd back
> An echo of the bark!

The poem went into a second edition in 1830, and Hood planned a companion piece on the Epsom Races. This idea was never realized, although Charles Clark published a feeble imitation of Hood's manner under the title of 'Epsom Races' and impudently signed it 'Thomas Hood the Younger'.

However, the main project that was occupying Hood's mind at this time was his *Comic Annual*, to which his major energies were to be devoted during the next decade, which was to put a tremendous strain upon his physical and mental resources, which was to make him a pioneer in a now familiar form of publishing, and which was to contain some of his cleverest work.

VI

Life at Lake House

HOOD's conception of a 'comic annual' was something new, even in an age that had more than its share of annuals and miscellanies that came and went with the speed of modern 'little magazines'. Journals and annuals had published comic verse and prose, including much by Hood himself, for some years, but a large, almost untapped audience lay ready for a publication that was wholly comic. Hood's *Comic Annual*, later merging into *Hood's Own*, was an original enterprise, the first of the many humorous journals of the century. As soon as the first number was published for 1830, it inspired imitations; the *New Comic Annual*, sub-titled *Falstaff's Annual*, a blatant copy of Hood's enterprise, came out in 1831, and was advertised misleadingly by the publishers along with Hood's authentic writings, while Louisa Sheridan's *Comic Offering* or *Ladies' Mélange of Literary Mirth*, which was to run to 1835, also attempted in the same year to cash in on Hood's success. The *Comic Offering* was a very close imitation of Hood's original, the same size, with similar binding, the same mixture of comic prose and verse, spattered with punning illustrations. The main difference, apart from that of quality, is that only a handful of pieces are by the editor herself. The poems copy Hood's punning closely, e.g.

> Ulysses was a tough old Greek,
> And cunning as a fox;
> And little cared for thumps and blows
> As Catholics for—Knox.

Naturally piqued at these flagrant copies, Hood responded with some wounded remarks in the preface to the 1831 *Comic*

III

Annual: 'Now, I do not intend, like some votaries of freedom, to cast mud on the muddy, nor dirt on the dirty—but while I am on the hustings, I will ask the Committee of that Uncandid Candidate, "The New Comic", whether it was quite honest to canvass against me under my own colours, and to pass off the enemy's poll-book as mine? . . . Were there no other and fitter labels extant than those close parodies of mine? For example, The Laughing Hyena—or the Merry Unwise—or The Main-Chance? The Old Brown Bear in Piccadilly is bearish perhaps—but he is original. . . .

'Fain would I drop the steel pen for a softer quill, to speak of an Editress who—distinguishing fair from unfair—has acted the perfect brunette towards me, and brought a heavy charge against me "for work done". In the Announcement of "The Comic Offering"—a little book chiefly remarkable for its coating of Damson cheese, seemingly equally fit, like Sheridan's poor Peruvians, for "covering and devouring",—it is insinuated that I am an author unfit for female perusal:—I, who have never in that respect infringed which, with me dwells "like fringe upon a petticoat". Miss Sheridan and modesty compel me to declare that, many Ladies have deigned to request for their albums some little proof of "the versatility" or prosatility of my pen:—yet what says the Announcement, or rather Denouncement: "But shall we permit a Clown or Pantaloon to enter the Drawing-room or Boudoir; no, *not even under a Hood!*. . . .

'I confess, besides, that on being so attacked by a perfect stranger, I did at first think it rather hard of her; but having now seen her book, I think it rather soft of her, and shall say no more.'

What irked him further was the fact that the *New Comic Annual* had been issued by Hurst, Chance and Co., who had printed the first volume of his own *Comic Annual*, after which the arrangement was terminated and the annual transferred to Charles Tilt as publisher. Hood regarded the imitation as a stab in the back. Most of all, he was offended by Mrs. Sheridan's suggestion that his annual was unsuited to the drawing-room. 'If she has heard of my indelicacy or vulgarity, it must have been from Sir Benjamin Backbite.' In fact, one of the reasons for the continued success of Hood's annual was its whole-

someness and its appeal to the family. As Hartley Coleridge
said to him in 1832, Hood had proved 'that there may be fun
without mischief, jest without malice, and wit without bawd-
dry'. At the beginning of the 1830's there was a reaction against
the cynicism of Regency times in matters of public and private
morality. Although still, in journalism, some of the old seami-
ness continued side by side with a new emphasis on the desir-
ability of decency in reading material for the family, the old
obscene ballads had largely disappeared from the streets, the
scandal-sheets that had flourished in Hood's youth had diminished in number, and, unsqueamish though they were, the
middle-class readers of the 1830's were seeking publications
that gave decent entertainment and information.

Charles Knight was busy carrying instruction to the people.
As superintendent of the Society for the Diffusion of Useful
Knowledge, he had established in 1827 the *Library of Entertaining Knowledge* and, in 1828, the *British Almanac* and its
Companion. In 1832, the *Penny Magazine*, which contained no
fiction, but merely information, appeared, selling 200,000
copies in weekly and monthly parts. The two decades from 1830
were, in fact, the heyday of informative periodicals and 'fun-
books', before the rise of the sensational type of cheap publication dealing with rogues, vampires, demons, freaks, atrocities
and murders, such as the *London Journal* and the lurid rubbish
spawned by G. W. M. Reynolds and Edward Lloyd, which
flooded the market just after Hood's death. But in the 1830's,
the *Comic Annual* and others like it filled the bill for respectable
entertainment. Without being prissy, it was clean; its humour
was often knockabout and elementary, but it avoided sexual
coarseness and innuendo; it was, in short, just the kind of
diverting reading the respectable middle-class reader was looking for; its general tone and decorum, before Queen Victoria had
made her influence felt on nineteenth-century mores, showed
that 'Victorianism' was something that preceded Victoria, and
that her reign served to hallow rather than to inaugurate.

During the ten years of the *Comic Annual*, its form changed
little. These well-bound, gilt-edged volumes, averaging 176
pages, $6\frac{1}{2}$ inches by 4 inches, contained a medley of comic
verse and prose, as well as fifty and more full-page plates with
some thirty head-pieces and tail-pieces. The lively illustrations,

which look forward to the modern joke-cartoons of *Punch* and the *New Yorker*, did much for the *Annual's* success. Often enough, the visual jests are rudimentary or naive, as in the illustration of a man being carried up high by an explosion and saying, 'It's all up with me!' or that of a miserable farmer standing by his stacks in the rain above the caption, 'Hey-day!'. But several of the engravings of Hood's own, or done by John Leech, George Cruikshank, John Wright and others to Hood's designs have a more nearly Goonish humour about them—the fat Dutchman smoking a pipe in a small boat, labelled 'Dutch Steamer' or the cymbal-player in action captioned 'The Music of the Spheres'. More than once, as we may expect, the drawings, like the text, have a macabre humour, strikingly like that of Charles Addams—five men on a gallows illustrating 'Going at five knots an hour', two natives over a steaming bowl saying to a passing Irish sailor, 'Come, eat some paddy', a picture labelled 'Lovers' Seat', showing a couple beneath a tree in what first seems an idyllic scene, until a closer inspection shows gnats buzzing round the man's head, and an adder entwined round his leg, while ants crawl up the woman's skirt, bees buzz behind her, a snail makes tracks up her dress and a frog investigates her hat on the ground. This kind of humour is 'sick' enough for any modern reader, especially in such engravings as that in the 1831 *Comic Annual* wherein two men about to be hanged look down from the gallows at a bull pursuing another man, one saying to the other, 'How lucky, Bill, we are up here!' Physical and macabre humour of this kind Hood's readers could take in their stride; only sexual innuendo repelled them, and in this he never indulged.

The first *Comic Annual* differed from the others in containing work by other hands, the faithful 'Edward Herbert' and Horace Smith among them, while 'the late John Keats' was represented by 'Sonnet to a Cat'. Hood, experienced now in the technique of soliciting contributions, wrote many letters in preparing this first number. To Scott, for instance, he wrote on September 3, 1829:

Dear Sir,

Not having had the honour of hearing from you, I have indulged in the hope that you meant to favour me with some little humorous anecdote for the Comic Annual, according to my late request. I need not say that after having been able to pride myself on your poem in the Gem, I am very anxious to have some such token of your kindness in an annual of my own. I do not desire a quantity, or to speak it reverently—*Scott v. lot*— a few lines only would suffice to make me as proud as the lady of Tilliehidlem, and I should be happy to acknowledge the obligation by note of hand—as well as heart. . . .

> Most respectfully and truly yours,
> Thos. Hood.

It must have cost Hood much time and effort to write such letters, and the harvest was, in any case, meagre enough. Scott could send him nothing suitable, and others were equally unhelpful. The trouble seems to have been that few could write successfully the kind of comic material Hood had in mind for his annual. So, after the first issue, which was dedicated to Sir Francis Freeling, the Postmaster-General and 'great Patron of Letters', and in which, in any case, the bulk of the matter came from Hood himself, he relied upon his own pen to fill the nine succeeding volumes, with perhaps occasional assistance from Reynolds.

The second annual, for 1831, dedicated to 'His Grace the Duke of Devonshire, the great comptroller of all public performers; kindly countenancing plays upon words, as well as plays upon boards;—the noble patron of the Italian, as well as of the present English opera', contains 31 pieces, all by Hood, of which 20 are comic verses, including 'I'm not a Single Man', 'My Son and Heir' ('My mother bids me bind my heir'), 'The Duel' (another comic ballad), 'Domestic Asides', 'Ode for St. Cecilia's Eve' (a clever parody of Dryden's poem) and 'French and English':

> Never go to France,
> Unless you know the lingo.
> If you do, like me,
> You will repent, by jingo.

The prose consists of comic stories, articles and reflections, much in the manner of *Punch* today. One especially interesting set of engravings are the 'Fancy Portraits', which construct the faces of well-known people out of objects associated with their trade or profession; for instance, Kirke White is shown as the end of a church with windows for eyes, nose and mouth and Sir Isambard Brunel, the great railway engineer, is depicted with a huge open mouth like that of a railway tunnel. Salvador Dali is not quite as original as some of his admirers imagine.

With the launching of the *Comic Annual*, Hood became identified for good and all in the public mind as a comic writer; except for one or two of his friends, those few who had read his serious poems quickly forgot that side of his genius. Hartley Coleridge, 'Barry Cornwall' and others lamented that he did not 'exert his best and noblest talent', but he could not afford to indulge himself in any more pleas of midsummer fairies, and set himself to hold fast to the ear of the public he had caught as a comic entertainer. So successful was he at obliterating the memory of his serious work that Henry Crabb Robinson could write in his diary on March 9, 1846, less than a year after Hood's death: 'Read at night Hood's serious poems. I had no notion of the earnest strength of his serious verses. I was aware only of his comic merit and chiefly as a punster.'

Hood was now established as a licensed jester, good always for a laugh, available always for a comic commission. The Duke of Devonshire, in accepting the poet's gift of the first *Annual*, requested his help in devising original inscriptions for the painted spines of a door of sham books at the entrance to a library staircase at Chatsworth. Hood quickly supplied him with two lengthy lists, containing, among others, these suggestions: 'Percy Vere. In 40 volumes; Lamb on the Death of Wolfe; Malthus's Attack of Infantry; McAdam's Views in Rhodes; Pygmalion. By Lord Bacon; Boyle on Steam; Bookkeeping by Single Entry; John Knox on "Death's Door"; Designs for Friezes. By Captain Parry; Peel on Bell's System; Cursory Remarks on Swearing; Shelley's Conchologist; Recollections of Bannister. By Lord Stair; The Scottish Boccaccio by D. Cameron; Cook's Specimens of the Sandwich Tongue.'

Only the first four volumes of the *Comic Annual* had personal dedications, that of 1832 to King William IV and that of 1833 to Lady Harriet Granville. The King received the dedication and a copy of the book with interest and pleasure and asked to see the author. As Hood's children relate in the *Memorials*: 'He accordingly called upon His Majesty by appointment at

116

Brighton. My Father was much taken with his Majesty's cordial and hearty manner, and I believe he was very well received. One thing I remember is the fact, that on backing out of the royal presence, my father forgot the way he had entered, and retrograded to the wrong entry. The King good-humouredly laughed, and himself showed him the right direction, going with him to the door.' Hardly a memorable or a world-shaking encounter evidently—in fact, it might almost have come from 'Beachcomber'—but at least the mark of royal favour showed how firmly Hood had established himself with his annuals.

While he was working on the early issues of the periodical, he was also active with contributions to the *Athenaeum* and other journals, and with his 'entertainments' and comic songs for Charles Mathews. The success of the entertainments possibly led to his being invited to write words to music by Jonathan Blewitt, which were sung by Mathews and published in 1830 as *Comic Melodies*, consisting of three parts with two songs each. One of these, 'Lieutenant Luff', a typical comic ballad on the tragic consequences of intemperance, contained a succession of such unblushing puns as:

> According to this kind of taste
> Did he indulge his drouth,
> And being fond of *Port*, he made
> A *port*-hole of his mouth!
> A single pint he might have supped
> And not been out of sorts,
> In geologic phrase—the rock
> He split upon was *quarts*!

(Of course, the puns are always italicized, lest the reader should miss one!) The songs apparently caught on, since Blewitt afterwards considered it worth while to write music for 'Nelly Gray', 'Sally Brown' and 'John Trot', and to publish them as numbers of *The Ballad Singer*.

In 1830, Hood's second daughter, Frances Freeling, known as Fanny, was born, and, unlike the first child, survived. Her godparents were Sir Francis Freeling and Mrs. Charles Wentworth Dilke, or Maria, one of the Hoods' closest friends. Their circle of acquaintance was not large at this time—the Dilkes, the Lambs, the Balmannos and one or two other people Hood had come to know professionally, such as John Wright, were those he saw most frequently. He and Jane were content with this restricted group, and had no desire to form part of the 'literary life' of London itself.

A disagreement with the landlord of Rose Cottage over repairs led to the Hoods leaving Winchmore Hill some time in 1832, and moving to Lake House, close to Epping Forest in Essex. This residence had been fabricated by additions to an old hunting-lodge belonging to Wanstead House. The House had been built in 1715 by Sir Richard Child, later Earl Tylney, and Louis XVIII and other exiled Bourbons had stayed there; it had been demolished in 1822, leaving the hunting-lodge solitary and part derelict. Tom Hood described Lake House thus: 'It was a beautiful old place, although exceedingly inconvenient, for there was not a good bed-room in it. The fact was, it had formerly been a sort of banqueting-hall to Wanstead Park, and the rest of the house was sacrificed to the one great room, which extended all along the back. It had a beautiful chimney-piece carved in fruit and flowers by Gibbons, and the ceiling bore traces of painting. . . . Several quaint Watteau-like pictures of the Seasons were panelled in the walls, but it was all in a shocking state of repair, and in the twilight the rats used to come and peep out of the holes in the wainscoat. There were two or three windows on each side, while a door in the middle opened on a flight of steps leading into a pleasant wilderness of a garden, infested by hundreds of rabbits from the warren close by. From the windows you could catch lovely glimpses of forest scenery, especially one fine aspen avenue. In the midst of the garden lay the little lake from which the house took its name, surrounded by huge masses of rhododendrons.' Anticipating Dickens's Mr. Wemmick and perhaps supplying a hint for the character, Hood installed a miniature cannon at Lake House and would solemnly fire 'salutes' on it to welcome visitors or celebrate anniversaries. He was fond of shooting and the rabbits that over-ran the estate provided him with plenty of targets from the portico.

Lamb's tart comment, already quoted, indicates that Hood intended to farm at Wanstead. Although it seemed a good idea at the time, as taking the Hoods into a healthful rural atmosphere, later events showed that the move to Lake House was most ill-advised, for not only was the dilapidated house uncomfortable and inconvenient, but it proved damp and unhealthy for one in Hood's precarious state. His years at Wanstead were punctuated by bouts of illness, which necessitated trips to Brighton and Ramsgate for recuperation. Financially the house proved ruinous in upkeep, and with the farming involved him in a heavy expenditure. There is evidence, too, to show that at Lake House Hood lived beyond his means, entertaining friends generously, and keeping several guests, while he postponed urgent assignments for the sake of conviviality.

It is not surprising that, given his state of health, Hood should sometimes have procrastinated, having at the last moment to drive himself frantically to write a promised contribution or to complete a Comic Annual, which nearly always appeared late, anyhow. He told Dilke in 1834, for instance, 'I am fagging hard at the comic. It's an ill fire that bakes nobody's bread, and the Great Conflagration [the burning of the Houses of Parliament on October 16] will make an excellent subject. I was up all last night, bright moonlight, drawing cuts and writing, and watching a band of gipsies encamped just out of my bounds. I saved my fowls, and geese, and pigs, but they took my faggots. However, I shot two cats, that were poaching. As Scott says "My life is a mingled yarn". Today, the man's missing. I'm afraid he's scragged.'

For all this, Hood's spirits remained high, and the records of the Wanstead period show him often engaged in one of his major diversions, practical joking, a recreation dear to his unsophisticated age. Jane had learned to tolerate such japes played on herself from the days of their honeymoon. She bore them good-humouredly, and, her children say, joined in the laugh against herself with great good humour. On their first trip to Brighton, in 1828, Hood warned the inexperienced housewife against buying plaice with red or orange spots 'as they are sure signs of an advanced stage of decomposition'. When the fisher-woman came to the door, Jane displayed her newly-acquired knowledge by fussily turning over the fish, finding them all spotted and rejecting them accordingly. To her doubts of their freshness, the fisher-woman asserted that they had been caught that very morning. Jane replied, 'My good woman, it may be as you say, but I could not think of

buying any plaice with those very unpleasant red spots!' The
fisher-woman shouted indignantly, 'Lord bless your eyes,
Mum! who ever seed any without 'em?', while Hood roared
with laughter on the landing above. As Mrs. Balmanno recorded: 'Sometimes, perhaps, the jest was pointed a little too
heavily, but never did the sweet face or gentle voice of Mrs.
Hood betray anything like a cloud or exasperation even when
put to tests that would have proved eminently trying to the
female patience of many modern Goddesses!'

At Lake House, Hood often practised the same kind of rudimentary fun. On one occasion, he caught some boys robbing
his orchard. They were led, trembling, into the house by Hood
and his gardener. George Reynolds, Hood's father-in-law, a
gentleman of imposing aspect, took the poet's broad hint, and
assumed the character of a country J.P. The offenders were for-
mally charged by Hood, and their pockets yielded evidence of
their misdoings. Reynolds, with a severe air, sentenced them to
immediate execution by hanging on the cherry tree. Prompted
by her father, little Fanny knelt down and begged for mercy
on the boys. They, too, dropped to their knees, and asked
clemency, vowing never 'to do so no more'. On this, Hood and
Reynolds solemnly pardoned the 'criminals', and they ran off,
to the hearty laughter of the men. A cruel jest, surely, and one
that it is hard nowadays to think of as quite as funny as the
Hood family found it or to associate easily with a man as capable of tenderness and compassion as Hood undoubtedly was.
Yet this was part of the temper of the age, in which lingered
something of the brutality of earlier times, an age in which
public executions were still held, when soldiers were flogged
for the most trivial offences, when small children and women
attached to iron girdles drew coal for sixteen hours a day in the
foul darkness of the coal-pits.

In such a time, humour, especially that of Hood, an invalid,
almost inevitably dwelt heavily on the physical—on illness,
mutilation and death, and practical joking, the most physical
and often the most brutal form of humour, was a popular form
of diversion. On another occasion at Lake House, Hood was
tipped by some friends into the lake in his grounds. When,
soaking wet, he made his way indoors, he began to complain
of agonizing cramps and stitches, and took to his bed; Jane, who

was in the joke, was not perturbed; but the friends became alarmed as Hood's groans and moans increased, especially as there was no doctor for miles. Assuming that he had got ague or fever, they milled about with improvised remedies—one brought up a tin bath, another a kettle of boiling water, the third the mustard. Hood, in a sepulchral voice, quavered that he was dying, and solemnly gave out a list of absurd last requests, which the friends were too agitated to recognize as legpulls. Finally, after the penitent gulls had begged forgiveness for toppling him into the water, he exploded the jest with a shout of laughter, which they at first took for a delirious frenzy.

He even played jokes on his children, such as painting Fanny's wooden doll with large pink spots which convinced her that the doll had caught the measles, or plastering a pinch of damp gun-powder round the wick of her candle just before she lit it to take to her bedroom. And to his friends he would often send hoaxing letters or illiterate ones pretending to come from readers of the magazines they edited. We may find it easier to excuse these frivolities if we realize that it was partly by such means, jests for pleasure rather than for payment, that Hood was enabled to face the grind of being a professional funny-man while his body was racked with pain. Like Mrs. Mopp, it was being so cheerful as kept him going. Just occasionally did a hint of a complaint break through, as when he wrote to Dilke, 'I am a little Job in afflictions, but without his patience.'

During 1833, a major project, which had been in his mind for some time, occupied a great part of his energies. This was *Tylney Hall*, a three-volume novel, Hood's first, and, in fact, his last.

Although announced for publication in January, 1834, *Tylney Hall* was delayed until the end of the year through a disagreement between Hood and the original publisher, Charles Tilt, who had issued the *Comic Annual* since 1831. When the novel did appear, it was published by A. H. Baily, who put out the *Annual* from 1835. Some causes of Hood's quarrel with Tilt were indicated by the poet in a letter to Dilke from Coblenz: 'And here as a corroboration of my notion of Tilt's villainy let me first mention the following. I sold 500 of my first annual (with Hurst & Chance) to America. Of the second I sold some more, having been applied to *myself*, for some. After that for three years I sold none, Tilt telling me there was no demand or that the Americans reprinted it. For the 6th annual, in Baily's hands, I have had a demand again for 500—& amongst the letters sent out to me is one from Philadelphia with an offer of money for *early sheets* to reprint in Knickerbocker's Magazine of New York. It says, "You are every where admired in the best parts of America and your puns and sayings are extremely quoted. I think that the advent of your annual is a matter of as much moment in this country as that of the President's message."—Coupling this with the late order for 500 and knowing the Americans cannot well reprint for want of woodcutters, I think 'tis at least a suspicious case.'

Hood's troubles with publishers were chronic. Some of the difficulty—as with Tilt—undoubtedly lay with the grasping nature of many bookseller-publishers at the time, their miserable royalties, their cheating of their authors and their ability to strike hard bargains with penurious writers like Hood, as well as with the hopeless inadequacy of the copyright laws. But part of the blame must lie with Hood. It was difficult enough for even a popular writer, sustained by a modest private income, to make a good living in Hood's time; it must have been almost impossible for him, with his own and Jane's bouts of illness, his constant need of recuperative vacations, and his ambitious attempt to maintain the shambling, ruinous Lake House. He suffered acutely, too, from the perennial author's suspicion that all publishers enrich themselves at the expense of their writers. Hood, so amiable a friend, so loving a husband and father, displayed in his dealings with publishers a sensitive temper which led him from one difficult situation to another.

In any case, *Tylney Hall* finally appeared on October 20, 1834. If there was one thing that the book demonstrated beyond doubt, it was that Hood was no novelist. A couple of months before he died, Lamb wrote, in one of his last letters, a friendly but not uncritical comment on it that shows no sign of the coolness of relationship that had earlier developed between the two:

Dr. H——,
I have been infinitely amused with 'Tylney Hall'. 'Tis a medley, of farce, melodrame, pantomime, comedy, tragedy,

punchery, what not? if not the best sort of novel, the best of its sort, as how could it fail, being the only one? 'The Fête' is as good as H[ogarth]'s Strollers in the barn.

For the serious part, the warning Piece shot over Raby's head is most impressive. Only Luckless Joe should not have been killed; his Fates were teazers, not inexorable Clothos; and the Creole should have been hang'd.

With kind rememb^{ces} to Mrs. Hood,

> Yours,
>
> C. Lamb.

turn over

The puns are so neat, that the most inveterate foe to that sort of joke, not being expectant of 'em, might read it all thro', and not find you out.

My sister I hope will relish it by and by; as it is, she tries to make it out, and laughs heartily, but it puzzles her to read above a page or so a day.

Lamb was right; the novel is 'a medley', and so most of the contemporary reviewers thought, as they praised the boisterous humour and the pathos, but were either cool to, or condemned, the romantic melodrama of the main plot. Dickens summed the book up neatly, when, writing to Forster in 1846, he said, 'I have been reading poor Hood's *Tylney Hall*; the most extra-ordinary jumble of impossible extravagance and especial cleverness I ever saw.' Hood's notion of romance and tragedy was of the most elementary, one might almost say, bourgeois, kind; the plot of his novel is in some ways reminiscent of Scott, but much more of the crude Gothicized melodrama of the con-temporary popular theatre, and it is presented in language of the deadest sort, with banal imagery and hysterical stereotypes in the dialogue. The 'serious' plot tells of the impact of Walter Tyrrel, 'the Creole', mysterious nephew of Sir Mark Tyrrel, of Tylney Hall, on Sir Mark and his family. Impelled by a weird gypsy, who is actually his mother in disguise, and who comes straight from the most naive shocker, Walter weaves a plot which brings about the death of Ringwood Tyrrel by the hand of his brother, Raby, who flees. When Raby is presumed dead, Walter takes over the title and Tylney Hall, but is re-jected by Grace Rivers, Raby's sweetheart. In the end, after the gypsy has died when spurned by her ungrateful son, and Walter has been killed in a duel with a squire, Raby returns, a sadder and wiser man, assumes the title and marries the faithful Grace.

The unoriginality of the plot, the two-dimensional characterization, and the total lack of distinction in the telling make the serious parts of *Tylney Hall* poor stuff indeed. Yet the novel was popular enough in its time, running into over ten reprints on both sides of the Atlantic, because of its other aspects—the wit, farce, knockabout humour and lively minor characters, owing something to Smollett, but also typical of Hood in that they are verbal parallels to his drawn caricatures. Tubbie Campbell, the volatile Scottish servant, Dr. Bellamy, or 'Old Formality', the portly apoplectic gentleman with the dress and manners of a past age, the fanatical Methodist Uriah Bundy, with eyes set on the destruction of the world, and the bluff Squire Ned, are all robust, broadly conceived characters in direct line of descent from those of the eighteenth-century picaresque novel.

The most interesting people in the novel are 'Unlucky Joe' and Thomas Twigg. Joe is a ragged pot-boy, born on a Friday, whose whole life is one long series of misfortunes, and who is unable to find a place in the world. Like Dickens's Jo in *Bleak House*, whom Hood's character anticipates, Joe is always being moved on, 'from village to village, and from town to town, with a curse sounding after me, like a kettle at a dog's tail', and he is killed at the end by a runaway horse, on Good Friday, having exemplified the saying, 'Friday's child is full of woe'. The mixture of comedy and pathos in Joe's character, if not as telling as in Dickens's similar creations, does produce some of the novel's most credible and moving moments. The Twiggs almost take over a large part of the book, to its advantage. Mr. Thomas Twigg, a retired ironmonger, who aspires to be a country gentleman, with his vaporous wife, nitwit daughter and prankish son, provide the happiest passages in the novel with their disordered household and well-meant pretensions. Their great *fête champêtre*, which Lamb praised, is a most delightful comic set-piece, and makes a modern reader wish that Hood had sacrificed his 'serious' plot to devote more time to the Twiggs and the other comic characters. It was thought by some critics at the time that Twigg was intended to be a lampoon on Thomas Tegg, a bookseller-publisher who wrote a reply to Talfourd's plea for new copyright laws, but apart from the similarity of name, there is no evidence that such was Hood's intention.

While *Tylney Hall* has its bright moments, however, they are all incidental ones; the melodrama and farce do not blend; ill-constructed and varying enormously in tone, the novel falls into fragments. Hood's punning style, too, acceptable enough in verse, and sometimes happily employed here, becomes wearisome and strained in the lengthy prose narrative.

Undoubtedly the inspiration for the book's title and some of its material came from the environment and history of Wanstead House, and Earl Tylney, its eighteenth-century builder. The career of William Pole Tylney-Long Wellesley, who married Katherine, daughter of Sir James Tylney Long and squandered her fortune, leading to the selling of the property and the demolition of Wanstead House, was supposed by some to have furnished Hood with elements of his 'serious' plot. But he strenuously denied this in the preface to the 1840 single-volume edition: 'It pleased some of those ingenious persons who pique themselves on putting this and that together, to discover a wonderful resemblance in "Tylney Hall" to Tylney Long; and to associate the author's then residence, Lake House, with a celebrated mansion formerly standing in the vicinity. From these *premises* it was inferred that, as sundry structures had been indebted for their building materials to the wreck of Wanstead House, even so the private histories of the Wellesley and Long families had furnished matter for this novel. . . . The truth is, the figures were not drawn, after the Royal Academy fashion, from living models. My friends and acquaintances will forgive me for saying that none of them had *character* enough—in the artistic sense of the word—to make good pen and ink portraits.' It is interesting, in view of other resemblances between Hood's work and Dickens's *Bleak House*, to note the similarity between the latter part of this disclaimer and Dickens's *All the Year Round* article protesting against the identification of Harold Skimpole with Leigh Hunt: 'He no more thought, God forgive him! that the admired original would ever be charged with the imaginary vices of the fictitious creature than he himself has ever thought of charging the blood of Desdemona and Othello, on the innocent Academy model who sat for Iago's leg in the picture.'

However, although Hood made money from *Tylney Hall*, he knew that it was not a genuine artistic success, and he wrote no further fiction like it. His other 'novels' or rather pseudo-novels, *Up the Rhine* and the unfinished *Our Family*, exploit the domestic and comic elements which constitute the best parts of *Tylney Hall*, and are, in consequence, much more successful than it was. He had too great a need of money to devote time and energy to the kind of book to which he could not be sure of a good public response; he was wise enough to learn from experience, and, as with *The Plea of the Midsummer Fairies*, *Tylney Hall* represented an experiment that was not repeated.

December, 1834, saw the death of Charles Lamb, in his sixtieth year. He had a serious fall in Church Street, Edmonton, just three days before Christmas and died of erysipelas on December 27. Lamb's dear friend, Samuel Taylor Coleridge, had died five months before, and the shock of this loss affected Lamb so deeply as to impair in him the wish to live. His sister, Mary, on Charles's death, passed into one of her spells of insanity that deprived her of any true awareness of the blow. Although, as we have seen, the earlier intimacy between Hood and Lamb had faded somewhat, they retained a mutual respect, and Lamb's last letter on *Tylney Hall* shows that he had forgiven Hood for the unwitting slight of 'The Widow'. Hood made one of the little group, which also included Procter, Moxon, Cary, and friends from the India House, who stood in the Edmonton churchyard on the bleak winter's Saturday when Lamb was laid in his grave in the spot where, on an afternoon's walk a couple of weeks before, he had indicated to his sister that he wished to be buried.

In his 'Literary Reminiscences', Hood paid a last tribute to his friend: 'To sum up his character, on his own principle of antagonism, he was, in his views on human nature, the opposite of Crabbe; in criticism, of Gifford; in poetry, of Lord Byron; in prose, of the last new novelist; in philosophy, of Kant; and in religion, of Sir Andrew Agnew. Of his wit I have endeavoured to give such examples as occurred to me; but the spirit of his sayings was too subtle and too much married to the circumstan-

ces of the time to survive the occasion. They had the brevity
without the levity of wit—some of his puns contained the germs
of whole essays. Moreover, like Falstaff, he seemed not only
witty himself, but the occasion of it by example in others. . . .

'It is now five years since I stood with other mourners in
Edmonton Church Yard, beside a grave in which all that was
mortal of Elia was deposited. . . . He had not died young. He
had happily gone before that noble sister, who not in selfishness,
but the devotion of a unique affection, would have prayed to
survive him but for a day, lest he should miss that tender care
which had watched over him upwards from a child. Finally
he had left behind him his works, a rare legacy!—and above
all, however much of him had departed, there was still more
of him that could not die—for as long as Humanity endures and
man owes fellowship with men, the spirit of Charles Lamb will
still be extant.'

The following year, 1835, was a crucial one for Thomas
Hood, a period of the most acute financial and domestic problems he had encountered thus far. It began with the birth on
January 19 of Tom, his son, to whom C. W. Dilke stood as
god-father. As with the previous births, this was a difficult one
for Jane, whose life was once more in danger, and who for
some weeks hovered on the brink of death. The child survived,
and was christened Tom Hood. In time, Jane fought her way
back to health, but meanwhile Hood found himself almost overwhelmed by misfortune. Apart from pressing money troubles
and business problems, he had been much upset by a quarrel
with his sisters-in-law, Marianne Green and Charlotte, who
had rallied to help Jane in her extremity and, distressed by
the obvious poverty of the Hood household and the decrepit
condition of Lake House, had taken out their indignation on
Hood, and blamed him, in large part, for Jane's enfeebled
state.

More than this, they were convinced that their sister was
about to die. Charlotte, whom Hood blamed as the real trouble-
maker, said to him once when Jane was sleeping, 'I hope
she will wake sensible, and then pass away quietly', and John
Wright, Hood's engraver friend, heard her say, 'What gives
me horror, is that if Jane had been left alone she would have
died days ago.' 'Damn such pestilential sensibility!' wrote

Hood. 'Does she want a dead sister to cry over, let her give her good wishes to Marian.' While the Reynoldses thus spread gloom through the household and accentuated Jane's state, Hood was sitting up night after sleepless night with his wife, holding her hand, and doing all in his power to nullify the depressing effect of the in-laws and to call his beloved one back from death.

When at last the family left, driven from Lake House by fear of catching the measles that Fanny had contracted, Hood sat down in these circumstances of extreme depression to pour out his woes to his dear friend, Dilke, on February 9, in a tremendous epistle. This is a deeply revealing, almost painfully personal letter, rambling, repetitive, in places almost incoherent, in which the writer bares his heart, proclaims his miseries, avows his deep love for his wife, alternately curses his fortune and gives thanks for what little solace he has obtained, and takes immense comfort from having a sympathetic ear into which to void his distresses. It is rarely in Hood's letters that he is so intimately self-revealing. He was never again to come quite so close to desolation and self-pity; only the tremendous accumulation of woes, to which there seemed no end, could have provoked from so normally sanguine a personality the naked expression of sickness of body and heart. Yet even here cheerfulness keeps breaking in. This letter is so important a personal disclosure that it must be quoted from at length:

My dear Dilke,

Here I sit, solus, in that large drawing-room, with a sick wife upstairs—a sick child in the next room to this—(Fanny has sickened with the measles)—and a fly-load of company has just departed, containing Mr. & Mrs. Green [Marianne] and Miss Charlotte Reynolds, the two children & nursemaid. As a true Philosopher, I have found comfort in the three predicaments—Jane is better, enough to atone for all the rest—but then poor Fanny is ill,—yet hath her illness this relief in it, that it hath hastened away the aforesaid fly with its living lumber,—The Greens, the Charlotte, the two young Greens & their nursemaid, no slight relief to the larder of a man whose poulterer hath today refused a pair of fowls—& those were people who would eat fowls if fowls were to be had. But that is a trifle to the load off my head. I have had misgivings whether my anxiety for Jane might not make me somewhat rough in my remonstrances, but in a case of such vital interest, a little hardness on my part might have been forgiven—but the manner of their departure reconciles me perfectly to what I have done, so as only to leave a doubt whether I went far enough. Only the old lady [Jane's mother] remains & if sometimes wrong headed she is always right-hearted, & I am sure forgives me for sometimes opposing the first characteristic. . . . My last words were, that as they had *given Jane over*, they would forgive me, any offence on my part if I should restore her whole to them—a contemptuous reply sealed my feeling towards them for ever, & I have whistled them down the wind.

Not one of them has worked the tithe of what I have—twice have I pitched headlong from my chair with extreme watching,—but still I am in heart & alert for the dear object of my efforts is I hope accomplished, yet what was done to oppress me in my sore time of trouble I cannot forgive or forget—it must be as endurable in my memory as 'The Most Terrible Ten Days of my Life'. How should I relish the comfort of true friends if I am not to feel & taste the baseness & bitterness of false ones. . . . My indignation has settled into deep disgust & we shall never be well again whilst I retain my nature. I can forgive their oblivion of me, the little credit I have obtained for efforts, superhuman, in proportion to my own exhausted strength, having just got through my two books,—though on the personal acct. I could never condescend to admit such on my list of friends—but I cannot forget that thro them or some or all of them my poor girl went thro all but the torments of hell. A curse I say on such selfish ones! Jane never saw *me* shed a tear or heard a misgiving word till given over,—that true tenderness will be called callousness,—my love to her will be called hate to them,—I know what I am to expect from the style of their departure. My comfort is I have real friends (as yourself) who know me better—& I can appeal to a very domestic life, in proof of my sincere love for Jane, & to unbiassed testimony in favour of my exertions 'not to be a widower before my time'. It relieves my jaded heart to throw itself thus upon yours,—to requite me for such unworthy treatment.—

There—I am better—& they are worse. What a world we live in!—I am quite convinced all my theories of laughter & tears, &c.—are gospel. . . .

An hour with you would do me good—but next to that, is this letter, wherein I do most cordially grasp your hand & grapple you into mine own heart with hooks of steel. But I am rambling as wildly almost as Jane has lately wandered,— you must allow for the revulsion of feeling that seeks this vent. Times of intense stealthy agony—hours of forced cheerfulness – long nights of earnest watching, of breath and pulse,—myself a very spider as it were on the fine spun web of life—lovings, sorrowings, hopings, despairings,—hope sometimes a comet, sometimes a fixed star—sometimes a shooting one, dropping suddenly from the seventh heaven—add every energy of mind concentrated to observe, understand, & discriminate the phe- nomena of a very nice case—the internal conflicts, the external skirmishes,—all these & more might be my excuses for a more than usual excitement, now that a favourable result has been obtained, after a storm, during which I had seen every hope but my own driven from its anchor—Oh My God Dilke if ever I fought the good fight of faith, or had any pretentions to a mind it was during that frightful struggle! There was a hope —but it was like Romeo awaiting the revival of his Juliet in a dank charnal, of bones hideous, chokeful,—musicked by a Choir of Ravens. Love, only, love, could have stood the ordeal & it did. *That* will be the blessing of my life. Come what may Jane & I henceforth must be dear above dear to each other! It will be as we had passed the tomb *together* & were walking hand in hand in Elysium! Out of the fullness of the heart and of the head I write—but I am dreadfully mistaken, if you do not under- stand me in every word—have no fear of my firmness of mind or self command—this is only a *relief*, which, if you have had as kind a friend as I write to, you have sometime or other, I guess, had reason to appreciate. . . . As I sat serene & silent in the darkest hour, & cheerful in the dreariest, so even now, with people round me in common converse, my heart is singing paens of joy for my Eurydice. It only grieves me that I cannot yet get her out of the accursed Cavern, of her Fears—to use her own words she 'still smells of earth'—a shovel-full of earth's dirtiest in the dismal faces that first planted that cruel terror!

She must have suffered terribly—I read most unutterable things in her face—& curst the spell that was laid upon her spirit. Think me not mad, my dear Dilke, but I am writing of things words cannot reach. Horrors, horrible, most horrible, must have been her portion. Still, I beg, let this not pass beyond ourselves, but when we meet I can circumstantially prove to you what I say—namely she was half-killed by fear, & her friends, if so to be called. You may suppose therefore that amongst the other Demons that beset & tormented me, Scorn, Indignation, anger, & I was going to say Hatred were not missing.

I have not written myself calmer for I began calmly—but it is time to talk of calmer things. My best, & dearest, has been composed all day, no rambling, but a doubt how to decide between me (Hope personified—but a unit) & 'her family'— as many Despairs as Members, *here*. I have as it were to clear the mire from her eyes, to take the dust out of her mouth—to restore her from among that marble multitude, in the Arabian Nights. But the sweet end is this—*all other* troubles disappear,— & come poverty, age [?], and all ills, with my wife & honour and poverty & my two babes, I still will love the world & thank its ruler. And now you know more of T. Hood than you could gather from a Comic Annual, or the whole series, or the Whims, or anything I have ever written, saving this letter,—& you will believe I am happy—tho much moved. . . .

Yours in confidence & in true & everlasting friendship.

Thos. Hood.

To this letter, of which I have given about two-thirds here,[1] there are appended two postscripts, together as long as the letter itself, in which Hood reiterates his 'devout love' for Jane and his relief at her steady recovery, and in which, later, he reports on her continued progress and further damns her family for their treatment of her and him. 'Sweet it is', he writes, 'to have been able to pay off a dividend of that tender care, nursing & devotion I owe of old to my most excellent Jane. There are harsh chords that will jar if touched upon, but others that discourse most excellent music, & those mute melodies are now

[1] The full text of this letter is to be found in *Letters by Thomas Hood from the Dilke Papers in the British Museum*, edited by Leslie A. Marchand, Rutgers University Press, 1945.

singing in my soul, lulling many worldly cares to sleep. Have
no care for me. My mind which has stood firm throughout
will not fail me *now*.' Much of what Hood wrote in this letter
about his in-laws may be discounted as the product of a hectic
reaction after the tension of the preceding weeks. A few years
later he was on cordial, if hardly intimate, terms again with
Jane's sisters. But this epistle plainly shows the kind of nervous
strain under which he laboured for most of his married life,
and it gives as well a clear impression of the close ties that
bound him to his dear wife.

Jane's illness was only one of the troubles pressing on him at
this time. At the beginning of 1835, his financial situation had
become desperate. What directly caused this is something of
a puzzle. Tom Hood says simply, 'At the end of 1834 by the
failure of a firm my father suffered, in common with many
others, very heavy loss, and consequently became involved in
financial difficulties.' Walter Jerrold in his biography of
Hood added to this a speculation of his own in referring to
'financial troubles said to be consequent on the failure of a
publishing firm'. And Jane Hood in some notes she wrote
on her husband's career said 'His money annoyances began
about 1833 or 4 caused by the failure of Mr. Wright', which
suggests that it is John Wright, their engraver friend, who is
referred to. There are no explicit references to this business
failure in the published or unpublished letters I have seen, but
a further detail is added by a reference in the unpublished
'Case of Mr. Hood', submitted by F. O. Ward to Sir Robert
Peel in 1844 in support of an appeal for a pension for Hood;
'He labours under pecuniary embarrassments occasioned not
by any imprudence or extravagance on his part, nor even by
any circumstances which he could foresee or control, but by
the bankruptcy of Messrs. Wright and Branston in 1833.'

The Branston here mentioned is almost certainly Robert
Branston, the wood-engraver, who with John Wright, executed
the engravings from William Harvey's designs for 'The
Dream of Eugene Aram'. Robert was a son of Allen Robert
Branston (1778–1827) a very distinguished engraver who, by
importing the techniques of his father, a copper-plate engraver,
into the medium of wood, helped his craft to gain ground at the
beginning of the nineteenth century. Robert, and his brother,

Frederick, both pupils of their father, made some mark on the craft in their time, especially the former.

Since Wright and Branston worked with Hood not only on 'Eugene Aram', but also on engravings jointly executed for his early *Comic Annuals*, it seems clear that they were the bankrupts concerned. Although there is no official record of the bankruptcy of a firm involving the two,[1] it is also probable that Hood, in view of his training as an engraver, could have been financially involved with the two men. One interesting possibility is suggested by the fact that Robert Branston is known to have invented a process for printing from casts in metallic relief taken from etched copper-plates, a process that was found to be uneconomic and clumsy.[2] It is tempting to speculate that Hood, whose youthful inventions showed his interest in such matters, helped to finance this project and lost his money on it, as Mark Twain lost his on the ill-fated patent type-setter; but in the absence of any evidence, this must remain pure conjecture.

On the other hand, the financial loss could hardly have been a serious one; for one thing, Hood did not leave England until 1835, for another, there are several friendly references to Branston in unpublished letters; e.g. Wright to Hood, May 31, 1837, 'Branston is fixed up (at ?) Lake House and has built a work-room over the stable', and Jane to Hood, October 1839, 'Branston has been over from Ireland to fetch his two little girls, and is going to marry an Irish widow with a little girl—the little girl is provided for but the widow has nothing they say—and he is very foolish to marry her.'[3]

---

[1] I have been unable to find any records of bankruptcy proceedings against Wright and Branston, Branston and Wright, or John Wright, engraver, for the years 1832–6 in the London Public Record Office. Nor is there any record of such a firm in the Department of Official Receivers in Companies Liquidation of the Board of Trade. If, however, as the evidence indicated shows, the Wright concerned was indeed Hood's friend, he was particularly unlucky in business. Wright is usually referred to (by Jerrold and by Marchand, for instance) as of 'Wright and Folkard, wood-engravers of Fenchurch Street', while handling Hood's affairs during the period of exile. But the *London Gazette* records on March 31, 1835, in the month that Hood left England, the dissolution of the partnership between William Armstrong Folkard and John Wright, with Folkard remaining as sole proprietor.

[2] *Treatise on Wood Engraving* by Jackson and Chatto, 1861.

[3] Bristol Public Library.

These references, and Hood's continued intimacy with John Wright, strongly suggest that, whatever the nature of Hood's financial relations with these two men, it was, in fact, other debts that brought him to ruin. Both Wright and Branston were able to remain at home while Hood, in exile on the Continent, told Betsy that he could not meet her while on a trip back to England in 1838, 'Dilke, Wright and Baily . . . were all the parties that were in the secret and if I had come to you I must have gone elsewhere and so increased the chance of the matter getting known.' It is odd, too, that Hood himself never refers to the failure of a firm, even in his full epistolary discussions of his affairs with Dilke. On the contrary, it is Lake House that is most in his mind. 'I do feel released', he writes to Dilke in January, 1836, 'from the overpowering cares of a heavy expenditure and the transition from a hopeless to a hopeful state.' The place clearly had many painful associations for him. He told Jane from Stratford in April, 1840, that when he paid a visit to Lake House, 'facing the front and looking up at that bedroom window the recollections of so much misery suffered there came over me like a cloud'. And for Wright, too, it held unpleasant memories: 'I went down one day,' he told Hood on May 31, 1837, 'but was miserable the whole time, and fancied I saw you up every turn I took. The place looks wretched, there has never been a shilling laid out on it, the garden looks as if it had not been touched since you left. . . . If any-one can make the place answer Branston will for he'll give nothing away and won't overburthen himself with visitors if he can help it.' [1]

All of this leads to the conclusion that, whatever Hood's family convinced themselves to be the origin of Hood's financial plight, it was, in fact, his injudicious farming experiments and his hospitalities at Lake House that were the main cause of his troubles. Charles MacFarlane, writing in the 1850's, gives what is doubtless a highly coloured version of the circumstances, but one that seems to contain an element of truth: 'Hood,' he says, 'had no head for business, no system, no management, and he spent the money as fast as he got it. For some time, he occupied a pleasant little cottage in the right pleasant

---

[1] It seems likely that Branston's occupancy of Lake House after Hood left it was in some way connected with their financial relationship.

valley of Winchmore Hill. . . . It was certainly house enough
for him; but Tommy did not think so, and all of a sudden he
was invaded by the insane fancy that he could save expenses
and even make money by farming—he who scarcely knew
grass-seed from gunpowder. So after a lucky hit with some book
or other, he went away and took a large house on the edge of
Epping Forest, quite a mansion and manor house, with extensive gardens and about eighty acres of land attached. As the
house was so roomy, he could give his friends beds, and as a
general rule those who went to dine stayed all night, and a part
of the next day.

'The house was seldom devoid of guests, the distance was so
convenient, and Tommy's cockney friends liked to breathe
country air, and took up quite a romantic passion for the
scenery of the Forest. His household expenses were treble what
they had been in the snug, pretty little cottage at Winchmore
Hill: and then the farm ran away with a world of money. It
may be imagined how a thorough cockney, one born and
bred in the Poultry, Cheapside, a poet and punster, would
farm! What with his hospitalities, and what with his agricultural expenditure, he became seriously embarrassed.' [1]

Making all allowances for the obvious prejudices in this
account, enough remains faithful to other facts about the Lake
House period to reinforce the idea that Hood, in the flush of his
successful publications, ambitiously saw himself as a country
squire, breaking out from the restricted social life of his earlier
manhood and from the restraints of city life into a more gracious
and expansive station, and unwisely undertook to establish
himself in a situation far above his means to sustain. There is
something not a little touching in the spectacle of this 'cockney'
aspiring, like his own Thomas Twigg, to a status and a way of
life so wholly different from the one he had previously known
and doing so in a way which, though humble enough, was
sufficient to ruin him for the rest of his life. His own sad comment to Dilke in January, 1836, after the disaster, shows him a
wiser man, 'The struggle to maintain caste is indeed a bitter
one and after all I fear we must say, "le jeu ne vaut pas la
chandelle".'

Whether through the failure of some project of Wright and

[1] *Reminiscences of a Literary Life, 1799–1858.* John Murray, 1957.

Branston, through his own mismanagement of Lake House or through a combination of both, Hood, in any case, found that, after the birth of young Tom, he had either to apply for bankruptcy or go abroad. A fragment of a letter written by him in the third person about himself and quoted by his children, says: 'Emulating the illustrious example of Sir Walter Scott, he determined to try whether he could not score off his debts as effectually and more creditably, with his pen, than with the legal whitewash or a wet sponge. He had aforetime realized in one year a sum equal to the amount in arrear, and there was consequently fair reason to expect that by redoubled diligence, economizing and escaping costs at law, he would soon be able to retrieve his affairs. With these views, leaving every shilling behind him, derived from the sale of his effects, the means he carried with him being an advance upon his future labours, he voluntarily expatriated himself, and bade his native land good-night.'

Whatever the degree of his blame for the crisis, Hood's decision was a commendable one. He could easily have elected bankruptcy, but instead chose the more difficult way of voluntary exile until he had earned enough to pay off his debts. It was an honourable act, but in more ways than one an unfortunate step, for the consequences to Hood's health were to be disastrous. However, he always preferred physical ills to sickness of conscience. He wrote later to Dilke, from the Continent: 'My struggles have been great & my sufferings unknown. . . . In spite of some sharp pangs in the process I am ready to confess that the crisis which sent me here was a wholesome one: although to do myself justice, I must say, that without the absolute necessity I should have adopted some other course than that I was upon. I have been blamed I think not deservedly about Lake House, by Judges from the event, but the truth is my prospects and standing were latterly completely changed—and I should have acted accordingly. . . . If not as a thoroughly independent man (I mean morally, for I am so here actually) I have felt at second hand the inestimable blessing of being *free*.'

The decision made, Hood left his affairs in the hands of Dilke and Wright, and his wife and children in the care of Dr. William Elliot of Stratford, who had attended Jane in her illness, and to whose care Hood, in great part, attributed her recovery, and, in March, 1835, set out for Coblenz, which Dilke had recommended to him, to spend there the first two years of a five years' exile.

VII

In Exile—Germany

FOR Hood, leaving England meant not only leaving behind his wife and family and facing up to an indefinite period of hard work; it also meant plunging into a strange, uncongenial and perhaps somewhat ridiculous environment. Few writers of his time were more stubbornly English than Hood; for him the wogs began at Dover. His knowledge of foreign languages was scanty; he had a little French, but he knew no German, and during his years up the Rhine, never bothered to learn more than a few phrases. If the 'musical, mystical Germans' were cloddish enough not to understand English, it was their loss. In both his voluminous letters home and in *Up the Rhine* itself, he treats the Germans with a mixture of amused tolerance, exasperation and assured ignorance not untypical of an Englishman of his class at the time—in decided contrast to the way in which the German reading public was later to treat him. It is abundantly clear that it was only the pressure of the most dire need that made him venture forth among the 'stupid Germans', like a traveller among the trolls, for, in his attitudes, his values and his attempt to establish himself solidly as a middle-class man in his native land, he was as insular as it is possible to imagine.

Saying good-bye to Jane and the children, he crossed to Rotterdam in March by the steamer, *Lord Melville*. It was a dreadful passage; on March 4th and 5th, the ship struck a terrible storm, which brought disaster to several other vessels off the Dutch coast. The *Lord Melville* survived, but Hood suffered such agonies during the trip that he afterwards blamed his subsequent ill health on the storm. 'I was *sea-sick* and frightened at sea for the first time,' he wrote to Jane from Coblenz a few days later, 'so you will suppose it was no trifle; in fact, it was unusually severe. I went up at midnight and found *four* men at the helm, hint enough for me, so I went down again, and in the morning a terrific sea tore the whole *four* from the helm, threw the captain as far as the funnel (twenty paces) and the three men after him. Had it not come *direct aft*, it would have swept them into the sea, boat, skylights, and everything in short, and left us a complete wreck. Eleven others miscarried that same night, near at hand, so you may thank the cherub I told you of: but such a storm has seldom been known. It was quite a squeak for the Comic for 1836.' Later in the same letter, he added, 'But it made me very ill, for it was like being shaken up in a dice box, and I have had a sort of bilious fever, with something of the complaint Elliot cured me of, and could not eat, with pains in my side, etc., which I nursed myself for as well as I could.'

On the ship, he had become friendly with a young man named Mr. Vertue, 'so you see my morals are in good hands'. He supped merrily at Rotterdam with Vertue and two of his friends on the evening after landing, and parted from them with an introduction to Vertue's father, a merchant with a large family who lived in Coblenz. At Nimeguen he embarked on the Rhine steamer, where he spent Saturday night; when they arrived at Cologne on Sunday, they were held up by an accident to the ship's paddle. On board he fell in with an old English General, Sir Parker Carrol, who coincidentally proved to be an old friend of the Dilkes. Together they saw the sights of Cologne—the Lions, the Cathedral and the Church of St. Ursula and the Eleven Thousand Virgins.

The latter, containing its piles of martyrs' skulls and the macabre display of their bones on the walls, naturally made a special appeal to him; as he wrote in *Up the Rhine*, the church was 'chock full of the relicks of morality'. Despite such jests and despite the ingenuousness he attributes to his young mouthpiece, Frank Somerville, in *Up the Rhine*, Hood seems to have been impressed by the Cathedral more than he would admit to himself. 'Its glorious builder must have had a true sense of the holy nature of his task. The very materials seems to have lost their materialism in his hands,' says Frank Somerville, 'in conformity with the design of a great genius spiritualized by its fervent homage to the Divine Spirit. In looking upward along the tall slender columns which seem to have sprung spontaneously from the earth like so many reeds, and afterwards to have been petrified. . . . I almost felt, as the architect must have done, that I had cast off the burden of the flesh, and had a tendency to mount skywards.'

This was Hood's first real contact with Catholicism, which was to remain a puzzlement to him in his years of exile, as his baffled comments in his letters home indicate. He took refuge from the slight disturbance Popery created in him by looking forward to its early demise. 'I have never had any of the vulgar insane dread of the Catholics,' he told Dilke in 1836. 'It appears to me too certain that they are decaying *at the core*, and by the following natural process—men take a huge stride at first from Catholicism into Infidelity, like the French, and then by a short step backwards in a reaction, attain the *juste milieu*.' For him, the *juste milieu* was the mild Broad Church humanitarianism of the Church of England, before the ungentlemanly vulgar enthusiasts of the Oxford Movement upset the whole apple-cart.

Dilke had advised Hood to walk along the Rhine, getting to know the countryside, and choosing a suitable place to live in. Accordingly, on the Tuesday, he set out, with the Rev. Mr. Clarke, a 'gentlemanly young man' he had met on board, for Coblenz, where they slept; on Wednesday they went to Mainz together. But the effects of the stormy voyage and the necessity of rising at five each morning to catch the steamer made the plan too much for Hood and he parted company with Clarke at Mainz and returned to Coblenz by boat. Here he was warmly received by the elder Mr. Vertue, who told him that he would have trouble in finding lodgings in any of the villages outside Coblenz. In any case, Coblenz appealed to him very much at first sight. 'It is a capital and clean town,' he told Jane, 'and does justice to Dilke's recommendation.' His first impression of the Germans, however, was anything but favourable; their constant smoking, guzzling and drinking had astonished him, and, although he found many reasons for mirth at their gastronomical excesses, he could not feel at ease until he had his family around him. 'I cannot, I would not forget I am an Englishman,' he avowed to Dilke.

So he urged Jane to start for Coblenz as soon as she felt well enough, optimistically certain that he would have a suitable house for her as soon as she arrived. 'With my dear ones by my side, my pen will gambol through the "Comic" like the monkey who had seen the world. We are not transported even for seven years, and the Rhine is a deal better than the Swan River. . . . My mind was never so free—and meaning what is right and just to all, I feel cheerful at our prospects, and in spite of illness have kept up. . . . I should like you to bring out six months money at least to place me above the thought of want in a strange land. . . .' And, towards the end of this letter, 'My love sets towards you like the mighty current of the great Rhine itself, and will brook no impediments.' He had already begun some 'Rhymes of the Rhine', most of which are addressed to Jane, like the sonnet that begins

> Think, dearest, if my lids are not now wet,
>   The tenderest tears lie ready at the brim,
>   To see thine own dear eyes—so pale and dim,—
> Touching my soul with full and fond regret . . .

A few days later, he followed his first letter with another, full of high spirits, telling Jane that, thanks to the help of the Vertues, he has installed himself in furnished rooms at the Widow Seil's at 372 Castor Hof.[1] 'There are three little rooms, one backward, my study as is to be, with such a lovely view over the Moselle. My heart jumped when I saw it, and I thought, "There I shall write volumes!" ' He gives Jane detailed instructions as to what to bring with her—a set of *Comics* for Vertue, the bound up *Athenaeums*, blocks enough for the whole *Comic*, and other volumes—and what to do on the journey: 'The "Batavier" is an excellent boat; have *porter* on board her, as you will get none after Rotterdam; up the Rhine take Cognac and water, not the sour wine. . . . Wrap yourself well up.' He is full of plans for the future: 'Get yourself strong, there is still a happy future; fix your eyes forward on our meeting,

---

[1] These lodgings have not survived two world wars. Although the historic church of St. Castor close by still stands, the Castor Hof itself is today a desolate, empty square.

my best and dearest. Our little home, though homely, will be happy for us, and we do not bid England a very long good night.' And he sows his letter with jests—'By the bye, Mrs. Dilke told me to keep my linen well aired. I suspect it was only her ignorance, and that she had taken what is up in all the packets—*Dampschiffe*—for damp shirts. It signifies *steam boats*—not an unnatural mistake.' He has particular fun at the expense of his inability to speak German—'My young landlady has paid me a smiling visit this morning, and we have had a little conversation in German and English, which neither of us understood'—and he ends with a bouncing confidence—'I am become quite a citizen of the world, I talk to everyone in English, broken French, and bad German, and have the vanity to think I make friends, wherever I go.'

On March 29, Jane left London with Fanny and young Tom. The weather on the trip was fair, and, although Fanny was ill for part of the voyage and the passage from Rotterdam to Cologne was disturbed by some noisy card-playing Prussian officers, they had a tolerable journey to Cologne, where Hood met them. He insisted on their spending a day there, to allow Jane to recover from the fatigue of the trip, and they saw the Cathedral together. Jane thought it impressive, but the famous masquerade room much less so. 'The idea is better than the execution. German wit and humour, Hood says, are like yeast dumplings a day old.' Coblenz, however, was up to her expectations. 'The houses are good,' she told Mrs. Dilke, 'the streets wide, airy, and clean, with here and there a bit of pavement in the English style, which I have always found attracted my weary feet as if it has been a loadstone.'

But she was shocked at the look of her husband, whose cheerful letters had concealed all traces of the disastrous effects of his voyage. 'When he arrived', she told Mrs. Elliot, 'I scarcely knew him, he looked so ill. . . . He is in a wretched state of health, he had been sadly overdone before he left England, and the storm he was out in completed the mischief.' Hood refused to see a doctor, but when, soon after the family reached Coblenz, he was seized with frightful spasms in the chest, Jane called in a Dr. Beerman, who had been recommended by the Vertues. The doctor's ministrations had some effect, although Jane, like Hood, was sceptical about the competence of German physicians. 'I wanted faith in our physician, but of course did not say so; their practice is so different to the English, they won't hear of calomel.' Thomas was clearly gravely ill. 'I cannot express how wretched, and terrified I was, for he said himself it was like being struck with death.'

The first attack was followed by other, slighter ones; for all Hood's doubts, Dr. Beerman knew what he was about. 'My Dr. certainly does me good,' Hood told Dilke, 'and, though a Jew, does not repeat his visits unnecessarily, but "waits till called for"; he talks a little English, and as Pope says I feel assured, "a little learning is a dangerous thing".' The doctor urged Hood to go to Bad Ems to convalesce, but the poet, desperately in need of funds and plugging away at the 1836 *Comic*, could not dream of a holiday.

Yet, in spite of the decline in his health, he felt that his major difficulties were behind him, and he was able to write pleasant lengthy letters to his friends at home. One of his epistolary habits which the tolerant Jane had to endure was that of inserting interpolations in her letters. She would write a paragraph or two at a time, and Hood would impishly add sentences and whole paragraphs of nonsense or puns, or alter some of the words she had already written, so as to make puns out of them. As usual, Jane seems to have taken this foolery in good part. Her letters are full of comments like this, after a particularly bad pun: 'Hood *again*! I will not quit this letter again till I have finished it, he has "interpret himself so".' Much of the matter in both Jane's and Thomas's letters concerns the comical implications of their lack of German. During his two years in Coblenz, the German language remained merely a source of jesting for the poet.

From the Vertues, the Hoods inherited a servant, Gretel— whose name they 'foneticized' to 'Gradle'; in a letter to Dilke Thomas inserts a little dialogue showing the problems of communication with her:

'Jane wanted a fowl to boil for me. Now she has a theory that the more she makes her English un-English, the more it must be like German. Jane begins by showing Gradle a word in the dictionary.

Gradle: Ja! yees—huhn—henne—ja!—yees.

Jane (a little through her nose): Hmn—hum—hem—yes—

yaw—yaw—ken you geet a fowl—fool—foal, to boil—bile—
bole for dinner?

Gradle: Hot wasser?

Jane: Yaw, in pit—pat—pot—hmn—hum—eh!

Gradle (a little off the scent again): Ja, nein—wasser, pot
—hot—nein.

Jane: Yes—no—good to eeat—chicken—cheeken—check-
ing—choking—bird—bard—beard—lays eggs—eeggs—hune,
heine—hin—makes cheeken broth—soup—poultry—peltry—
paltry!

Gradle (quite at fault): Pfeltrighchtch!—nein.

Jane (in despair): What shall I do! and Hood won't help me,
he only laughs. This comes of leaving England! (She casts her
eyes across the street at the Governor's poultry-yard, and a
bright thought strikes her.) Here, Gradle—come here—comb
hair—hmn—hum—look there—dare—you see things walking
—hmn, hum, wacking about—things with feathers—fathers—
feethers.

Gradle (hitting it off again): Feethers—faders—ah hah! fedders—ja, ja, yees, sie bringen—fedders, ja, ja!

Jane (echoes): Fedders—yes—yaw, yaw!

Exit Gradle, and after three-quarters of an hour, returns
triumphantly with two bundles of stationers' quills!!! This is a
fact.'

The family had a great stroke of luck, however, a couple of
months after Jane's arrival. While they were walking through
the streets of Coblenz one evening, a young officer, overhearing
them talking in English, introduced himself to them as Lieutenant Philip de Franck of the 19th Polish Regiment of the
German army. De Franck, whose mother was English and who
had been educated in England, spoke English and German
fluently. He had been fourteen years in the Prussian service,
but still retained a nostalgia and affection for England. 'In
truth', wrote Jane to Mrs. Elliot, 'we were equally glad to give
him change for his English, which he declared he had had by
him till it had become burdensome.' De Franck, who was
stationed close across the Rhine at Ehrenbreitstein Fortress,
proved to be the only intimate friend the Hoods made among
the Germans in Coblenz; he became their interpreter, counsellor and close companion, to whom Hood later wrote immense,

jocose letters, and as he was unmarried, a frequent and welcome visitor to their home for a game of cribbage, a chat and a practical joke or two at Jane's expense, such as changing her cards and moving her pegs while she was out of the room.

Jane, who was still suffering from the weakness following the birth of young Tom, was at first somewhat depressed in the new and alien environment. She missed her friends at home, and the facilities of an English household. 'The comforts the English miss,' she sighed to Mrs. Elliot, 'are not very portable, or they might bring them out, for instance—a four-post bed, a Rumford stove, a kitchen range, and a carpet. But use reconciles, we almost feel native, and "to the manner born" so don't pity us, for we don't pity ourselves.'

As her health improved, so her spirits rose. Yet things remained difficult for the Hoods in Coblenz, cut off as they were from social intercourse by language barriers, the need for rigid economies and unpredictable health. There were English people to be met at the Bellevue Hotel in Coblenz, where Hood sent his copies of the *Athenaeum* when he had finished with them, but the other English abroad were not exactly to his taste: 'At the table d'hôte,' he told Dilke, 'the English are fond of copying foreign customs and manners. First pull out the crumb of your roll, about half of which roll up, and work between your fingers (if snuffy the better) into little balls as big as marbles. They will not look exactly like Wordsworth's White Dough but rather dirty putty. When you have used your quill toothpick, stick it up, bolt upright, in one of those dirty balls, a little flattened beneath, as you may see candles stuck in extempore clay candlesticks at an illumination. Should it (the tooth-pick) want cleaning, furbish it with the other dirty bread balls; then it will be ready for further use!'

In fact, little as Hood cared for the Germans, he had hardly more time for the English traveller, as witness many passages in *Up the Rhine* and in 'The Schoolmistress Abroad'. In the latter, for instance, the schoolma'm gives vent to such sentiments as: 'Then to allude to indiscriminate conversation, a great part of which is in a foreign language, and accordingly places one in the cruel position of hearing, without understanding a word of, the most libertine and atheistical sentiments. Indeed, I fear I

have too often been smiling complacently, not to say engagingly, when I ought to have been flushing with virtuous indignation, or even administering the utmost severity of a moral
reproof. I did endeavour in one instance, to rebuke indelicacy;
but unfortunately from standing near the funnel, was smutty
all the while I was talking, and as school experience confirms,
it is impossible to command respect with a black on one's
nose.'

The only near acquaintance, apart from De Franck, the
Hoods had in Coblenz was an Italian teacher of languages,
Ramponi, with whom Thomas talked in French, and with
whom he fought over again the Battle of Waterloo. 'But the
forms this jealousy takes are so ludicrous it provokes as much
laughter as spleen and I enjoy the conflict.' Ramponi was
anxious to go to London to teach French, Spanish and Italian
there. Hood did not offer him much encouragement, pointing
out that Ramponi did not know the language of his proposed
pupils. 'I told him moreover that we had such swarms of
refugees of education and rank even I feared language masters
must be drugs with us.' Thanks, largely, to the companionship
of the Anglophilic De Franck, whom Hood initiated into the
mysteries of fly-fishing, and who, in his cheerful evenings with
the pair, gave them the illusion of being home again, Hood
came to reconcile himself to his present circumstances.

Nevertheless, loneliness often weighed in on him. 'I *miss
home*—old friends—books, the *communion of minds*.' He obtained
some relief from this feeling of being shut off by letters of almost
stupefying length, to the Dilkes, the Elliots, and John Wright,
who was looking after the mechanical side of the *Comic Annual*
for him. As he said to Dilke in a letter of July, 1836, 'The truth,
is, I have not many correspondents, nor many conversibles; so
that I select you, both to write to and talk to on paper—for
fear I shall die of that most distressing of complaints, a sup-
pression of ideas. I do not, however, though I am in Germany,
pretend to open a regular account of debtor and creditor, and
expect you to liquidate every letter of mine, as if it were a
foreign bill of exchange, by an equivalent upon your own side.
I know your time is too valuable to be so drawn upon, and so
is mine too; but, then, for me to write to you is matter of
recreation. You have *too* much of that of which I have too little

—society: so that if I choose to call on you, or leave my card, *i.e.* letter, I do not peremptorily expect your returning my visits!'

More letters have been preserved from this period than from any other of Hood's life; as a whole, the correspondence forms an engagingly personal series of impressions of German life, people and places, full of humour and bright anecdotes, puns, jests and comic dialogues, interspersed with serious passages of reflection, plans, self-analysis, even some self-pity, and much irony and insular comment at the expense of his Teuton hosts. Although often fatiguingly long, the letters have undeniable charm and are sometimes very shrewd in their assessments.

Here is a handful of brief, but characteristic, excerpts from the Coblenz letters, on a variety of subjects:

'Jane in bed, smothered in pillows and blankets, suffering from a terribly inflamed eye. In rushes our maid and without any warning, suddenly envelopes her head in a baker's meal-sack hot out of the oven! prescribed as a sudorific and the best thing in the world for an inflamed eye by the baker's wife (there's nothing like leather!). What between the suddenness of the attack and her strong sense of the fun of the thing, Jane lay helplessly laughing for awhile and heard Gradle coax off the children with "Coom schon babie—coom schone Fannische—mama kranke!" Encore! I sent a pair of light trousers which were spotted with ink to be dyed black; after six weeks they came back like a jackdaw, part black, part grey. I put my hands in the pockets like an Englishman, and they came out like an African's. I think seriously of giving them to a chimney-sweep who goes by here; full grown, long nosed, and so like the devil I wonder Fanny has never dreamed of him. There were two; but the other was starved to death the other day at our neighbour the general's. They lit a fire under him when he was up. Our Dr. Beerman, who was sent for, told me gravely, that he could not revive him, for when he came, the man was *"black in the face"*!' (To Wright, November 3, 1835.)

'Above all they are dreadfully beastly filthy horribly dirty and *nasty*. I have some stories on this head to tell you *orally* that will disgust but make you laugh. Then they are stupid and like all stupid people intensely obstinate. . . . I will give you a laughable instance of their dullness. The general opposite had ordered some great poplars in his yard to be cut down and we saw the whole operation. Each tree was nearly *cut thro* with the hatchet some ten yards from the ground by a fellow in a ladder which rested against the stem a dozen feet *above* the cut. I expected an accident every moment. The head gardener, pipe in mouth, looked on and superintended. The first tree all but lashed them in its fall—there were twelve men and four trees and 'twas a two days' job. At last came one of the biggest poplars in its turn. I saw even from my window and predicted that the rope would break—there was a join in it—a knot, with a streamer of loose tow hanging from it—that could not be mistaken. Down they all went accordingly on the rugged stones—pipes and all —from which they got up looking very foolish and rubbing their behinds. However they only tied another knot and tried again; the head man, and one or two who had looked on lending a hand. Down again—as a matter of course. Jane and I shrieked with laughter and they evidently heard us. Well, what does a foggy headed fellow do, but go into the house and bring out a coil of literal *cable* fit to pull down a church with, and what do they do with it, but tie it at the end of the old rotten rope, and then haul away again! Twas a miracle they had not a third summerset—but the tree thought proper to give away— there were a dozen heads together, in spite of the proverb no better than one!' (To Dilke, January, 1836.)

'There is all along shore here, now-a-days at least, a sharking grasping appetite, which growing by what it feeds on, has become ogre-like; and knowing the English to be rich, they have not known where, prudently, or with good policy, to stop. There was a colonel here, the other day only, crying out, naturally, at being charged in this *cheap* country five shillings for a bed; the landlord of the hotel in question, chose at the Carnival to burlesque an English family travelling; he has told me, the English are by far his best customers, but the ridicule was congenial to the spirit of the inhabitants. The truth is, we are marked for plunder; and laughed at, for the facility with which we are plucked, as if it were a matter of difficulty to cheat those, who in some degree confide in you—for we do generally set forth with a strong prepossession in favour of German honesty.' (To Dilke, June 20, 1836.)

'We have several little excursions, one to the Laacher Zee,

amongst the volcanic mountains. We went on Whit-Monday, but it ought to have been *Ash*-Wednesday, considering the soil of the road we went through. Their proper scavengers would have been Cinderellas. The walls and houses thereabouts are built with lava, and the lake itself is supposed to occupy an extinct crater. What a lovely, little secluded lake it is, embosomed in trees, and perched on the crest of a mountain; not like an eagle's nest, but a water "Roc's". It is said to be, in the middle, 200 yards deep, and the water is supernaturally clear. We fished, but of course could catch nothing, though there be huge Jack and Perch; in truth, as I could see my line from the top, they could see it at the bottom. There is a decayed church and cloisters, and the monkery and gardens afford delightful residence. . . . It is a delicious spot. I honour the olden monks for the taste with which they pitched their tents. Methought as I walked in their cloisters I could have been willingly a Benedictine myself, especially when I saw a pair of huge antlers over one of the doors—like a sign of "good venison within".' (To Dilke, June 20, 1836.)

In the summer of 1835, the Elliots came to spend a brief holiday at Coblenz, much to the Hoods' joy. Jane and Thomas took them to the Mozelweis tea-garden where they all drank punch and ate cold plum-tart, and later, on the way back, were able to provide them with a dinner from their own tiny kitchen. But, despite Hood's constant pleas to the Dilkes to visit Germany, they went to Margate for their holidays. Hood expressed his disappointment by putting a burlesque meditation into Dilke's mouth: 'Upon my soul, Maria, this is a delightful place! So like Coblenz! So you call this Margate, do you, my beauty? Well—' (a grunt like a paviour's) 'and I suppose you call that the fort—humph! Considering we might have stood before Ehrenbreitstein instead of it—hah!' (a sigh like an alligator's) 'My God!—that we could be so insane!— how any Christian being could stay a month in it!—why, I should hang myself in ten days, or drown myself in that stinking sea yonder!'

At this time Hood felt more cut off than ever, since De Franck had left with his regiment for Posen at the end of September. He sought distraction in work, flinging himself into the preparation

of the *Comic Annual* for 1836. He told Wright, 'I have been so
unwell, I am down, and diffident in what I do,' but Jane and he
had brought some material for the annual from England, he
worked hard at it even when he was in bed, and despite the
problems involved in working from abroad and in getting
blocks through the Customs, he succeeded, thanks to Wright's
help on the English end, in getting the book out on time. The
material in the *Annual* itself is a little tired in places; Hood was
holding back most of his comic verses and prose observations on
the Germans for *Up the Rhine*, which he already had in mind.
But there is at least one gem in the 1836 *Annual*—a long
narrative poem, 'Love and Lunacy', a farcical piece of great
animation suggested to Hood by a joke De Franck told him. It
is a measure of the distance he had moved from the influence of
Keats that now he can write in a manner that is pure parody
of the Keatsian romantic style:

> Heav'n bless the man who first devised a mail!
>   Heav'n bless that public pile which stands concealing
> The Goldsmith's front with such a solid veil!
>   Heav'n bless the Master, and Sir Francis Freeling,
> The drags, the nags, the leading or the wheeling,
>   The whips, the guards, the horns, the coats of scarlet,
> The boxes, bags, those evening bells a-pealing!
> Heav'n bless, in short, each posting thing, and varlet,
> That helps a Werter to a sigh from Charlotte.
>
> So felt Lorenzo as he oped the sheet,
>   Where, first the darling signature he kiss'd,
> And then, recurring to its contents sweet
>   With thirsty eyes, a phrase I must enlist,
>   He gulp'd the words to hasten to their gist;
> In mortal ecstasy his soul was bound—
>   When lo! with features all at once a-twist,
> He gave a whistle, wild enough in sound
> To summon Faustus's Infernal Hound.

Towards the end of the year, De Franck returned to Coblenz
and took Christmas dinner with the Hoods. This provided Hood
with the chance for another of his practical jokes, which he
recounted to Mrs. Dilke early in the New Year. De Franck had
so enjoyed the Christmas pudding that Jane made another one
especially for him to take back to camp and share with his

fellow-officers. 'We had bought a groschen worth of new skewers that very morning,' Hood relates. 'I cut them a little shorter than the pudding's diameter and poked them in across and across in all directions so neatly that Jane never perceived any outward visible sign of the inward invisible wood, although she stood and admired it for five minutes next morning before she sealed it up in white paper and sent it to Ehrenbreitstein. The next time Franck came he praised it very highly—I asked him if it was not well trussed—and he answered "Yes" so gravely that I thought he meditated some joke in retaliation and kept on my guard. At the ball the truth came out—he actually thought it was only some new method of making plum puddings and gave Jane credit for the wood-work.' Jane didn't think very much of this jest. Telling Mrs. Elliot of it herself, she ended, 'Now was not this an abominable trick,' while Hood said to Mrs. Dilke, 'You may guess I caught a rare scolding— not only at home, but when we went out it lasted all the way up Nail Street—to the text of "practical jokes are the lowest things in the world".'

The ball Hood spoke of was a 'grand New Year's Eve Ball' at the Casino to which he was invited to meet 'all the rank, fashion and beauty of Coblenz'. He enjoyed himself with a party of De Franck's fellow-officers, drinking 'Cardinals' and deriving much patronizing amusement from the frantic waltzes, the booking for dances, the plain belles of the ball, and the public effusiveness of the Germans, which he felt to be decidedly unEnglish. 'Exactly at twelve—bang went a minor cannon in an adjoining room and the waltz instantly broke up, and the whole room was in motion—everybody walking or running about to exchange salutations, and kisses and embraces with all friends and acquaintance male or female—Such *hearty smacks*— such hugs—and handshakings—to the chorus of Proast Ni Yar! Proast Ni Yar! Some of the maidens methought kissed each other most tantalizingly on the lips and neck, and languished into each other's arms—I am afraid because so many nice young men and gay officers were by to see it—but then their fathers and mothers were as busy too kissing and bekist.'

The winter was a severe one; the Rhine was frozen over, and the narrows at St. Goar, which De Franck took the Hoods to see, were blocked up with huge waves and furrows of ice. The two exiles suffered greatly from the cold, finding German stoves unsatisfactory substitutes for a good English fire. Yet Thomas was cheerful, and told Dilke that he had regularly progressed in health and that he had never completed the Comic with such ease and satisfaction. 'Except that I am more in figure a Greyhound I came in like a Spaniel winning the Derby, fresh and full of running.' But his letters are still dotted with grumbles about the Rhinelanders—their manners, their cheating of foreigners, their loudness, their funny, incomprehensible language, their gastronomic habits, their terrible food. 'The French are *artists*, the Germans are *daubers* in cookery. They are (in all that is grub-berly) lubberly, blubberly and, in regard to cleanliness, not over scrubberly.'

Much of the Hoods' indignation vented itself on 'Gradle', the domestic, who was accused of all kinds of misdemeanours, such as swindling the family on household expenses, taking young Tom for a walk without a coat, having a follower, 'Joseph the Carpenter', who couldn't be shifted from the kitchen, and, above all, inability to understand Jane's 'Germanized' English. Matters came to a head in January, 1836. The Hoods had allowed Gradle, a Catholic, to go to Mass every other Sunday, 'if *convenient*'. On one particular Sunday, after she had attended Mass, a request came from the parish priest to visit him. The Hoods, however, told Gradle to take the children for a walk in a particular direction. She set off, but retraced her steps and went towards the church. The six-year-old Fanny, who alone of the family understood German, 'did not choose to be diddled out of her walk and remonstrated with all her German might in the Vicar's presence—whereupon Gradle brought my little Protestants home again under a pretense that it rained'.

A sizzling row broke out, with little Fanny self-righteously reporting some of Gradle's less discreet complaints about her employers. De Franck was called in and after 'hearing the case', said to Gradle, 'On the first of *February*—March!!' 'But do not grieve for us,' Hood said to Mrs. Dilke, '—we shall get a better and a cheaper by 1/3.' 'It is too certain,' he avowed later to Dilke, 'the dear departed made a per-centage on everything she bought for us. I declined to sign a certificate of honesty Vertue had given her, so she cast her eyes on Joseph, the carpenter, whom she got to marry her, induced by the fortunes of a "Bibi" two years old, and 150 dollars saved out of the 60 she received from Vertue and us.'

Soon after changing their servant—who, poor thing, deserves some at least of our sympathy for having to endure the incomprehensible commands of a family whose head treated her as if she were a character in one of his own burlesque stories—the Hoods changed lodgings. They did not part from Miss Seil 'without some serio-comic originality in her struggles between extortion and civility', after which they took up residence 'at Herr Deubel's, 752 Alten Graben, Coblenz' (which Hood translated as 'At Mr. Devil's in the Old Grave'). This was near the Moselle bridge, with some fine views, and just three minutes' walk from the country. Although the new lodgings cost no more than the old ones, the Hoods felt the need to economize. 'We have changed our butcher, and gained a penny per pound; ditto laundress, and saved nearly a dollar a week.'

Hood's health remained moderately good, and he was able to go on various fishing expeditions, which he loved, to Lahneck and the Laacher Zee, with De Franck and his German friends. He also got much pleasure from wood-carving and making small objects for use and amusement. Most of all he liked making things for Tommy and Fanny. He bought a small toy theatre, and drew, painted and cut out the characters and scenery for a tragedy, *Paul and Virginia*, a spectacle, *St. George and the Dragon*, and a pantomime. For years afterwards, the theatre used to be brought out on high days and holidays, and Hood would perform the pieces to the delight of the children, their friends and their parents. He used to extemporize the dialogue. 'His stage management, properties and machinery were capital,' his son recalled in later years, 'and I can still remember the agony with which I used to see the wreck in "Paul and Virginia" break up by degrees, and the bodies of the lovers washed in over the breakers.' With the toy theatre, and a magic lantern, for which Hood painted the slides himself, he did his best to keep the children amused during the long winter's evenings.

In the autumn of 1836, the Dilkes yielded at last to Hood's lengthy importunities, written, many of them, in 'crossed letters', for economy's sake, with the original text crossed at right angles with further text in red ink. They agreed to come across for a brief holiday at Coblenz. It was the time of the army manœuvres, when the various regiments crowded the villages around the town. There was a great camp established on the plain across the Rhine between Coblenz and Andernach, together with a fair with booths for the sale of fancy goods, for refreshment, and for dancing and entertainment. The Crown Prince spent three days there reviewing the troops and shortly afterwards there was to be a mock attack on the village of Bassenheimer, about eight miles away.

The Hoods had engaged a carriage well in advance, but, unfortunately, Dilke himself fell ill, and the carriage remained unused until the day of the mock battle, when Dilke insisted on Jane and Thomas going alone. The 'stupid people of Coblenz', in Jane's words, did not care to travel so far, so the Hoods were the only spectators present, and had a splendid, unobstructed view of the skirmish. Hood was thrilled by the spectacle and, as Jane told Mrs. Elliot, 'on talking it over with De Franck, he was astonished to find how clearly he had seen it all, and pointed out how one side lost the vantage ground, and ultimately was conquered by that oversight'. This review inspired Hood to invent another pastime for his children, a war game, with toy soldiers, painted in their precise colours, tents and accoutrements, cannon, baggage-waggons and so on, ranged in two armies and manœuvred, by rules like those of chess, over a field supplied with villages, bridges, forts and churches.

The Coblenz manœuvres had excited in the frail Hood an enthusiasm for the soldier's life; when De Franck's regiment, the 19th Polish Infantry, was ordered to march to Bromberg, in German Poland, and Hood was invited to accompany them, he accepted with alacrity. The invitation had come from the Colonel, who was something of an intellectual, and who had translated 'Eugene Aram' into German. The only thing that held Hood back was the presence of the Dilkes; but it was agreed that he and Jane should stay with their friends until the last moment, and then catch up the regiment by coach at Eisenach, after which Jane would return to Coblenz, leaving her husband to ride with the soldiers as far as Kustrin.

At length, saying good-bye to the Dilkes, the Hoods set off and made contact with De Franck at a village near Langen

Salza, where they were billeted on a Saxon peasant. Jane was somewhat perturbed at the sleeping arrangements. The first bedroom 'had two beds for Mr. Franck and a brother officer, and the inner one, which was also the sitting-room, had one for us; this was rather unpleasant, but if I had been a princess I could not have commanded any better, so I treated it in the best manner I could'. Hood found the coaches trying. 'Myself taken very ill in the night; but had some illness hanging about me brought to a crisis by being stived up, all windows shut, with four Germans stinking of the accumulated smoke and odour, stale, flat, and unprofitable, of perhaps *two* years' reeking garlic and what not, besides heat insufferable.'

The next morning, the pains were still severe, so he did not dare to ride the horse he had purchased to keep up with the regiment's foot-marching, and, with Jane, he went back to a quiet inn at Saxe Gotha, where he rested. Soon he was feeling better, attributing his seizure to 'cold in the muscles of the chest', although this was far too favourable a piece of self-diagnosis, and set off to rejoin the regiment at Halle, after seeing Jane back to Coblenz in an '*old, old* diligence'. Before Jane saw the Dilkes again, she was involved in an accident. A wheel came off the coach, which overturned, trapping Jane inside. She was dragged out, protesting, by a young German, who left her perched on the top. Fortunately, while she was still sitting bruised and crying in this precarious position, she heard a voice say, 'Don't be alarmed, let me assist you down'. 'Thank God, that's English!', she said, and scrambled down, assisted by her fellow-countryman. She transferred to the Frankfurt diligence, which was just as well, since the one in which she had been travelling overturned twice more and was delayed for three hours.

Hood had been working at the 1837 *Comic Annual* before he left Coblenz, but time was pressing; in fact, he should have finished the material by September. So he took some uncompleted poems with him to finish on the march, hoping to turn out other things as well. After Jane left him at Gotha, he spent two days there, working on the Annual, resting and consulting a doctor, who assured him that he had only caught a cold and ought to wear red flannel on his chest. Then he set off by coach to meet the regiment and pick up his horse at Halle. He received a warm welcome from the officers, and mounted his animal, which proved gratifyingly docile. 'Tell Fanny he walks after Franck and knows him like a dog; I expect to be equally good friends with him, by feeding him with bread. Fanny herself might ride him.' Although he knew that the march was to be a strenuous one, he was enjoying himself greatly. 'For some distance,' he told Jane, 'I rode between the captain and a gentleman in plain clothes; it turned out he had formerly been a soldier in the battalion, and is now a Professor, and there was I the author turned soldier!'

His letters home to Jane are full of high-spirited descriptions, gossip and declarations of tender affection. They give a pleasant running commentary on various stages of his journey; it is astonishing how he could have found the time to write them, for the days' marches were fatiguing, and the evenings were generally divided between convivial encounters in the mess and busy work on the Annual. He sent the writing for the *Comic* to Jane so that, for safety's sake, she could forward copies to the publisher. From Potsdam, where the regiment had proceeded by way of Wittenburg, he described the progress of the march. Wrapped in a military cloak, and riding his horse, which still bore the cloths of its former owner, an army captain, he would join the French-speaking officers among those at the front or rear of the regiment. He was often taken for the regiment's doctor or chaplain, and passed through the toll-houses without paying. The regiment rose at four each morning, and set out about five or half-past, in the dark; Hood marched on foot until he could see the road, then mounted. Breakfast was taken sitting by the roadside, each contributing to a kind of picnic whatever he could find. Hood learned to forage, and produced such things as a couple of cold pigeons and a loaf split and buttered; he always cleared the table at his quarters into his pocket.

His billets were often curious—a ball-room at Pruhlitz, and a miller's shed at Schlunkendorf ('what a name!')—and De Franck more often than not slept in straw to let his friend have the only available bed. Hood was greatly entertained on the way with the various people he encountered, and delighted in his old game of gentle hoaxing. He persuaded the Burgomaster of Nichel that he himself was an English burgomaster, and told a woman at Schlunkendorf that he had come 50,000 miles, was married at 14, and had 17 children: 'and as I was in yellow boots, and Mrs. D.'s present of a robe, and really looked a Grand Turk, she believed me like Gospel'. His health kept up, and he told Jane from Potsdam, 'I seem to have scarcely had an inconvenience, certainly not a hardship, and it will ever be a pleasant thing to remember. I like little troubles; I do not covet too flowery a path.'

He had intended to go with the 10th Company to Kustrin and to return to Coblenz via Frankfurt/Oder, Breslau, Dresden and Mainz, but his march ended at Berlin on October 29. He had stayed a day over in Potsdam, and when he rejoined the soldiers at Berlin, he found that De Franck had been invited by Prince Radziwill to stay with him for two or three weeks. Military exigencies were forgotten; De Franck stayed over, and, since he was the pretext for Hood's journey, the poet could not well go on without him. In the capital, Hood enjoyed himself with sight-seeing and attending the opera—*Undine*, which he liked, for it was 'full of fairy work'. He was flattered to be invited to dine with Prince Wilhelm Radziwill and his family. He discovered, to his gratification, that most of the family knew and admired his writings, were particularly fond of the *Comic Annual*, the latest number of which they begged him to send them, and had even read *Tylney Hall*. 'They say no man is a prophet in his own country,' he exulted to Jane, 'and here literature certainly came in for its honours.'

After a few days, he decided to return home. The weather had turned bad; it was snowing and the roads were 'covered with genuine *London*-like mud'. And with the change in the weather, he began to feel unwell again. So he abandoned his plan to return by a leisurely route and made his way to Coblenz as directly as possible. On the journey the coach broke a pole on the rough road at the top of a bleak hill, and he travelled to the next station in an open wagon. This, and the night journey in an open coupe from Frankfurt to Mainz in the keen wind and the bitter cold, brought on a severe chill. When he arrived back in Coblenz, he was coughing fearfully and spitting blood. He could no longer conceal from himself the fact that his illness was something more than a 'cold in the chest muscles'. 'I suspect this time', he wrote to Dilke who, also unwell, had returned home, 'it was a touch on the lungs, which were never touched before, being indeed my strongest point.'

He had to take to his bed at once, but this meant no rest for him. As the material for the *Comic* was still not finished (he had lacked his 'papers and lists' in Berlin) he had to push on with it. At the same time, he began putting together the impressions he had been collecting in Germany, and especially on the march, for the 'German book' he had in mind, and the proceeds from which he hoped would go a long way towards dissolving his debts. Despite delays and the problems of transport, the *Comic Annual* for 1837 came out as usual, in time for Christmas 1836, even though it was not nearly as early as Hood had hoped. But he was so greatly relieved to get it off his shoulders that he celebrated the despatch of the last box of drawings and manuscripts to England by a gay supper for the family. Fanny, who was then seven, always remembered being taken up almost at dawn, rolled in a huge shawl, and installed in an arm-chair for the occasion, while her father, free from anxiety now and brightening up through all his fatigue, laughed and joked merrily. Each following year, the completion of the *Comic Annual* was celebrated by one of these jolly finishing suppers.

For all the hold-ups caused by the march, Hood's illnesses and procrastinations, the 1837 Annual was one of his best productions to date. In it something of a new note is sounded—a political one. Hood apologized for not seasoning the *Comic* with more 'political pepper and spice', but pleaded that, living abroad, he was out of touch with recent developments. 'I might have been getting up an urgent call for the Repeal of the Corn Laws—when the Corn Laws had been regularly outlawed, at the poetical petition of Ebenezer Elliott and Corney Webbe. At the same hour, whilst I was writing a deprecation of Sabbath-Bills, and Parliamentary Piety—Sir Andrew had, perchance, embraced Judaism, and exchanged Sunday for Saturday.' Nevertheless, some of the content of the Annual indicates that this preface is largely ironical, since in it Hood reveals a political awareness somewhat unexpected from him, and couched in the humanitarian terms of his more celebrated later poems. 'Agricultural Distress', subtitled 'A Pastoral Report', is a most interesting and shrewd comment on the effects of the new Poor Law. In turn, six rustics give their

definitions of 'Agricultural Distress', the first five interpreting
it as meaning farm accidents, until Colin gives his explanation:

> '. . . Why, farming is to plough and sow,
> Weed, harrow, harvest, reap and mow,
> Thrash, winnow, sell,—and buy and breed
> The proper stock to fat and feed.
> Distress is want, and pain, and grief,
> And sickness—things as wants relief;
> Thirst, hunger, age and cold severe;
> In short, ax any overseer. . . .
>
> There's no distress in growing wheat
> And grass for men or beasts to eat;
> And making of lean cattle fat,
> There's no distress, of course, in that.
> Then what remains?—But one thing more,
> And that's the *Farming of the Poor*!'
>
> Hodge, Dickon, Giles Hob, and Simon:
>
> 'Yea!—aye!—sure*ly*! for sartin!—yes!—
> *That's* Hagricultural Distress!'

Apart from the aptness of its social comment, this poem exhibits
a tidy craftsmanship, catching the cadence of the speaking
voice and anticipating similar dialogues by William Barnes.

The 1837 Annual also contained a lively Ode to Dr. Hahnemann, the homoeopathist, which makes fun of the crank-
theories of German doctors, and turns Hood's own painful
experiences at their hands into a jest that, at the same time, has
its undertones of pain:

> But, zounds! each fellow with a suit of black,
> And strange to fame,
> With a diploma'd name,
> That carries two more letters pick-a-back,
> With cane, and snuff-box, powder'd wig, and block,
> Invents *his* dose, as if it were a chrism,
> And dares to treat our wondrous mechanism,
> Familiar as the works of old Dutch clock.

So, too, with 'The Desert Born', another of his elaborate pieces
of anti-climax, in which the poet imagines himself lashed,
Mazeppa-like and helpless, on the back of a great Arabian
horse racing across the shifting sands. The last line, intended to

dissolve the whole poem into a joke, reveals that the dead horse that falls on him at last was a 'Night Mare on his chest'; but the sense of mental strain and physical pain in the poem, as in:

My scanty breath was jolted out with many a sudden groan—
My joints were rack'd—my back was strain'd, so firmly had I clung—
My nostrils gush'd, and thrice my teeth had bitten through my
  tongue . . .

plainly reflect his ill health and the agonizing pressure on him of the claims of his work. As he puts it in his Preface: 'Judge then, courteous reader, with what gladness of heart I am now penning the last sentence of a book which, if it will not knock my tormentor on the head quite so effectually as Sinbad brained his back-fare with a great stone, will at least stun and confound him for three moons to come.'

Yet this was merely a pious hope, for he turned at once to the completion of his 'German Book', and rained drawings and narrative sections of it on Wright. His health was so bad that he had ventured out of doors scarcely half a dozen times between his return to Coblenz and the end of April, 1837, when a long letter to De Franck begins, 'Aren't you glad to hear now that I've only been ill and spitting blood three times since I left you, instead of being very dead indeed.' The winter had been all but intolerable; Hood and Jane, for all their good intentions of learning German and seeing more of the country, found the people no more congenial than they had at first; they were both home-sick, Hood especially yearning for a sight of the sea.

Matters came to a head over the despatch of his material to London. There were delays of a month in sending books, clashes with officious Customs men; on one occasion Hood was charged for *plumbing*, that is, putting leaden seals on a box, which had none on it, and had in any case been opened already at Emmerich. 'However,' said Hood, 'I shall have my revenge: the materials of my book are in London, and so let the Rhine-landers look out for squalls.' These exasperations determined him to quit Coblenz for Ostend, where he would be near the sea, and close enough to England to visit it when he was well enough. The two years' exile in Germany was drawing to a little-regretted close.

VIII

In Exile—Belgium

ALTHOUGH Hood had decided to quit Germany early in April, he was unable to leave until some weeks later. He was suffering so badly from rheumatism and chest trouble that he dared not touch the 'good English porter' at the Trèves Hotel. 'It is miserable work,' he wrote to De Franck, 'to be such a shattered old fellow as I am' [he was 38] 'when you, who are in years my senior, are gallivanting and like a boy of nineteen!' His condition was aggravated by home-sickness. Letters from the Dilkes and the Elliots telling of common friends, visits to the opera and musical evenings, and urging him to gather all the money he could and fly home to his own hive, deepened his desire to come back to his English fireside. Above all he missed the society of the faithful De Franck, with whom he carried on a prodigious correspondence mingling the grave with the facetious. De Franck was usually addressed as 'Tim says he', an allusion to a comic Irish dialogue they had laughed at together, while Hood was addressed, enigmatically, as 'Johnny'. The matter is complicated by Hood's writing at least one letter to De Franck, signed as if by De Franck himself and addressed to 'Mr. Wood' in jest at De Franck's poor memory for names! The correspondence between them is full of such schoolboyish jokes, as frequent on De Franck's part as on Hood's.

Hood wrote much to De Franck about their common interest in angling (although he was not sure now how his chest would stand up to casting), and generally let down his hair. 'I am almost melancholy,' he wrote on April 23, 'for I never had any serious fears about my health before; my lungs were always good. But now I think they are touched, too.' To Dr. Elliot he gave a more detailed description of his symptoms, ending, 'I look more like the Rueful Knight than a Professor of the Comic.' Yet, even in letters like the 'selfish egotistical ones', as he called them, he found room for jokes, puns, lively anecdotes and an optimistic hope that, once he was free of the climate of Coblenz and poor German food and heating, and able to inhale the bracing sea breezes, all would be well.

One of the last pieces of writing Hood did before he left Germany was a series of three long letters for the *Athenaeum* on 'Copyright and Copywrong'. Sergeant Talfourd had raised in Parliament the question of the unsatisfactory nature of the Copyright Law of 1814, and, as one whose whole income came from writing, Hood had a strong personal interest in the issue. His Letters vibrate with powerful feeling and the conviction that comes from direct experience; they are eloquent and forceful, but they also make out a logical case.

He deplores the low standing of writers in the eyes of the law and the community. 'We have no more caste than the Pariahs. We are on a par . . . with quack doctors, street-preachers, strollers, ballad-singers, hawkers of last dying speeches, Punch-and-Judies, conjurers, tumblers, and other "divarting vaga-bonds". We have neither character to lose nor property to protect. We are by law—outlaws, undeserving of civil rights. . . . The title of a book is, in legal phrase, the worst title there is. Literary property is the lowest in the market.' Writers, he points out, have no protection against piracy, not only abroad, but even in their own land; they are the prey of dishonest publishers and booksellers.

In the second letter, Hood describes the lack of recognition of literary worth by public honours and employments; Society, he says, regards literature 'as a vanity or luxury rather than as a grand moral engine, capable of advancing the spiritual as well as the temporal interest of mankind'. And in the last, he challenges the common view of writers as eccentrics, scamps, and libertines, deplores the submission of their character after death to a 'sort of Egyptian post-mortem trial', and shows the unfortunate situation of a writer's family and heirs unable to profit by the fruits of his genius. 'Learning and genius,' he writes, 'worthily directed and united to common industry, surely deserve, at least, a competence. . . . The more moderate in proportion the rate of their usual reward, the more scrupulously ought every particle of their interests to be promoted and protected so as to spare, if possible, the necessity of private benefactions or public collections for the present distress, and "Literary Retreats" for the future.'

It was a long time before Talfourd's campaign bore fruit, and Hood's ideal of perpetual copyright is farther away today than ever, yet the latter's eloquent testimony undoubtedly played its part in bringing about copyright reforms later in the century. Talfourd acknowledged the value of Hood's advocacy and, in the published edition of his speeches on copyright in the House of Commons included a petition by Hood, saying that, although it was 'thought too richly studded with jests to be presented to the House of Commons', 'its wit embodies too much wisdom to allow of its exclusion from this place'.

At last the time came when the Hoods could move from Coblenz. Towards the end of June they left 752 Alten Graben: 'The farce did not, like many modern ones, fall off at the end. We had a famous row with our landlord. He rushed up his own stairs, and shouted from the top, "Dumme Englander". And then Jane had a scrimmage with him. . . . Finally, just on the gunwale of the packet, as it were, they gave us a finishing touch; for Jane called to pay a bookseller on the road, and he made her pay for a number more than she had had.' They travelled down the Rhine to Cologne, then by coach to Ostend by way of Liége, Brussels, and Ghent, arriving on June 23. The weather was fine, but Thomas and Jane arrived exhausted by heat and fatigue.

They settled in at 39 Rue Longue, Ostend, and Hood's spirits perked up at once. 'The Esplanade is very fine,' he told Wright, 'and the sands famous for our brats, who delight in them extremely . . . it is such a comfort to think of only that strip of sea between us, quick communication by packets, and posts four times a week, that I feel quite in spirits as to my work, and hopeful as to my health.'

Many letters to Wright survive, in one of which Hood tells how he contemplates an ode to Queen Victoria for the *Athenaeum*. He and Jane found Ostend cleaner than Coblenz. 'It is quite a treat to see the clean faces and hands. I *could* kiss the children here about the streets—and the maids too. I think the German men kiss each other so because, thanks to dirt, there is no *fair sex* there.' They also got on a good deal better with the Flemish than with the Germans; yet they found themselves almost as badly off as in Germany for society, for though there were plenty of English about, they were 'such English—broken English and bad English—scoundrelly English!' But as almost every Fleming they met spoke English 'more or less', they fitted in 'very smoothly and as contentedly as we can be abroad'. And, although Hood was astonished that Ostend was so full of cabals and that duelling was prevalent, he thought the people civil and obliging and not 'malicious, like the Rhinelanders'.

In these conditions and with his health benefiting from the change, he took up his pen again. One of the first fruits of Ostend was the magnificent 'Ode to Rae Wilson, Esq.' which appeared in the *Athenaeum* on August 12. Wilson, a Scottish lawyer of narrow religious views, and a writer of ineffably dull travel-books, had been assailing Hood for some years as one of a group of writers whose work was, in his opinion, full of 'profaneness and ribaldry'. Hood was informed by friends that Wilson's latest book, *Notes Abroad and Rhapsodies at Home*, contained a shocked assault on him for an image in 'The Blue Boar', a poem in the 1837 *Comic Annual*. The offending lines, describing a pig:

> Whilst, from the corner of her jaw,
> A sprout of cabbage, green and raw,
> Protruded—as the Dove, so staunch
> For Peace, supports an olive branch—

were, claimed Wilson, a blasphemous reference to the Holy Ghost. This stupidity aroused Hood to a rare fit of anger.

In the introductory note to the Ode, he wrote: 'It is the female swine, perhaps, that is profaned in the eyes of the Oriental tourist. Men find strange ways of marking their intolerance; and the spirit is certainly strong enough, in Mr. Wilson's works, to set up a creature as sacred, in sheer opposition to the Mussulman, with whom she is a beast of abomination.' The Ode itself is a sheer delight, a fervent attack on canting bigotry, which Hood's generous heart instinctively hated, and of which he had had some slight experience among his own relatives. Apart from some passages in Byron, and Burns's incomparable 'Holy Willie's Prayer', there are few poems in English that so pungently and wittingly demolish the 'self-elected saints' and those

> Censors who sniff out moral taints,
> And call the devil over his own coals—
> Those pseudo Privy Counsellors of God,
> Who write down judgments with a pen hard-nibb'd;
> Ushers of Beelzebub's Black Rod.

Mingled with pleas for toleration, defence of the sincerity of Papists, affirmations of Hood's own 'blue-domer' latitudinarianism, 'Making all earth a fane, all heav'n a dome', and a scathing attack on mere formularies in religion, are pointed and searing lines on that form of bourgeois hypocrisy by no means peculiar to his own day:

> Behold yon servitor of God and Mammon,
> Who, binding up his Bible with his Ledger,
>   Blends Gospel texts with trading gammon.
> A black-leg saint, a spiritual hedger,
> Who backs his rigid Sabbath, so to speak,
> Against the wicked remnant of the week,
> A saving bet against his sinful bias—
> 'Rogue that I am,' he whispers to himself.
> 'I lie—I cheat—do anything for pelf,
> But who on earth can say I am not pious?'

The puns, while sometimes brilliant, are strictly rationed, mere facetiousness rarely intrudes, and the tone of indignation carries the whole thing along to make it Hood's most biting poem; edged with righteous force, and not with personal malice, it sums up a good deal of his spontaneously warm-hearted feeling for decent, humane values.

In the autumn, John Wright and the Dilkes visited the Ostend exiles, and brightened their lives considerably. Meanwhile Hood pushed on with the *Comic Annual* for 1838, which came out in reasonable time. He told Elliot in December, 1837: 'I have done the "Comic" with an ease to myself I cannot remember before. . . . But who would think of such a creaking, croaking, blood-spitting wretch being the "Comic"?' The number, while amusing enough and containing several things of interest, such as a prose lampoon on the fashionable cult of Animal Magnetism, and the entertaining, if too lengthy, 'Hit or Miss', was a rather unexciting one, with no really substantial item.

In October, Wright suggested that Hood should capitalize on the success of the Annual by re-issuing selected parts of its contents in monthly parts, a move prompted perhaps by the wide public response to Dickens's *Pickwick Papers* in parts. At first Hood was doubtful; he did not see his way clear, he had the German book on his mind, he would have to be two issues ahead, his health might not stand it, and so on. But finally he agreed, and in January, 1838, Baily published the first issue of *Hood's Own* or *Laughter from Year to Year, Being Former Runnings of His Comic Vein, with an Infusion of New Blood for General Circulation*. The thirteen numbers duly printed contained mostly material from the Annual, with occasional additions of new pieces, such as the 'Literary Reminiscences'. These were written at the request of the publishers to accompany a portrait of Hood by George Robert Lewis, who travelled to Ostend to paint it. The portrait, which admirably catches the blend of seriousness, tenderness and fun in Hood's character, was reproduced in the July, 1838, issue of *Hood's Own* and as a frontispiece to the first collected volume of the monthly in 1839. The new venture was an unqualified success, and the collected volume of 1839 and a subsequent one compiled by Tom Hood in 1861 were the main publications that kept Hood's name alive during the Victorian age.

Despite Hood's optimism, his health remained poor. Late in December, 1837, he visited London for the first time since his exile, and stayed for three weeks with the Dilkes; he still mistrusted the ministrations of Continental doctors and wanted to consult his old friend, Dr. Elliot. After a thorough examination, Elliot pronounced Hood's lungs to be perfectly sound, and said that the real trouble lay in the liver. Reassured, for that was his own conviction, Hood returned to Ostend to press on with his writing, and, inevitably, to battle with weakness and exhaustion. For instance, on February 24, 1838, Jane told Mrs. Dilke that her husband had been prostrated again. The German doctor, wiser than Thomas gave him credit for being, said the main cause was extreme exhaustion, 'for the cold weather, want of air and exercise, acted upon by great anxiety of mind and nervousness'. Nor was Jane's health any better. Writing to his sister, Betsy, in January, Hood confided to her that Jane had recently had a miscarriage, 'brought on by alarm and exertion at my last attack', and was still weak from the disaster.[1]

The jocose correspondence with De Franck continued to flow, full of references to the joys of angling and boating. Hood had hired a boat built under the supervision of an old English ship-master 'all snug, safe, and handy', and whenever the weather and his health allowed, enjoyed himself 'as a marine'. Unhappily, Jane and the children, who had not his head for the sea, had been so terrified by one experience on a rough sea with three lubberly Flemings for a crew, that they would not accompany him again, 'which is very hard', said Hood, 'as I cannot take out any other ladies without Jane, the place being rather apt to talk scandal—and one of our female friends is very fond of boating'.

Scandal-mongering seems to have been a favourite pastime with the English residents of Ostend. Hood had several brushes with a certain Mrs. F.—who refused to set foot in his house again after he had lectured her on character-assassination. 'I had a little duel of messages with my "scandal-mongering" acquaintance the other day. "Pray tell Mr. Hood," says she, "that I have no doubt but his complaint is a *scurrilous* liver" (schirrous). So I sent her my compliments, and begged leave to say that was better than a "cantankerous gizzard".'

De Franck, on his part, lamented that he was forced to leave Bromberg, where he had expected to stay for six years, for Posen, where a review of the army was to take place, and later from Posen that he had had an illness that necessitated having his head shaved. Hood ragged him unmercifully about this. 'Of course, the Radziwills, who made you so retrench your moustaches, will be quite content with you now: but I hope you will not be slack in your correspondence in consequence, although I must expect to have more *balderdash* out of your own head.' One reason, apart from that of genuine friendship, for Hood's keeping up his voluminous correspondence with De Franck was the officer's frequent farcical anecdotes which more than once gave Hood a hint for a comic piece.

Typical of De Franck's little stories is this, from a letter

[1] Bristol Public Library.

167

written from Bromberg on February 4, 1838: 'At a grand battue (at Posen) several cockneys attended, one of them could not keep his dog quiet which must be at a battue as the sportsmen must stand very still and wait till the game stirred up by the drivers comes within shot. At last he tied the dog with a cord to the button-hole of his breeches pocket where, as he thought, he had him quiet at last. Unfortunately for our cockney a hare soon came towards him at which he fired as soon as he got sight of her, but the dog twigged her too and so with the shot he darted off tearing away the whole front part of our hero's inexpressibles, and made off after the hare. It was a most ridiculous scene to see the dog running through the wood with a pair of breeches trailing after him, with the cockney's long face, and better still, to see him obliged to ride home half a Sansculotte.' [1]

About June, Jane paid a brief visit to England for a change of scene and to visit friends. She told Elliot of Hood's continued debility; Hood passed on his verdict to De Franck in words that show the extraordinarily even temper of his acceptance of his lot: 'The danger of the case was gone, but that as I had never been particularly strong and sturdy, I must not now expect to be more than a young old gentleman, but I will be a boy as long as I can in mind and spirits, only the troublesome bile is apt to upset my temper now and then.'

He was most gratified to learn that his name was very much alive in Britain; he told De Franck that a friend of Byron's as well as Long Wellesley, the Duke of Wellington's nephew, who had been Hood's landlord at Lake House, had sought him out in Ostend. He and Jane were much less isolated than at Coblenz and though they still had their troubles with servants— one letter to Wright tells of the dismissal of a frivolous maid, Mary—they had settled into a pleasantly quiet home routine. Hood, plagued with a 'sort of bastard gout . . . as if I were an aristocrat at times, limping about, and in and out of bed with various afflictions', told De Franck wryly, 'Sickness is selfish, and invalids never feel acutely for each other,' adding, 'My domestic habits are very domestic indeed; like Charity I begin at home, and end there; so Faith and Hope must call upon me, if they wish to meet.'

[1] Bristol University Library.

He had plenty to keep him busy, with the 1839 Annual to prepare, *Hood's Own* to keep going and the German book to finish. The *Comic* came out in time, although Hood's hand ached with drawing and he felt that, while the Annual was always 'a lay miracle', this time it had got done by a 'special Providence'. This, the tenth and last volume in the series, contained much the mixture as before, with the brightest spots perhaps a celebration of the abolition of slavery in 'The Doves and the Crow', and 'Rural Felicity', a sprightly variant on the old theme of the townsman experiencing the terrors and discomforts of the country.

In February, 1839, Hood travelled to England, in part to have Elliot re-examine him, but mainly to look into his affairs with Baily. He had for some time been suspicious of his publisher's integrity; but, as he wrote to Dilke soon after reaching Coblenz in 1836, 'I am in his [Baily's] power—and I believe he in money matters to be safe.' But his three weeks' visit proved very upsetting with 'a number of vexatious and unjustified delays in business'—('all booksellers are alike'), he told Elliot. He felt that Baily's accounts were dubious, that he was cheating him, and being evasive about actual sales of his work, and his long-standing doubts about his publisher flamed up into a strong disagreement, which seemingly resulted in Baily refusing to issue any more numbers of the *Comic Annual*, although he remained bound by a contract to issue the German book.

Back in Ostend, sick and worried, Hood turned again to the latter work, on which his hopes were set, although, as he told Wright, 'I have found more difficulty in inventing than in executing, my state allowing of the mechanical, but not of the imaginative.' To Elliot, he said, 'I am not desponding, but such annoyances as the present, weaken, and lower, and worry me, particularly as I have as much to do as a strong person could get through.'

In April, 1839, the Hoods moved to more suitable lodgings at La Rhétorique, Rue St. François, Ostend, and the small circle of English friends they had made in the town provided them with amicable company. Perhaps because Hood could get by in French, his Ostend letters, unlike the German ones, contain few verbal caricatures of the locals and their customs, and both he and Jane appear to have been free from the petty domestic worries that had plagued them at Coblenz. Thomas told De Franck on May 23, 1839, the day of his fortieth birthday, 'I think my liver complaint is tolerably cured, and I have not spit any blood for a very long while, but the *curing* has half killed me. I am as thin as a lath, and as weak as plaster. Perhaps I have no blood left to spit. . . . Another year will set me up, or knock me down—the wear and tear of my nerves, &c, cannot last longer. . . . But then I am two score, and sometimes am ready to call them the Forty Thieves, for having stolen away my youth and health.'

But one misfortune after another was to follow in the ensuing months. *Up the Rhine*, as the 'German book' was now called, was well ahead, and as Wright, who had been so assiduous in Hood's interests, had fallen seriously ill, Jane left for England in October both to visit her family, whom she had not seen for almost five years, and to do what she could to shepherd the book through the press. While she was there, Wright died, thus removing one of Hood's most loyal friends, who had been, in effect, his business manager during the exile. Jane, who had as close an interest in the details of publishing as Hood himself, wrote to him to say of Baily, 'from what I can already gather I fear he is as false as we think him'.[1]

While she was away, Hood had an exceptionally severe attack of rheumatism, which he blamed on the very sudden change to bitterly cold weather. 'I groaned all the night through in agony, without intermission; and on Thursday morning about ten, put on leeches which relieved me a *little*. Soon after, from sheer exhaustion, I fell asleep; but almost immediately woke up again with a most violent cramp in the leg. . . . You may suppose the double anguish was intolerable,— in fact it quite convulsed me;—and when the cramp was over I had the other pain all day, with only one short doze.' Anxious not to alarm Jane, however, he added, 'I seem doomed to have the trial once a year—thank God, it only comes like Xmas. But I am not out of spirits for in other respects I have been unusually well and getting on.' He is also solicitous for her: 'I do beg you will see Elliot, it is of as great concern as anything else, and you are apt to forget *yourself*, dearest, when other matters are in

[1] Bristol Public Library.

hand.' He ends with a comic attempt to minimize his seizure. 'It was *cruel* suffering but I could not describe it to them without laughing, that cramp, for I was pirouetting about on one leg and the other drawn up in such a twist, as only Grimaldi was able to effect. Or remembering I was only in my shirt I must have been somewhat like Oscar Byrne in his short tunic and making as many grimaces. Luckily I was alone, for I must have bundled out of bed had Hannah More been present.' [1]

Thanks in large part to Jane's efforts, *Up the Rhine* was published by Baily in December, 1839, with an 1840 imprint, and at once met with even more than the success Hood had hoped for it. It pleased critics and public alike, and the first edition of 1,500 copies was exhausted in a fortnight. A second edition, with a preface dated January, 1840, followed, and another, printed at Frankfurt, likewise sold well. Altogether, this book, which had been so long in the making, had the best reception of anything he had so far published. It was a hybrid, part travel-book and part novel, which unashamedly imitates *Humphrey Clinker*, as Hood acknowledges in the preface: 'To forestall such Critics as are fond of climbing up a Mât de Cocagne for a Mare's Nest at the top, the following work was constructed, partly on the ground-plan of Humphrey Clinker, but with very inferior materials, and on a much humbler scale. I admire the old mansion too much to think that any workmanship of mine could erect a house fit to stand in the same row.'

As with Smollett's novel, *Up the Rhine* is told in the form of letters, and even the major correspondents are modelled upon Smollett's—Richard Orchard, the hypochondriacal bachelor uncle, Mrs. Wilmot, his widowed sister, with a marvellous capacity for the misunderstanding of simple problems, Frank Somerville, the easy-going, intelligent nephew, and Martha Penny, the mis-spelling and malaproping maid—'For my own part, instead of objection to a Catholic, I should feel my Christian duty to embrace him, as perhaps the happy Instrument, under Grace, of making him a convict.' In their letters back home, the four travellers up the Rhine describe the odd characters they meet, the customs of the Germans, the churches and villages, and have many adventures, mostly comic, sometimes serious. Throughout the novel are interspersed stories, usually as loosely

[1] Bristol University Library.

relevant as those in *Pickwick Papers*, and light-hearted poems, several of them parodying medieval beliefs and legends in the manner of Barham's *Ingoldsby Legends* of the following year, and Mark Twain's *Innocents Abroad*, although without the crude vulgarity of the latter—'The Knight and the Dragon' and 'Our Lady's Chapel' among them. One poem has the inevitable pun on 'eau de Cologne'; another sums up Hood's views on the rapacious Germans:

> Ye tourists and Travellers, bound to the Rhine,
> Provided with passport, that requisite docket,
> First listen to one little whisper of mine—
> Take care of your pocket! Take care of your pocket!

Much of *Up the Rhine* reproduces material found in Hood's letters home, often in almost identical words, such as the account of the New Year's Ball at Coblenz, and the book ends, up in the air—for there is no plot—with a full description of the march with De Franck, and it is the 19th Infantry with which Frank Somerville travels. There is excellent reportage, especially of such things as the Cologne Cathedral ('a miracle of art—a splendid illustration of transcendentalism') and some shrewd observations on, for instance, the violent anti-semitism, which was something new to him. 'As for his Fatherland,' Frank Somerville writes, 'a Jew may truly say of it as the poor Irishman did of his own hard-hearted relative—"Yes, sure enough he's the parent of me—but he treats me as if I was his son by another Mother and Father!"' Richard Orchard, too, reflecting Hood's own tolerance, rebukes a bigoted fellow-Englishman in the Catholic church: 'It's my notion that all Christians are of one family, and as such, I can't understand how a friend to family worship can want to narrow the circle by shutting out any of his relations.' There is, of course, much fun at the expense of German eating and drinking habits, especially among the Rhinelanders, whom Hood found much less attractive than the Saxons and Brandenburgers, a shocked meditation on the German suicide-rate—'This propensity to suicide is a reproach which the Germans have to wipe away before they can justly claim the character of a moral, religious or intellectual people'—a dialogue on angling, some satire on Dr. Hahnemann and German quacks, and anecdotes—the quill episode with Gradle, for instance—from his own experience. Hood himself appears under the name of Mr. Markham, an invalid living abroad for economy's sake, from whom come sober opinions almost identical with the author's own in his letters, although tempered with some restraint, for, as he told Dilke, 'I do not want, like Jonathan in England, "a war, and all on my own account", nor Irish-like to whiten the English by blackening the Germans.'

Up the Rhine is a readable, light-weight effort; it is easy to understand its appeal both at home and abroad, at a time when travel-books tended to be stodgy, rhapsodic, and dull, and there is much in it that remains lively. But, on the whole, it is a fragile thing, showing signs of having been flung together, shapeless and superficial. Hood had found much to delight his eye in Germany, but neither the country nor the people were congenial to him, and for all the good temper and restraint of caricature in the book, this feeling is plain in the absence of coherent plan and inner substance in *Up the Rhine*.

Still worried about his affairs with Baily, Hood travelled again to England in January, taking young Tom with him. He spent five weeks there this time, staying with the Dilkes in Grosvenor Place and dividing his time between arguments with his publisher and trying to decipher 'very ill-kept and tardily-rendered accounts', which doubly irked one whose own accounts were at least neat, and looking around without success for some really profitable literary job to help him clear off the last of his debts. He returned to Ostend much depressed about his health and that of Jane, 'her anxiety and fatigue about me are against her', yet still capable of joking about it. 'I was amused by a remark of old Dr. Jansen's,' he told Elliot on March 1, 1840. 'I said my sedentary profession was against me. And when he understood it was literary, "Ah!" said he with a glance at a thin, yellowish face, "a *serious* writer, of course." Akin to this, I one day overheard a dispute between Tom and Fanny as to what I was. "Pa's a literary man," said Fanny. "He's not!" said Tom. "I know what he is!" "What is he, then?" "Why," says Tom, "he's not a literary man—he's an invalid." ' Several letters to Elliot show him still stubbornly clinging to his belief that his lungs were sound but that 'the mischief is in the stomach or liver'. Increasing lassitude and langour he tended to attribute to the damp climate—'At three o'clock the whole place was wrapped in a white mist, and our paved yard as wet as after rain. . . . You literally see the damp ascend, step by step, until the whole flight is wet. To natives and residents in health this may not prove so obviously injurious; but to invalids, and especially coming into it at this season, its effects are very marked.'

The state of Hood's affairs as well as his health must have formed a principal topic in his letters to his old friend and collaborator, John Hamilton Reynolds. Reynolds himself had not been damned by Hood in the quarrel with Jane's sisters in 1835, and the two men continued their relationship for some years. Unfortunately, the correspondence between them, which, according to Hood's children, was extensive, has disappeared. When Tom and Fanny were compiling the *Memorials*, Reynolds' widow, having some unknown reason for rancour against the family, refused to allow them access to the letters, and it is now unlikely that more than a few will ever turn up. From the evidence that remains, it is clear that, having for some years played with equal levity at both law and letters, and earned a reputation as one over-fond of convivial company, but liable to antagonize friends and clients by his ready tongue, Reynolds found that, while his early promise in literature had not been fulfilled and money from journalism, once elegantly scorned, was scanty in time of need, he had reached his early forties without advancing in the law either, and with his fair share of money troubles. Wright in a letter to Hood on September 6, 1837, confides, 'I have been sorry to hear that John Reynolds is in some scrape about Price's affairs. I don't know how but hear that he had become possessed some time since of 7 or 800 pounds in the business, which the creditors now claim to be divided. It was money in Chancery and paid over by the Court I believe to John, and he now has to refund it.'[1] Two years later, Reynolds was declared bankrupt.

One surviving letter he wrote to Hood in Ostend, dated March 13, 1840, shows the change in temper such misfortunes had wrought in the once ebullient John Hamilton. Asking Hood for a promised paper for the *New Sporting Magazine*, which Reynolds was helping to edit, he says, 'I do seriously

[1] Bristol University Library.

believe that the months are very unlike cherubs, and consist *only* of *latter ends*'; and he grumbles about the 'industrious crawlers' who 'go ahead without a head, whilst we are limping along with down-at-heel shoes—and hats with the lids off.'[1] He acted as Hood's solicitor on occasion, the last time being during the dispute with A. H. Baily in 1840. In the middle of the affair, however, Reynolds was replaced as Hood's legal representative by a Mr. St. P. B. Hook, after which no further contact between the two men can be traced. It may be that some disagreement about Reynolds' handling of Hood's affairs led to a lasting breach between them. A disappointed man, virtually forgotten by his contemporaries, and remembered only by some as an associate of Keats, Reynolds became increasingly cynical and frustrated, and died in 1852 at Newport, in the Isle of Wight, few of the islanders knowing that he had any literary claims whatever.

Hood's references in his letters to his worsening condition made Elliot press him to return to England for a further personal examination. Arriving in London in April, 1840, Hood first stayed a week with the Dilkes, then moved to Elliot's at Stratford, where he had a violent attack, spitting blood profusely. Dr. Elliot tended him with great care, and was not convinced, at that stage, that the poet's trouble was 'aggravated by largeness of my heart'. From his bed, Hood told Jane, 'He is very earnest for my returning to England, as the best climate for both mind and body, and at this moment, there are many inducements literally *before my eyes*. It is a lovely, sunny day. Imagine me in bed, with the windows open, looking over their garden across the country, so green with its meadows and hedges, and Shooter's Hill so beautifully blue in the distance. It looks lovely and yet "my heart's in the *low*lands—my heart is not here", and I feel how many other conditions are necessary to my living in England.' Yet, in spite of the other conditions, mainly financial ones, Hood knew in his heart that he would have to return to England permanently, if only to die there. 'There is no country like England, no people like the English after all', he affirmed to Jane in a letter written on Good Friday. At first, he advised her to remain in Ostend, but as the weeks crawled by, and he mended only slowly, his need of her

[1] Ibid.

showed so plainly in his letters that in the middle of May she came post-haste to Stratford, leaving the children in the care of a friend in Belgium. She found Thomas much rested and improved under Elliot's care, and her own arrival contributed to further improvement.

But, although Elliot had warned Jane solemnly that much of her husband's condition was the result of mental anxiety and nervous strain, this was a time when his mind was clouded with the complexities of an action against Baily. Dissatisfied with Baily's accounts, he had decided to remove his works to another publisher. But Baily retained them all, in Jane's words, 'On the plea that he had a quarter share of *one*—The "Hood's Own"—instead of a quarter share of the *profits only*'. Hood brought a legal action against the firm of A. H. Baily and Co. which dragged on interminably, and was, in fact, settled in his favour only four years later, by which time the cost of litigation had exceeded the value of the property. In the meantime, the profits on *Hood's Own* and on the second edition of *Up the Rhine* were tied up pending settlement of the suit. To add to Hood's troubles, one of his English creditors had seized the stock of his works still in Baily's hands. The cumulative effect of these difficulties is reflected in an exchange of letters in the *Athenaeum* during October, 1840, an exchange distinguished by an unusual acrimony on Hood's part.

Baily had announced him as a contributor to the *Sportsman's Oracle and Almanac of Rural Life*. In high dudgeon, Hood wrote to the *Athenaeum* to point out that the work from his pen to be included was only the reprint of an article written in 1838 for Nimrod's *Sporting*. 'I am the more anxious', he wrote, 'to disavow any such imputed contributionship, because it would imply the continuance of a Connexion renounced by me six months hence, as religiously as one renounces the devil and all his works.' The following week, Baily replied, claiming that on the contrary it was he who had repudiated Hood because his popularity as an author was declining 'and the consequent diminished sales of his works not realizing the money I had been in the habit of advancing to him', adding a blow distinctly below the belt, 'and to the fact that a heavy stock of his last works, which remained in hand, having been seized by his creditors, I am to attribute an animosity the exhibition of which has, however, recoiled upon himself'. He added that the copyright of the article in question was his, anyhow, and that for it, 'I some time ago gave Mr. Hood much too large a sum.'

Hood's lengthy reply showed him stung by Baily's tone, and especially resentful at 'the publication of my private affairs'; he asserted that the article had been written at Baily's request for a sum suggested by him, that the connection had been broken in March by Hood, not Baily (he quotes from the correspondence to prove it) and that it was a creditor, not 'creditors' who attached the works, and that after proceedings had been begun by Baily. 'Any man', writes Hood, 'who has so long borne his burden in secret and silence, and with so cheerful a spirit—bear witness for me, my humble works—will not be confounded with a suppliant for the world's pity or assistance. One who seeks his happiness in the domestic affections, and who has a home and a family circle—whose favourite pursuits are his profession—can neither be poor nor feel so—and, least of all, if he happens to have before his eyes some signal example of poverty, nay utter destitution, of all enjoyments, moral or intellectual. Be it known, then, to the world—since such is Mr. Baily's *pleasure*—that, self-banished, I have been struggling abroad to retrieve my affairs, and to acquit myself honourably of all claims upon me,—a consummation once quite in the foreground of my prospects, but rendered remote by the sudden breaking up of my health, after a stormy passage to Rotterdam. I can adduce medical testimony that my literary exertions have been fully as great as could be expected under the circumstances of my case; indeed, I will venture to say in my own behalf that, taking both effusions together, no gentleman alive has written so much Comic and spitten so much blood within six consecutive years.'

Baily did not reply to this broadside, which was just as well, for Hood's situation was even more desperate than his letters reveal. He and Jane, after leaving the Elliots, had settled at Camberwell, initially at 8 South Place, then, after a couple of months, at 2 Union Row, High Street. In May, they sent for their children from Ostend, to discover, to their horror and distress, that Tom and Fanny were detained there pending Hood's settlement of outstanding debts in Belgium of something over £100. Desperate, Hood turned to the publisher,

Richard Bentley, and offered him the copyright to *Tylney Hall* in exchange for a sum needed for an 'indispensable purpose'. When Bentley pressed him for a reason, Hood replied in June, 'The main fact is that since I saw you my children (for whom I sent) have been detained in Belgium, for some debts owing there—which could have been paid out of the means in Baily's hands. Neither my wife nor myself can return there, both being liable by the Belgian law—and I only ascertained yesterday that our ambassador has no power to interfere—. . . . It was never thought possible that a boy and girl of five and nine years old could be detained—it is not perhaps legal—but they are in the people's power and I am doomed just now to feel how might overcomes right. It has become therefore a matter of strict necessity for me to seek for present money to release my children.' [1]

Presumably Bentley advanced the sum required, for he issued *Tylney Hall* in July with a new preface by Hood, and in the same month Jane and Thomas travelled to Belgium to retrieve the young ones. Elliot had warned Hood that his health would suffer further unless he remained in England, so they decided to stay home this time. The years of exile were at an end; their legacy was a sad one—Hood's health had seriously deteriorated, to the stage where he was a perpetual invalid, his finances were little better than when he had left England, and his mind was weighed down with cares heavier than any he had known before.

[1] Bodleian Library.

IX

'Miss Kilmansegg' and Others

BACK home, it became more urgent than ever for Hood to plunge into action with his pen. As a comic writer he had become popular; and it was as a comic writer he would continue to earn his daily bread, although old friends like Allan Cunningham continued to lament the submergence of the serious strain in him. Acknowledging receipt of a copy of *Hood's Own* in May, 1840, Cunningham wrote, 'At this cold and distant hour it is almost ungraceful to say how much amid your mirth and fun your unexpected touches of true pathos and moral seriousness affected me; nor how welcome were your recollections of the Taylor and Hessey days when Lamb scattered his bright though dilatory jokes about and Hazlitt sat with his foxlike eyes looking direct at nothing and yet seeing all!' Now that the *Comic Annual* had concluded, periodical contributions became Hood's main source of income. In August, he produced for the *New Sporting Magazine* two entertaining pseudo-Waltonian pieces on 'Fishing in Germany', which included some of De Franck's angling experiences at Bromberg, and in November, for the *Athenaeum*, he wrote a most appreciative review of Dickens's *The Old Curiosity Shop*, at that time being published serially as part of *Master Humphrey's Clock*.

The character of Little Nell made a deep impression on Hood, as it later did on many other eminent Victorians, and he rhapsodized over her: 'How sweet and fresh the youthful figure! . . . How soothing the moral, that gentleness, purity and truth, sometimes dormant, but never dead, have survived, and will outlive fraud and force though backed by gold and encased in steel.' He complained of the contrived framework of the story, but admired Quilp as a 'highly-wrought character', and recognized a particular significance in Dickens's presentation of 'Worth in low places'. 'Above all,' says Hood, 'in distributing the virtues, he bestows a full proportion of them among a class of our fellow creatures who are favoured in Life's Grand State Lotteries with nothing but the declared blanks. . . . The poor are his especial clients.' This review pleased Dickens enormously, and was the beginning of the contact between the two men that produced a generous correspondence and led to mutual respect and something like friendship. Dickens wrote to thank Hood for his review, and Hood replied in November: 'As to the Review—as in the Grand Reviews at Coblenz—the beauty of the country that was passed over was a sufficient reward. That it was written with a kindly feeling towards you, is true: for books which put us in a better humour with the world in general must naturally incline us towards the Author in particular. . . . In the meantime, I heartily grasp and shake the hand you autographically hold out to me, and embrace your friendship with my whole heart. A friendship that promises to endure, if from nothing better, thro' the mere difficulty of falling in, and consequently out, with each other.'

Dickens carried his appreciation further. In the preface to the 1848 edition of *The Old Curiosity Shop*, he referred to an essay of which Little Nell was the principal theme, 'so earnestly, so eloquently and tenderly appreciative of her, and of all her shadowy kith and kin, that it would have been insensibility in me, if I could have read it without an unusual glow of pleasure, and encouragement. Long afterwards, and when I had come to know him well, and to see him, stout of heart, going slowly down into his grave, I knew the writer of that essay to be Thomas Hood.' Years later, when Dickens published the first instalment of Mrs. Gaskell's *Cranford* in *Household Words* in 1851, he changed what he felt to be too frequent complimentary references to himself and his books to 'Hood' and his works. Mrs. Gaskell, by no means pleased, altered the names back when her novel came out in book form in 1853.

Hood met Dickens presumably through common friends like 'Barry Cornwall', Richard Monckton Milnes and C. W. Dilke.

In 1841, he was able to say to De Franck: 'Didn't you enjoy Pickwick? It is so very English! I felt sure you would. Boz is a very good fellow, and he and I are very good friends.' Although they saw each other seldom, Hood found Dickens an excellent counsellor, and was not slow to seek the younger man's advice on dealings with publishers and finding new engagements. This advice Dickens gave generously and considerately. There is no doubt that, while he thought little of Hood's gifts as a writer of fiction, he responded warmly to his talents as a writer of comic and grotesque verse and admired both Hood's prodigious inventiveness and his curious fancy. It is more than likely, as we shall see, that Dickens took several hints from Hood's works for elements in his later novels.

In addition to his prose pieces for various journals, Hood in 1840 began writing for the *New Monthly Magazine*, then under the editorship of Theodore Hook, and including among its contributors such writers as Lady Morgan, Mrs. Trollope, Mrs. Catherine Gore, Horace Smith and Douglas Jerrold. In this company, Hood stood out brightly. For all his illness and misfortune, he was entering one of his most brilliant and productive periods. He began with a series of comic and satirical verses entitled 'Rhymes for the Times and Reason for the Season', the first of which was another of his broadsides against Phariseeism and rigid Sabbatarianism, entitled 'An Open Question'. This dealt with the closing of the Zoological Gardens to the public on Sundays

> To me it seems that, in the oddest way,
>   (Begging the pardon of each rigid Socius)
> Our would-be Keepers of the Sabbath-day
>   Are like the Keepers of the brutes ferocious—
> As soon the Tiger might expect to stalk
>   About the grounds from Saturday till Monday,
> As any harmless Man to take a walk,
>   If Saints could clap him in a cage on Sunday—
> But what is your opinion, Mrs. Grundy?
>
> Spirit of Kant! Have we not had enough
>   To make Religion sad, and sour, and snubbish,
> But Saints Zoological must cant their stuff,
>   As vessels cant their ballast—rattling rubbish!

Once let the sect, triumphant to their text,
    Shut Nero[1] up from Saturday till Monday,
And sure as fate they will deny us next
    To see the Dandelions on a Sunday—
But what is your opinion, Mrs. Grundy?

Another *New Monthly* contribution was 'The Tale of a
Trumpet', a perhaps over-lengthy (some 800 lines) but animated comic narrative about a deaf old lady who buys a wonderful ear-trumpet from a pedlar (who is obviously no friend to
mankind) finds she can overhear all the gossip and malice of the
village, retails it all, and is drowned as a witch. The moral is

There are folks about town—to name no names—
Who much resemble that deafest of Dames!
    And over their tea, and muffins, and crumpets,
Circulate many a scandalous word,
And whisper tales they could only have heard
    Through some such Diabolical Trumpets!

The most substantial work he provided for the *New Monthly*,
however, was 'Miss Kilmansegg and Her Precious Leg', which
ran from September to November, 1840. This marvellous extravaganza, Hood's masterpiece of grotesque satire and comic
morality, is a quite extraordinary feat for a man enfeebled of
body and crushed by financial cares. With prodigious facility,
sustained brilliance of invention and of daring, but triumphant
rhyming, unexpected imagery, dazzlingly clever shifts of
thought, lively wit and a wide range of feeling from pathos and
poetic sweetness to corrosive satire and slapstick fun, it sweeps
along almost breathlessly through its 2,388 lines. The rush of the
verse, the ingenious but not too thickly piled puns, and the
hustle of clever rhymes do not conceal the fact that this is not
primarily a comic poem. Rather is it a skilful attack on the Victorian worship of money as embodied in the new race of wealthy
Philistines, whom Dickens was later to satirize in the Veneer-
ings and Mr. Podsnap. The poem is, in Hood's wry description,
'a Golden Legend', but one which instead of medieval romanticism offers a sordid tale of the corrupting power of gold. And
it is one of the strengths of this remarkable poem—a 'sport', if
ever there was one, among the works of its age—that this theme

[1] A lion.

is never lost sight of; 'gold', the dominant motif, weaves in and out of the poem, the word itself and its derivations, repeated again and again produce at the end an almost oppressive sense of squalor and aversion. The tone, a mixture of savagery, bitter raillery and *saevo indignatio*, perhaps lacks the consistently high indignation necessary to really deadly satire, and it is possible to feel that, while the poem has plenty of creative energy, it has not quite enough moral energy to be thoroughly effective. Yet it has an astonishingly original grotesque atmosphere, a mixture of seriousness and savage comedy that is surely unique in its age.

Miss Kilmansegg, the heiress, is born to immense wealth. At her christening:

> Gold! and gold! the new and old,
> The company ate and drank from gold,
>   They revell'd, they sang, and were merry;
> And one of the Gold Sticks rose from his chair
> And toasted 'the Lass with the golden hair'
>   In a bumper of golden Sherry.

> Gold! still gold! it rain'd on the Nurse,
> Who—unlike Danae—was none the worse!
>   There was nothing but guineas glistening!
> Fifty were given to Doctor James
> For calling the little Baby names,
>   And for saying, Amen!
>   The Clerk had ten,
> And that was the end of the Christening.

Surrounded by golden ornaments, playing with golden toys, educated 'with a book of gold leaf for a primer', she grows up arrogant and spoiled:

> They praised her falls, as well as her walk,
> Flatterers made cream cheese of chalk,
> They prais'd—how they prais'd—her very small talk,
>   As if it fell from a Solon;
> Or the girl who at each pretty phrase let drop
> A ruby comma, a pearl full-stop,
>   Or an emerald semi-colon.

When she is a young girl, Miss Kilmansegg loses a leg as a

result of a hunting accident, and insists that it be replaced by a golden one:

> So a Leg was made in a comely mould,
> Of Gold, fine virgin glittering gold,
>   As solid as man could make it—
> Solid in foot, and calf, and shank,
> A prodigious sum of money it sank;
> In fact, 'twas a Branch of the family Bank,
>   And no easy matter to break it.

The golden leg extends her fame far and wide; the leg becomes both symbol and centre of her pride; even when she appears at a ball as Diana, her tunic is

> loop'd up to a gem in front
> To show the Leg that was Golden!

She is courted by men of all stations and incomes:

> She was follow'd, flatter'd, courted, address'd,
> Woo'd, and coo 'd, and wheedled, and press'd
> By suitors from North, South, East and West.

It is, however, a swarthy foreign Count of suave manners who wins her hand: they are married on a day of glorious sunshine:

> Gold above, and gold below,
> The earth reflected the golden glow,
>   From river, and hill, and valley;
> Gilt by the golden light of morn,
> The Thames—it look'd like the Golden Horn,
> And the Barge, that carried coal or corn,
>   Like Cleopatra's Galley!

Before long, the golden heiress finds that the Count is a rake and a spendthrift, actually penniless, who neglects her while he gambles her money away. Even when she weeps in her misery, her tears are described in terms of alchemical imagery:

> The waters that down her visage rill'd
> Were drops of unrectified spirit distill'd
>   From the limbeck of Pride and Vanity.

Having run through all her money, the Count tries to persuade
her to give up the precious leg to him so that he may realize
more capital on it; there is a terrible quarrel, and then she goes
to bed, overwhelmed with chagrin:

> How little she saw in her pride of prime
> The Dart of Death in the Hand of Time—
> The hand that moved on the dial!

That night the Count beats her to death with the Golden Leg,
and vanishes, taking the limb with him:

> Gold!—still gold! it haunted her yet—
> At the Golden Lion the Inquest met—
> Its foreman a carver and gilder—
> And the Jury debated from twelve till three
> What the Verdict ought to be,
> And they brought it in as Felo de Se,
> 'Because her own Leg had kill'd her!'

Subtleties and incidental felicities are many, such as the
comical rhapsody on doubles that accompanies Miss Kilmansegg's marriage, and the grim echo later:

> As she went with her taper up the stair
> How little her swollen eye was aware
> That the shadow which followed was double!

and the incredible number of variants played on the idea of
gold. The occasional macabre flippancy only enhances the
underlying seriousness, the contempt and the bitter social
comment of the whole piece. While Hood's own money
troubles certainly contributed something to the theme and tone
of the poem, it is lifted far above the personal by its metaphorical vigour and imaginative grotesquerie. And it all ends
with the crashing moral driven home by the reiterated rhymes
on 'gold' falling like hammer-blows:

> Gold! Gold! Gold! Gold!
> Bright and yellow, hard and cold,
> Molten, graven, hammer'd and roll'd;
> Heavy to get, and light to hold;
> Hoarded, barter'd, bought and sold,
> Stolen, borrow'd, squander'd, doled:

Spurn'd by the young, but hugg'd by the old
To the very verge of the churchyard mould;
Price of many a crime untold:
Gold! Gold! Gold! Gold!
Good or bad a thousand-fold!
　　How widely its agencies vary—
To save—to ruin—to curse—to bless—
As even its minted coins express,
Now stamp'd with the image of Good Queen Bess,
　　And now of a Bloody Mary.

Dickens, it seems to me, was one of the many who felt the striking originality of 'Miss Kilmansegg'. The literary influences that operated on the great novelist, or rather that he digested into his own obsessive vision, were many and various, but Hood must take his place as one of them. It is possible, as Alvin Whitley has suggested,[1] that there is some relationship between Dr. Bellamy, 'Old Formality', the pompous old gentleman with the stately manners of a past time, in *Tylney Hall*, and Dickens's Mr. Turveydrop in *Bleak House* and between Hood's 'Unlucky Joe' in the same novel, who is always being moved on, and poor Jo the crossing sweeper in Dickens's book. Much else, too, in Hood may have given hints to Dickens—Eugene Aram's self-analysis suggests the introspective self-dissection of murderers and dreamers like Jonas Chuzzlewitt (whose Doppelganger side is likewise intimated in 'Miss Kilmansegg') and Bradley Headstone; the old Hall in 'The Haunted House' is a counter-part to the shadowy staircase in the Dedlock mansion, and to Mr. Tulkinghorn's chamber.

Much more significant, to my mind, are the resemblances between Dickens's last completed novel, *Our Mutual Friend* and 'Miss Kilmansegg and her Precious Leg'. The dominant idea in both works is man's corruption by wealth; in his novel, Dickens brings to a focus the main themes of his later works: gold and what men do to attain it, the worship of money in a venal society, marriage and betrayal for money, the sham of a society professing all the moral virtues but driven only by the lust for gain—these are ideas that both works share, but in themselves they are too general to allow us to establish definite links. It is in

[1] 'Two Hints for "Bleak House" ', *The Dickensian*, Vol. LII, No. 320, September, 1956, pp. 183-4.

the use of gold as a recurrent motif throughout *Our Mutual Friend*, the powerful symbolic significances that Dickens develops around the word, and the whole savage tone of contempt for wealth, that we can catch resemblances, suggesting that Hood's poem sank deep into the novelist's mind and, perhaps unconsciously, helped to shape the mood and substance of at least one later novel.

When we look for detailed resemblances, it is surprising how many there are. The opening verses of 'Miss Kilmansegg' are full of anticipations of Dickens; the celebrated description of the fog at the beginning of *Bleak House* has affinities with the first stanza of Hood's poem:

> To trace the Kilmansegg pedigree
> To the very root of the family tree
>   Were a task as rash as ridiculous:
> Through antediluvian mists as thick
> As London fog such a line to pick
>   Were enough, in truth, to puzzle Old Nick;

and the elaborate burlesque genealogy that opens *Martin Chuzzlewit* resembles the content and tone of the next eight stanzas, beginning

> It wouldn't require much verbal strain
> To trace the Kill-man, perchance, to Cain,

which recalls Dickens's words 'It is remarkable that as there was, in the oldest family of which we have any record, a murderer and a vagabond, so we never fail to meet, in the records of all old families, with innumerable repetitions of the same phase of character.'

Dickens's description of the Veneering household with its vulgar display of conspicuous wealth and its plate that says 'I'm so many ounces of precious wealth worth so much an ounce,—wouldn't you like to melt me down?' is very like Hood's description of the Kilmansegg mansion:

> Gold, and Gold! and nothing but Gold!
> The same auriferous shine behold
>   Wherever the eye could settle!

> On the walls—the sideboard—the ceiling-sky,
> On the gorgeous footmen standing by,
> In coats to delight a miner's eye
> With seams of the precious metal;

the central symbol of the dust-heaps in *Our Mutual Friend* has its parallel in Hood's

> Gold, still gold—it flew like dust!
> It tipped the foot-boy, and paid the trust;
> In each open palm it was freely thrust;
> There was nothing but giving and taking;

there is an anticipation of Mr. Podsnap in a phrase that is typically Dickensian:

> Seemed washing his hands with invisible soap
> In imperceptible water;

(as, indeed, Hood's 'Ode to Rae Wilson, Esq.' is a full-length portrait of a hypocrite remarkably like the unborn Mr. Pecksniff).

Miss Kilmansegg herself has many of the coquettish traits of Bella Wilfer, the murderous Count resembles Dickens's odious, dapper usurer, 'Fascination' Fledgeby, Silas Wegg, the avaricious plotter, has only one real leg, like Miss Kilmansegg, herself, and the final lines of the poem, quoted above, are the best possible epigraph for Dickens's novel. These resemblances, together with the similarity in tone, one of a peculiar comic savagery, between the two works, suggest to me a closer relation between Hood's poem and Dickens's novel than may be explained away by similar temperaments, the use of similar themes and the inheritance of a common tradition.

Despite the quality of the work Hood was producing at this time his fortunes were in no better state. In fact, his financial situation was so desperate that, in January, 1841, R. H. Barham brought his plight to the attention of the General Committee of the Royal Literary Fund. Dilke, in supporting Barham's testimony, asserted that 'within these few days he has been in want of even a few shillings'. The Committee at once granted Hood a sum of £50, but, when it arrived, the poet was able to decline it. He told Dr. Elliot on February 1, 1841, 'You will be gratified to hear that, without any knowledge of it on my part, the Literary Fund . . . unanimously voted me £50, the largest sum they give, and, setting aside their standing rules, to do it without my application. I, however, returned it (though it would have afforded me some ease and relief) but for many and well-weighed reasons. I am, however, all the better for the offer, which places me in a good position. It was done in a very gratifying and honourable manner, and I am the first who has said "*no*". But I am in good spirits, and hope to get through all my troubles as independently as heretofore.'

In a dignified letter to the Committee, thanking them for their consideration, and declining the money, Hood said, 'I am too proud of my profession to grudge it some suffering, I love it still, as Lord Byron loved England "with all its faults", and should hardly feel as one of the fraternity, if I had not my portion of the calamities of authors. . . . Indeed, my position at present is an easy one, compared with that of eight months ago, when out of health and out of heart, helpless, spiritless, sleepless, childless. I have now a home in my own country, and my little ones sit at my hearth, I smile sometimes and even laugh.' He ended his letter: 'Fortunately, since manhood I have been dependent solely on my own exertions—a condition which has exposed and inured me to vicissitude, while it has nourished a pride which will fight on, and has yet some retrenchments to make ere it surrender. I really do not feel myself to be yet a proper subject for your bounty, and should I ever become so, I fear that such a crisis will find me looking elsewhere—to the earth beneath me for final rest—and to the heaven above me for final justice.'

Unhappily, Hood's brave gesture proved premature.[1] Circumstances worsened so much in the ensuing months, with the lawsuit against Baily still tying up his major source of income, and no regular revenue anywhere in sight, that, in May, 1841, he was forced to recant, and appeal to the Committee for that help he had so proudly declined in the previous year. On the 25th of that month, he wrote: 'You may conceive the extreme pain with which I revoke my former decision. My views and feelings as then expressed are still unaltered, but unexpected

---

[1] K. J. Fielding, 'The Misfortunes of Hood', *Notes and Queries*, December, 1953, pp. 534–6.

combinations have occurred which compel me for the sake of others to seek and accept the aid you so handsomely offered.' At a meeting on June 9, the Committee was prompt to re-affirm the original grant. On being notified of their decision, Hood wrote:

Gentlemen:

The feelings I endeavoured to express when you so generously tendered me your assistance have left me little to add on the actual receipt of your bounty. Pray accept, once more, my most grateful thanks for your kindness, and your continued good will towards me. It cannot but be gratifying to find that so many strangers are my friends, at a time when friends are proverbially apt to degenerate into acquaintance, and acquaintance into strangers.

The present opportunity tempts me to explain why my former renunciation of this money should have been followed so speedily by an application so much at variance with my professions. There was, however, no affectation of independence—indeed, during the last 12 months my earnings will cover my very economical expenditure. The truth is, that an unforeseen case occurred when the sum would be of service so important as to overcome my scruples—or rather it made their sacrifice a matter of duty towards others. But my former sentiments and views remain unaltered—for my vessel is no crazier, my clouds no blacker, and my sea of troubles no rougher than before. It is true that I have heard from Leicestershire that I am in prison—and from Brussels that I am insane. My difficulties have been again paragraphed in public journals—and my 'destitution' has been cried about on the Exchange, or rather in the neighbourhood of Cornhill. Nevertheless, I am happy to assure you Gentlemen, that as yet my only confinement has been to my bed, and that my madness must have originated in some other brain, or at least Head.

What the particular occasion was that caused him to change his mind we do not know; it may have been the sudden swoop of a forgotten creditor. He can hardly be blamed for revoking his refusal, in the desperate circumstances of his existence at that time, especially when it was done with such dignity and engaging candour. Yet, through all these trials, his spirit was uncrushed. A letter to De Franck, dated April 13, 1841, refers only glancingly to his illnesses, and is full of optimistic plans—a two-volume novel and a new series of the *Comic Annual*, jokes, puns, leg-pulls, comment on the translation into German of 'Eugene Aram' which De Franck and a Herr von Rühe had undertaken, and remarks on fishing. It was about this time, too, that he vented his hatred of Phariseeism and narrow religious bigotry in a prose work he called 'My Tract'.

He had been visited at Camberwell by a former acquaintance, a woman of the 'unco' guid' kind who had irritated him in earlier years by forcing her religious opinions on him. On returning home, she sent him some tracts accompanied by a letter in which she attacked his religious views and his publications. What good, she asked, would his *Whims and Oddities* do for his immortal soul? What would he think of his literary levities on his death-bed? With the same grim relish with which he had answered Rae Wilson, Hood wrote a vigorous affirmation of his religious beliefs and an appraisal of hers which makes a most effective onslaught on canting bigotry, while giving some insight into his own inner convictions.

'The cool calculations', he wrote, 'you have indulged in on my desperate health, probable decease, and death-bed perturbations must have afforded you much Christian amusement, as your ignorance must have derived infinite comfort from your conviction of the inutility of literature and all intellectual pursuits. And even your regrets over the "Whims and Oddities that have made thousands laugh" may be alleviated, if you will only reflect that Fanaticism has caused millions to shed blood, as well as tears; a tolerable set-off against my levities. For my own part, I thank God, I have used the talents He has bestowed on me in so cheerful a spirit, and not abused them by writing the profane stuff called pious poetry, nor spiritualized my prose by stringing together Scriptural phrases, which have become the mere slang of a religious swell mob. Such impieties and blasphemies I leave to the Evangelical and Elect; to the sacrilegious quacks, who pound up equal parts of Bible and Babble, and convert wholesome food, by their nauseous handling, into filthiest physic; to the Canters, who profane all holy names and things by their application to common and vulgar uses; and to the presumptuous women, who I verily believe with the Turks, have no soul of their own to mind, and therefore set themselves to patch and cobble the soul of the other gender. . . . I thank God my pen has not been devoted to such serious compositions, that I have never profaned His Holy Name with common-place jingles, or passed off the inspirations of presumption, vanity, or hypocrisy, for devout effusions. My humble works have flowed from my heart as well as my head and, whatever their errors, are such as I have been able to contemplate with composure when, more than once, the Destroyer assumed almost a visible presence. . . .

'Whatever may be your acquaintance with the *letter* of the New Testament, of its *spirit* you are as deplorably ignorant as the blindest heathen Hottentot, for whose enlightenment you perhaps subscribe a few Missionary pence. I implore you to spend a few years, say twenty, in this self-scrutiny, which may be wholesomely varied by the exertion of a little active benevolence; not, however in sending tracts instead of baby-linen to poor lying-in sisters, or in volunteering pork chops for distressed Jews, or in recommending a Solemn Fast to the Spitalfields weavers, or in coddling and pampering a pulpit favourite, but in converting rags to raiment, and empty stomachs to full ones, and in helping the wretched and indulgent to "keep their souls and bodies together"! '

He ends with the following stinging lines: 'Your mode of recalling yourself to my memory reminds me that your fanatical mother insulted mine in the last days of her life (which was marked by every Christian virtue) by the presentation of a Tract addressed to Infidels. I remember also that the same heartless woman intruded herself, with less reverence than a Mohawk Squaw would have exhibited, on the chamber of death; and interrupted with her jargon almost my last interview with my dying parent. Such reminiscences warrant some severity.'

One weakness of such utterances of Hood is that there is always in them less of the positive assertion of specific Christian principles than the denunciation of abuses of Christianity; his religion was almost entirely a matter of sentiment, of decent feelings and instinctive humanitarianism. It was that form of humanism at that time close enough to Christianity to show the derivation clearly, but later in the century to become divorced from religious principle. But his reprobation of cant, hypocrisy

and the cruder forms of ostentatious Evangelical piety proceeded from a genuine disgust at the soiling of religious values,
and from a spontaneous sense of what is truly charitable in
human conduct. In this, as in much else, he closely resembles
Dickens, and the terms in which he urges the recipient of 'My
Tract' to the exercise of some active benevolence are so like
those with which Dickens anatomizes Mrs. Pardiggle in *Bleak
House* that it is hard not to believe that the novelist did not have
the opportunity of reading Hood's broadside.

It was not very long after this that the Hoods had their first
real stroke of luck for many years. Theodore Hook died on
August 24, 1841, and Frederick Shoberl, the *New Monthly's*
chief sub-editor and its co-founder with Colburn, invited Hood
to take over the editor's chair. The Hoods were overjoyed. Jane
wrote to Mrs. Elliot in great delight, 'I have scarcely wits to
write to you; but you, our kindest and best friends in adversity,
must be the first to rejoice with us at better prospects.' Hood
hardly dared believe his good fortune, yet he was not too overcome not to bargain over his salary. Hook had received £400 a
year; Colburn, aware of Hood's need and hoping, perhaps, to
get him on the cheap, offered him £200; Hood, however, stuck
out for more, and by September 17, it had been agreed that he
was to be editor at £300 a year, any articles he might write to
be paid for separately. He took full advantage of the proviso,
and during his two years' editorship was one of the *New
Monthly's* most frequent contributors. In November, 1841, the
1842 *Comic Annual* was published, the intended forerunner to a
new series, but because of Hood's latest commitments, it had
no successor. It was one of the best, if not the very best, of the
Annuals, containing the pieces written for the *New Monthly* in
1840 and 1841, which included 'Miss Kilmansegg and her
Precious Leg', 'A Tale of a Trumpet', 'The Open Question' and
'Pompey's Ghost'.

With the prospect now of some measure of security, the
Hoods moved, towards the end of 1841, to an agreeable house at
17 Elm Tree Road, St. John's Wood, overlooking Lord's
Cricket Ground. The only disadvantage, Hood said, was that he
could so often see people at play while he was at work. But, at
St. John's Wood, almost for the first time since the early days
of their marriage, Jane and Thomas were able to enjoy some

tranquillity and simple peace. Occasionally they were able to have modest dinners, to which their intimate friends were invited. As young Tom later wrote, 'Though the boards did not groan, sides used to ache, and if the champagne did not flow in streams, the wit sparkled to make up for it.' Hood kept up his practical joking, writing nonsensical glosses to Jane's words in letters to De Franck, and essaying hoaxes on his friend. One such was an imitation gold-fish, intended as bait, but made of glued wood; when immersed in water, one half was intended to float away, leaving the other attached to the line with 'Oh, you April fool!' scored on it. It later struck Hood, when De Franck did not refer to the bait again, that his friend must have given the unique bait to one of the Princes as a gift, ignorant of its true character!

Thomas began his work for the *New Monthly* in October, 1841. In 'A Tête-à-Tête with the Editor', he depicts Advice as a garrulous old woman bent on instructing him in his duties: 'I recommended your nurse—and I was the cause of your being vaccinated instead of inoculated—and of your going to Alfred House instead of Eton; and of your visit to Scotland, and your residence in Germany; and that you wore flannel next to your skin, and shoes with cork soles; and have left off fermented liquors. In short, it is through me that you are what you are. My name is Ad——'

' "Vice", said I, recollecting her features in a moment.'

He followed this up with regular contributions, mainly in prose, some of them stories in several parts, such as 'The Schoolmistress Abroad'. During this time, he also wrote on occasion for the *Athenaeum*; on June 11 and June 18, 1842, he again took up the matter of copyright with two new, eloquent letters on 'Copyright and Copywrong'.

Hood proved to be an efficient editor; the *New Monthly* kept up its standard in 1842 and 1843, with contributions from many of the most popular writers of the time, such as Douglas Jerrold, Mrs. Trollope, Lady Morgan, Horace Smith, Mrs. Katherine Gore, and others. With frequent encounters with these and visits to and from old friends of the *London* days, like Henry Francis Cary, the translator of Dante, the Dilkes and the Elliots, the Hoods were living as social a life as they had ever had the chance of living. And their two children were growing up into pleasant youngsters, seemingly robust enough, although the strains of their peripatetic life and of their father's invalidism must have made Tom and Fanny's childhood difficult. As Tom wrote, 'My mother was always careful to keep my father free from any anxiety and worry that she could, and we children were brought up in a sort of Spartan style of education, and taught the virtues of silence and low voices.'

During this placid period, Hood's friendship with Dickens continued. He had written a most appreciative notice of *Barnaby Rudge* in the *Athenaeum* for January 22, 1842, and when Dickens sailed for America in the same month, he wrote a punning verse valedictory, 'To C. Dickens, Esq.' On Dickens's return from his tour, Hood was one of those invited to a welcoming dinner at Greenwich. Among those present on this extremely convivial occasion were R. H. Barham, W. H. Ainsworth, Charles and Thomas Landseer, William Jerdan, Bryan Waller Procter, George Cruikshank, 'Father Prout', and Monckton Milnes.

Hood was asked to take the chair, but begged off, and Captain Marryat presided instead. 'Well, we drank the "Boz" with a delectable clatter,' Hood told Mrs. Elliot, 'which drew from him a good warm-hearted speech, in which he hinted the great advantage of going to America for the pleasure of coming back again; and pleasantly described the embarrassing attention of the Transatlantickers, who made his private house, and private cabin, particularly public. . . . He told me that two American prints have attacked me for my copyright letters in the *Athenaeum*. . . . Then we had more songs. Barham chanted a Robin Hood ballad, and Cruickshank sang a burlesque ballad of Lord Bateman; and somebody, unknown to me, gave a capital imitation of a French showman. Then we toasted Mrs. Boz, and the Chairman, and the Vice, and the Traditional Priest sang the "Deep deep sea" in his deep deep voice, and then we drank to Procter, who wrote the said song; also Sir J. Wilson's good health, and Cruickshank's and Ainsworth's; and a Manchester friend of the latter sang a Manchester ditty, so full of trading stuff, that it really seemed to have been not composed, but manufactured.'

For Hood, the highlight of this pleasant evening was the proposing of his health by Monckton Milnes, which met with a warm response and a display of respect that touched him very deeply. 'I ascribed the toast to my notoriously bad health, and assured them that their wishes had improved it—that I felt a brisker circulation—a more genial warmth about the heart, and explained that a certain trembling of my hand was not from palsy, or my old ague, but an inclination in my hand to shake itself with every one present. Whereupon I had to go through the friendly ceremony with as many of the company as were within reach, besides a few more who came express from the other end of the table. *Very* gratifying, wasn't it?'

A further recognition of the esteem in which Hood was widely held came a little later when Douglas Jerrold dedicated his collected volumes of *Cakes and Ale* 'To Thomas Hood, Esq., whose various genius touches alike the springs of laughter and the source of tears'.

The friendship with Dickens was maintained chiefly by letter, for the two men's work kept them in different fields. At the beginning of October, 1842, Hood asked Dickens for an early copy of *American Notes*. Dickens replied on October 13, 'I can (and will) give you a copy of the American book, next Monday. It will not be in the hands of any other friends I have, until Tuesday night. I will bring it myself about noon on Monday: and with it, if you will let me, Prof. Longfellow of Boston (whose poetry you may have seen) who, admiring you as all good and true men do, wants to know you.'[1] Hood enthusiastically summarized the book in the *New Monthly* for November, 1842, under the title 'Boz in America'. 'I could not pretend to a review or to extract much,' he told Dickens, '—the dailies and weeklies having *sweated* your *Notes* as if they had been *Sovereigns*.' The promised visit by Longfellow duly took place, and J. T. Fields records that Longfellow described Hood as appearing at that time as 'a small, thin man, looking very pale and worn, not saying much himself, but listening to Dickens with evident affection and respect'.

On December 6, Dickens, who had long promised to do so, attended an evening party at the Hoods. He brought with him his wife and Georgina Hogarth, as well as Daniel Maclise, whom he had described to Hood as 'a very unaffected and

[1] This letter is in the possession of the editors of the Pilgrim Edition of Dickens's letters.

ardent admirer of your genius, who has no small portion of that commodity in his own right'. Among others present were Dr. William Elliot and his brother, Dr. Robert Elliot, who assisted Dr. William as Hood's physician, W. H. Ainsworth, R. H. Barham, John Forster and Rev. James Hewlett, otherwise 'Peter Priggins', a popular contributor to the *New Monthly*.

In March of the following year, Hood, with Douglas Jerrold and John Forster, attended the Printers' Pension Fund dinner in support of Dickens who was chairman, and in July, Dickens enlisted Hood's services as patron of a Bazaar organized for the benefit of the Manchester Athenaeum. Hood wrote a supporting letter, recording his 'deep obligations to Literature', which was printed and sold at the Bazaar in aid of the cause. Dickens, in fact, on other occasions, felt that he could count on Hood's support in good causes. One of these was to help with a fund Dickens had established to assist the insane wife and five children of the celebrated actor, William Elton, drowned at sea in July, 1843.[1] Hood readily responded, and composed an 'Address' spoken by Mrs. Warner at a benefit performance at the Haymarket Theatre and later sold as a pamphlet.

During this period, the health of both Jane and Thomas fluctuated. De Franck, writing from Hamburg on February 10, 1842, says, 'I am sorry indeed to hear that you have been so ill, my dear Mrs. Hood, though I may now hope, thank God, that you are perfectly recovered.' He also tells his friends that he applied 'to be dismissed from active *Service*, and to change into the Gensd'armerie so Tim says he, good bye to drilling recruits and more quizzing from that quarter'.[2] There are fewer references to ill health in Hood's letters; perhaps he had come to accept his chronic invalidism as normal, perhaps, too, the easing of financial anxiety and the return to familiar places had meant some corresponding physical relief. At the same time, he was busy. He told De Franck on August 14, 1843, 'Seriously, my dear Johnny, you cannot imagine the hurry I live in, like most of my contemporaries, but aggravated in my case by frequent illness, which makes me get into arrears of business, and then, as the sailors say, I have to work double tides to fetch up my lee-way.' The pressure of work, in fact, fatigued him so greatly that,

[1] Ibid.
[2] Bristol University Library.

in September, 1843, he decided, on impulse, to take a short holiday in Scotland, some twenty-five years after his first visit there.

Remembering what Dundee had done for his health as a youngster, he returned there, taking Tom with him. At first he was disappointed, for the city had changed, 'owing to the march of manufacture', many of his old cronies were dead, Robert Miln and Patrick Gardiner were not to be found in their offices, and the friends who remained, says Alexander Elliot, 'scarcely recognized in the pale, cadaverous, consumptive-looking man, whose hollow eyes shimmered through his spectacles, the bright, cheery laughter-loving friend of their youth'. But when he sailed across the Tay to South Ferry and Tayport, his aunt, Mrs. Keay, received the two Toms with open-hearted warmth. Ancient disagreements were forgotten in a lavish display of Scottish hospitality. Captain Keay, now retired, was living with his wife in Rose Cottage, high on the braes of Scotscraig, with a view of the whole Tay estuary. Here Hood felt that the 'bracing breezes' would do him much good. 'I eat and drink pretty well,' he wrote to Jane, 'but sleep badly still. However, the time is short as yet for much improvement.' He visited Dundee from Tayport almost daily, and, through an old acquaintance, Frederick Shaw, now a prosperous bookseller, met several Dundee literary and business men. Unhappily, his old friend, George Rollo, was away from Dundee, and Hood saw neither him nor Robert Miln, who was gravely ill, and, in fact, died on September 21, while Hood was still in the city. He was only forty-four years of age, and Hood, conscious perhaps of the likelihood of a short span for himself, took Miln's death very much to heart. A man who was introduced to Hood at Tayport told Alexander Elliot that he looked twenty years older than his actual age. He was pale and weary-looking and seemed weighed down with physical suffering; he spoke very quietly and in tone sounded 'far awa' ': he was dressed in black surtout and low hat, and wore spectacles; his clothes hung loosely on his meagre frame.

In later years, young Tom remembered, 'He used at hotels always to go into the public coffee-room, where his genial disposition and courtesy invariably got him a good reception. I dare say there are still many living who remember that thin, serious-looking gentleman, who often set the table "on a roar" by an unexpected turn or a dry remark, and who was so fond of a certain brown-skinned urchin, much given to the devouring of books.'

After a week in Dundee, Hood and Tom sailed for Leith and Edinburgh. Dickens had given him letters of introduction as a 'personal friend . . . whom I greatly value' to John Wilson ('Christopher North'), Macvey Napier, Lord Jeffrey, and D. M. Moir ('Delta'). The two former were away, but, as Hood wrote to Captain and Mrs. Keay, on October 5, after returning to London, 'I had an invitation from Lord Jeffrey, and dined with him at his country seat, Craigcrook, about three miles from the city. I also rode out with Tom to Musselburgh, and made acquaintance with D. M. Moir, a surgeon and well-known author. I was very much pleased with him and his family, and there were some fine boys with whom Tom was very soon quite at home.'

He spent the remainder of his week in Edinburgh sight-seeing—the Castle, the Advocates' Library, the Old Parliament House, and, characteristically, the Anatomical Museum—and looking longingly up at Salisbury Crags and Arthur's Seat, and wishing he could climb them. His son, who was already adept with the pencil, almost filled his sketch-book after his own fashion.

Hood returned to London at the beginning of October, much strengthened. He needed to be, because he was in the middle of another crisis in his affairs, one which was to put him once more at the mercy of various publishers and booksellers.

X

The Poetry of Conscience

DURING 1843, Hood found increasing difficulty in his relations with Henry Colburn, the proprietor of the *New Monthly*. The causes of the disagreement were various. As we have seen, Hood's illnesses, combined with his long-standing distrust of 'publishers and sinners', as he called them, may not have made him easy to deal with, although he carried out his editorial duties conscientiously and enriched the pages of the *New Monthly* with his own excellent contributions; he had also incurred the dislike of the trade by his vigorous support of Talfourd's attempts to reform the Copyright Laws. 'There are plenty of the trade would object to *me*,' he told Dickens in 1843, 'for I have published what I thought of them. Colburn as likely as any, who on the publication of my *last Copyright letter* attempted to call me to account for writing in the Athm. I had all along told him I should write there, and had done so, *till then* without an objection.'

More immediately to the point was Colburn's habit, in common with other publishers of the time, of not drawing a fine enough line between legitimate advertising and reviewing, and 'puffing', that is, sponsoring or commissioning favourable reviews, and using unethical means of pushing forward his own publications. This especially angered Hood, who regarded puffing as a prostitution of the profession of letters. In a letter to Hannah Lawrance marked 'Confidential', he wrote, 'I write in haste a few lines to put you on your guard by telling you of the arrangements for reviewing in the Magazine. I undertook to review all books except Colburn's own with the puffing of which I of course desired to have no concern. They are *done* by the persons of the establishment, Patmore, Williams or Shoberl. If you see the Mag. you will know what wretched things these reviews are.' Peter George Patmore, O. E. Williams, who wrote a life of Sir Thomas Lawrence, and Shoberl were all employed by Colburn as sub-editors, and Hood, who felt that, as editor, he should have complete control of the paper, resented the fact that Colburn's insistence on his printing their puffs degraded his own status and associated him, unwillingly, with a discreditable practice. After his resignation from the *New Monthly*, he told Dickens, on October 19, 1843, 'The result shows that from the beginning the Patmore, Shoberl and Williams trio had resolved on being sub-over-editors—and that if I had not resigned, I should have been resigned.'

One matter that especially rankled with Hood was the affair of *The Tuft-Hunter*. This novel, allegedly the work of Lord William Pitt Lennox, a dandy and writer of trashy fiction, was 'puffed' by Colburn, who published it in 1843, and even submitted it earlier to Hood with a request that he write a preface for it. Hood found it one of the 'grossest cases [of plagiarism] possible', from Scott's *The Antiquary* and *St. Ronan's Well*, and from his own *Tylney Hall*! He suspected Frederick Shoberl of being the real 'author', and applauded Dilke's scathing review in the *Athenaeum* of February 25, 1843. 'Lord L. is a fool,' he wrote to Dilke, 'but the other is a thorough rogue, and double traitor—the *system* deserves denouncing—however, I have thundered a bit at the attempt to connect me with it—and am having my fun out of Colburn.' But the fun, which consisted of the insertion of cryptic gibes in the *New Monthly*, had turned sour before Hood took his holiday in Scotland. He could stand Colburn and his associates no longer, and resigned from the magazine.

Colburn was so angry at Hood's leaving him that, like Queen Victoria on another occasion, he pretended later that the offensive person didn't exist. Three letters addressed to Hood at the office were returned to the senders, marked 'Not Known to Mr. Colburn'; one of these coming into Hood's hands, he sent the following lines to Dilke:

> For a couple of years in the columns of Puff
> I was rated a passable writer enough:

But, alas! for the favours of Fame!
Since I quitted her seat in Great Marlborough Street,
In repute my decline is so very complete
That a Colburn don't know of my name!

Now a Colburn I knew in his person so small
That he seemed the half-brother of nothing at all,
Yet in spirit a Dwarf may be big;
But his mind was so narrow, his soul was so dim,
Where's the wonder if all I remember of him
Is—a suit of Boys' clothes and a wig!

Hood was now high and dry again, with his regular source of
income cut off, and as soon as he returned from Scotland, he
began looking for another editorial post.

He had kept Dickens informed of his position throughout the
last difficult weeks on the *New Monthly*, and Dickens, who had
himself a good business head, wrote to his friend on September
12, 1843, 'There can be no doubt in the mind of any honourable man that the circumstances under which you signed your
agreement are of the most disgraceful kind, in so far as Mr.
Colburn is concerned. There can be no doubt that he took a
money-lending, bill-broking, Jew-Clothes-bagging, Saturday-
night-pawnbroking advantage of your temporary situation.' He
also suggested to Hood that he should try to get a position on
Ainsworth's Magazine, although he was under a false impression
that Ainsworth himself was no longer editor. Hood at once
wrote to the publishers, Cunningham and Mortimer, offering
his services. To his surprise, Ainsworth himself, who was still
editor and owner, replied in person, very cordially offering
Hood 16 guineas per sheet, 'the highest terms the Magazine can
afford', adding, 'Indeed, I may mention confidentially that
there will, ere long, be a dissolution of the firm of Cunningham
and Mortimer: but this will not effect the Magazine, or its
arrangements'. But Hood, who had hoped for a more per-
manent appointment, declined, salving his embarrassment by
telling Ainsworth that the terms were not adequate, and 'besides, to be candid, I do not quite like the unsettled state of the
establishment'. He also confided to Dickens that he felt Blanchard, one of Ainsworth's sub-editors, was 'very much in with
Colburn, Patmore, and the Marlboro Street gang'.

His next attempt to find a position was a bold one. He had three years before found himself unable to fulfil a commission for the publisher, Richard Bentley; and Bentley had taken Hood's letting him down rather badly. But, hearing that *Bentley's Miscellany* was without an editor, he wrote on October 21 to the publisher offering himself, hoping that, not only would by-gones be by-gones, but that his own prestige would get him the job. Bentley replied with a terse note pointing out that he had a perfectly good editor, Mr. Wilde, and, while feeling obliged by the offer Hood was so good to make, had not 'the remotest idea of making any alteration with regard to the Editorship of that publication'. This left Hood under the awkward obligation of explaining that he had no intention of trying to do Wilde out of his daily bread.

Frustrated on all sides in his attempts to find an editorial chair, Hood was driven once more to rely wholly on his own resources. He would start his own periodical—*Hood's Monthly Magazine and Comic Miscellany*—and be both editor and author as with the *Comic Annual* and *Hood's Own*. His plans were laid in early November, soon after the rebuffs from the other magazines, and he wrote in terms of high excitement to tell Elliot that he had financial backing for it, and that the first issue would appear on January 1. But, before *Hood's Magazine* was launched, he was to write his most famous poem, 'The Song of the Shirt', and thus begin his new venture on a wave of publicity and an accession of fame such as he had never experienced before.

He had other things in mind as well. His contributions to the *New Monthly* Colburn had engaged to publish in book form, and the project was duly carried through 'after tedious waitings on Colburn', as he told Elliot. The two volumes of *Whimsicalities*, dated 1844, appeared in December, 1843; they contained his *New Monthly* pieces, with one or two additions, and illustrations by John Leech and Hood himself. Since all the work therein was written before 'The Song of the Shirt', they merit a word or two first. The greater number of the pieces are in prose, and amply represent Hood's characteristic manner in his briefer prose works. We can detect four main influences on him— those of Lamb, of Sterne, of Smollett, and of the Gothic novel. The latter form is represented by such 'straight' stories as 'The Tower of Lahneck', crisply told, of two women, one English, one German, who climb to the top of a lofty castle-tower, then, when the stone staircase crumbles behind them, are marooned there; one leaps to her death, the other dies of starvation. Also in the Gothic vein are such less serious pieces as the deliberately and tantalizingly unfinished 'A Tale of Terror'. The relaxed conversational, gently humorous style of pieces like 'The Happiest Man in England' and 'The Omnibus' indicate something of his debt to 'Elia'; the rough-and-tumble incidents and the energetic physical humour of 'Mr. Chubb: A Piscatory Romance' and the comic epistolary method of 'News from China' and 'The Earth-Quakers' show the enduring impression of Smollett on him.

Most of all, it is Sterne who seems to have played the greatest part in shaping Hood's periodical prose. The mixture of sensibility, sentiment and comedy in Sterne accorded with Hood's own temperament, and the informal discursive method of *Tristram Shandy* he found especially suitable for improvised prose pieces written off the top of his head, sometimes while the printer's devil was waiting for copy. So we find *New Monthly* contributions like 'The Grimsby Ghost', 'Mrs. Gardiner', 'The Confessions of a Phoenix' and others, full of irrelevant interpolations, dialogues between the author and imaginary interjectors (in the 'Beachcomber' manner), tiny essays, comic meditations, single sentence chapters, and so on. 'The Longest Hour in My Life', a prolonged account of a fictitious encounter between Hood and a tiger, is spun out cleverly with such devices, and with disquisitions on the nature of Time, which not only recall *Tristram Shandy* and the Lockean theories of Time on which it is based, but specifically refer to it. 'Apropos of Time and his diverse paces,' begins Chapter III, 'he notoriously goes slowly—as Sterne vouches—with a solitary captive.'

References to Sterne and his work, in fact, are commonplace in Hood, who never hesitated to acknowledge his debt. His first prose publication, as we have seen, was 'Sentimental Journey from Islington to Waterloo Bridge', and he later wrote, 'A Friend in Need: An Extravaganza *after* Sterne', while 'English Retrogression' describes a pilgrimage to Calais in search of the hotel room where Sterne had the interview with the Franciscan, and ends with the hotel proprietor exclaiming, 'Sterne?—Diable l'importe!—it is de oder Hotel. Mon Dieu!

c'est une drôle de chose—but de English pepels when dey come to Calais, dey always come *Sterne foremost!*'

If any doubts remain as to Hood's devotion to Sterne, such a typical beginning as that to 'The Grimsby Ghost' should dispel them:

'In the town of Grimsby—

' "But stop," says the Courteous and Prudent Reader, "are there any such things as Ghosts?"

' "Any Ghostesses!" cries Superstition, who settled long since in the country, near a church-yard, on a *rising* ground, "any Ghostesses! Ay, man—lots on 'em! bushels on 'em! sights on 'em" ', and so on. Hood's prose has not the delicacy, the learning and the intellectual sophistication of Sterne's, nor its sense of high comedy, but it has a virtuosity, a racy tone and good-humoured note which a certain journalistic carelessness mars little.

Among the humorous poems written for the *New Monthly* were such delightful *jeux d'esprit* as 'No!':

> No warmth, no cheerfulness, no healthful ease,
>   No comfortable feel in any member—
> No shade, no shine, no butterflies, no bees,
> No fruits, no flow'rs, no leaves, no birds—
>   November!

and serious ones like 'The Elm Tree'. Hood was particularly fond of this poem, and told Dickens that he intended to issue it as a separate work, with illustrations by William Harvey, whose drawings for 'Eugene Aram' had helped to establish its popularity. This project remained unrealized. Hood's partiality for 'The Elm Tree', which is a rather inflated piece, again betrays his constant awareness of mortality. Sub-titled 'A Dream in the Woods', it is a meditation, suggested by the sighing of a decaying elm, on the dying of the forest, and its felling by a muscular woodman. When the elm is felled, Death takes the place of the woodman, and, gloating over the 'conscious, moving, breathing trunks' he lays low, says that the elm will in the end house all human kind. And the poet ends with an intimation of his own death:

> A secret, vague, prophetic gloom,
>   As though by certain mark

I knew the fore-appointed Tree
Within whose rugged bark
This warm and living frame shall find
Its narrow house and dark.

The *Whimsicalities* were well enough received, but before the collection appeared, Hood had made an indelible mark in a field new to him. *Punch* had been established in 1841, as 'a refuge for destitute wit; an asylum for the thousands of orphan jokes that are now wandering about', as its original advertisement said. Taking some of its character from Hood's *Comic Annual* and his *Magazine*, *Punch* dealt in broad, obvious humour and outrageous puns, but also, and most characteristically, it was a tartly satirical journal. Under its first editor, Mark Lemon, assisted by such gifted wits and commentators as Thackeray, Henry Mayhew and Douglas Jerrold, it mocked the social pretensions of the time, fearlessly lampooned political stupidity, hidebound Toryism and rentier complacency, and stood up courageously as a defender of the poor and the underdog. There was need for such an advocate at this time, when the effects of the industrial revolution were beginning to show themselves in the growth of slums, in starvation, miserable wages and appalling destitution.

Hood's own temperament attracted him to *Punch*. Although his need to earn a living and his health made it impossible for him to play any active part in social reformism, he had long had a keen interest in social conditions. Apart from his articles on copyright, and the prominent role he took in the forming of the Association for the Protection of Literature in 1843, his readiness to respond to appeals for literary work for special distress funds, the consistent tone of humane compassion in his writings, and his several attacks on canting Pecksniffs and Sabbatarians, he had done little more than glancingly refer to social matters in such poems as 'The Assistant Drapers' Petition' before 1843. The satire of 'Miss Kilmansegg' is moral and general rather than particular, and, although in its attack on the love of money, it does pinpoint the principal Victorian vice, it is sufficiently broad and grotesque to apply to 'the other fellow'. It was through *Punch* that Hood undertook a new kind of expression, one that was to carry his name to the very ends of Europe—that of humanitarian verse. If we ask why this came as the final phase of his work, there can be many answers—the serious type of utterance was scarcely suited to the pages of his jocular journals, social conditions had worsened in the 1840's to a degree that made it impossible for a man of Hood's sensibility not to be moved by them, and his own life-long suffering had given him the experience essential to the writing of such poetry.

His first contact with *Punch* was not a happy one. Picking up the initial issue, of July 17, 1841, he found a jest using his name, on page 2: 'Mr. T. Hood, Professor of Punmanship, begs to acquaint the dull and witless, that he has established a class for the acquirement of an elegant and ready style of punning.' Hood was upset by this, which he thought a lapse of taste. But a couple of years later, he had become an occasional contributor of jokes and punning riddles to *Punch's* pages. In the number for November 18, 1843, he essayed a different genre with 'A Drop of Gin', the first of his humanitarian poems. Rhetorical and declamatory, it is a warning on the evils of gin, but it does not make the mistake of confusing the symptom with the cause of the disease, as so many temperance reformers did. What other consolation, says Hood, has the 'ragged pauper, misfortune's butt' but the oblivion of gin?

> Then, instead of making too much of a din,
> Let Anger be mute,
> And sweet Mercy dilute,
> With a drop of Pity, the Drop of Gin!

The piece goes vigorously along, as so many of Hood's poems do, on a refrain, 'Gin! Gin! a Drop of Gin!', but it fails, largely because he has unsuccessfully married the kind of rhymes and rhythms he used in his comic verse to a serious subject. He did not make the same mistake with 'The Song of the Shirt'.

This poem was inspired by an article in *Punch* itself, for November 4, 1843, called 'Famine and Fashion', probably written by Douglas Jerrold. A poor woman, named Biddell, with two children to support, was charged with having pawned articles belonging to her employer. In the course of the proceedings, it was disclosed that she received sevenpence a pair for making trousers, and that the most she could make in a week, working fourteen hours a day, was seven shillings. *The Times* had a blistering editorial on the case, and *Punch* vigorously took up the cue. Profoundly stirred by the *Punch* article, Hood wrote 'The Song of the Shirt' at once, at a single sitting, and sent it to *Punch*. As he posted it off, Jane said to him, 'Now mind, Hood, mark my words; this will tell wonderfully. It is one of the best things you ever did.' She was right. Although Hood was afraid that the poem would not be quite in *Punch's* line, Mark Lemon, excited by its power, printed it anonymously in the Christmas (December 16) number, and was rewarded with a trebling of the circulation of his journal.

To say that the success of 'The Song of the Shirt' was tumultuous would not be to exaggerate. It ran through the land like a hurricane. *The Times* and numerous other papers reprinted it; Mark Lemon dramatized it as *The Sempstress*, first produced at the Theatre Royal, Haymarket, on May 25, 1844; it was translated into German, Italian, French and Russian and in both Russia and Germany did much to inspire native poetry of social consciousness. Dickens and others, who were quick to penetrate the author's anonymity, were loud in their admiration. But, much more importantly, this poem struck down below the levels of professional appreciation to plant itself deep in the hearts of the English people. Printed on broad-sheets and cotton handkerchiefs, sung on street-corners and on the stage, recited at popular gatherings, read from pulpits, and learnt by heart by illiterates, it became one of the genuine songs of the people, an inspired cry from Hood's heart made their own by the sweated and exploited who had no voice to protest against monstrous injustice.

In time, Hood publicly acknowledged the open secret of his authorship. Much touched by the popularity of the poem, he was chiefly moved by hearing that the 'poor creatures', as his son said, 'to whom he had given such eloquent voice, seemed to adopt its words as their own, singing them about the streets to an air of their own adaptation'. By its stirring of the sluggish conscience of the British people, 'The Song of the Shirt' did more than thousands of newspaper leaders and reams of political propaganda. In the line of Ebenezer Elliott, it was more potent than anything the 'Corn-Law Rhymer' wrote; Gerald Massey, himself in his social poems a disciple of Hood, recognized its power, and James Russell Lowell acknowledged its force in his lines:

> Here lies a poet. Stranger, if to thee
>> His claim to memory be obscure,
> If thou wouldst know how truly great was he,
>> Go, ask it of the poor.

A poem so well known—surely one of the best known in our language—has put itself almost beyond criticism. But we may note that it is characteristically Hood's—in the direct simplicity of its language, such a simplicity as is at the command only of those with a rich and varied vocabulary, in its effective use of repetition and refrain (has any English poet used repetition more skilfully than Hood?), in its concreteness, in its use of the unadorned substantive, in the touches of imaginative richness that light up more than one stanza, driven home by a happy use of internal rhyme:

> And a wall so blank, my shadow I thank
> For sometimes falling there.

It is Hood's, too, in the almost inevitable reference to Death, 'the Phantom of Grisly bone', and in the notion of duality, and of that reality that mocks the appearance, which shows itself both imaginatively, in his favourite idea of the 'double':

> Sewing at once, with a double thread,
> A shroud as well as a Shirt;

and verbally, with an unexpected and wholly successful pun, placed and used as few other poets would dare; and revealing, perhaps better than anything else in Hood, the poet in the punster;

> Work—work—work,
> In the dull December light,
>> And work—work—work
> When the weather is warm and bright—
> While underneath the eaves
>> The brooding swallows cling,
> As if to show me their sunny backs
> And twit me with the spring.

In the same issue of *Punch* which presented 'The Song of the

Shirt', appeared another poem by Hood in the same vein, 'The
Pauper's Christmas Carol', with an effective sardonic tone and
use of the refrain, 'Christmas comes but once a year':

> Full of drink and full of meat
> On our Saviour's natal day,
> Charity's perennial treat,
> Thus I heard a pauper say:—
> 'Ought I not to dance and sing
> Thus supplied with famous cheer!
>   Heigho!
>   I hardly know—
> Christmas comes but once a year.'

But, although its heart is in the right place, this poem lacks the
drive and passion of 'The Song of the Shirt'.

At the end of 1843, the Hoods left their lodgings at Elm Tree
Road, and moved to a house of their own again at 28 New
Finchley Road, in St. John's Wood. In affectionate memory
of the consideration of his patron, the Duke of Devonshire,
Hood named the house Devonshire Lodge. It was to be his last
home.

The new year began with the first issue of *Hood's Monthly
Magazine and Comic Miscellany*. The backing for this came originally from one Edward Flight. Things looked promising. The
Magazine followed the formula which Hood had already found
to be so popular. As his amusing prospectus put it: 'One
prominent object . . . will be the supply of harmless "Mirth for
the Million" and light thoughts, to a Public sorely oppressed . . .
by hard times, heavy taxes, and those "eating cares" which
attend upon the securing of food for the day as well as provision
for the future. . . . For the Sedate there will be papers of becoming gravity; and the lovers of Poetry will be supplied with
numbers in each Number. As to politics, the Reader of *Hood's
Magazine* will vainly search in its pages for a Panacea for Agricultural Distress, or a Grand Catholicon for Irish Agitation.'

The recipe worked again; the first number, which came out
on January 1, sold 1,500 copies. For *Hood's Magazine*, the editor
had gathered round him some of the most famous names of his
time. But almost half the material in this first issue was written
by Hood himself. Amongst this was 'The Haunted House'—

'one of the truest poems ever written', said Edgar Allan Poe—
'one of the *truest*—one of the most unexceptionable—one of the
most thoroughly artistic, both in its theme and in its execution'.
It is, in fact, as good a poem as Poe himself ever wrote on the
kind of theme he favoured.

Apart from Browning's 'Childe Roland to the Dark Tower
Came', I know of no other nineteenth-century poem that so
taps the springs of unnamed terror. Hood had never before
written with such sustained artistic tact, such allusive assurance,
and such a firm control over form. The poem may have been
suggested by a fine steel engraving by J. Cousen, after Thomas
Creswick, which Hood used as a frontispiece for the number. It
is a relentless piling up of the details and images of decay and
desolation in an old mansion where some terrible, never explained crime has been committed, a wonderful evocation of the
mood of nightmare dread, unmarred by facetiousness or false
notes. The total impression is built up with precise strokes and
careful selection of detail:

> With shatter'd panes the grassy court was starr'd;
> The time-worn coping-stone had tumbled after:
> And through the ragged roof the sky shone, barr'd
> With naked beam and rafter.
>
> O'er all there hung a shadow and a fear;
> A sense of mystery the spirit daunted,
> And said, as plain as whisper in the ear,
> The place is Haunted!

The latter verse, which, with variations, recurs nine times at
irregular intervals throughout the poem's 88 stanzas, again
shows Hood's mastery of insistent effect, while the cunningly
built stanza, with its final emphatic brief line and the echoing
double-syllable rhymes, create a curiously portentous impression.

The form of the poem bears a remarkable resemblance to the
slow, deliberate movement of a tracking camera in the hands of
an Alfred Hitchcock or an Ingmar Bergman. The speaker, as in
a nightmare, approaches the deserted mansion through its un-
hinged gates, past the crumbled pedestals, through the neglected gardens, choked with weeds and over-run with tangled

flowers, where birds and rabbits throng undisturbed, through the abandoned orchard where

> on the canker'd tree, in easy reach,
> Rotted the golden apple;

past the shaggy yew and dry fountain to the portal. Then, by stages, through the slowly gaping door, past startled bats, down halls and corridors given over to insects and decay:

> The subtle spider, that from overhead
> Hung like a spy on human guilt and error,
> Suddenly turn'd and up its slender thread
> Ran with a nimble terror.

> The very stains and fractures on the wall
> Assuming features solemn and terrific,
> Hinted some tragedy of that old Hall,
> Lock'd up in Hieroglyphic.

through rooms stifling in mould and must, up the dreary stairs, to more dank rooms where the heraldic symbol of the Bloody Hand keeps its colour where all else has faded, and on the hangings, everything is eroded

> save one ragged part
> Where Cain was slaying Abel,

and where the Death Watch Beetle ticks behind the panelled oak, to the chamber where no life flourishes:

> Across the door no gossamer festoon
> Swung pendulous—no web—no dusty fringes,
> No silk chrysalis or white cocoon
> About its nooks and hinges.

> The spider shunn'd the interdicted room,
> The moth, the beetle, and the fly were banish'd,
> And where the sunbeam fell athwart the gloom,
> The very midge had vanished.

Here, at the end of the quest is the poisonous centre of the whole web of decay, the mysterious and terrible room, where the only traces of the crime that has tainted all around it, is a series of fading spots from bed to door.

'The Haunted House' is a *tour de force* of the imagination.

What gives it its particular atmosphere is the very precision of the details, which, paradoxically, invest the whole thing with the air of nightmare. The opening verses hint that it is a dream; 'in the spirit or the flesh I found | An old deserted Mansion'; yet the first verse says, 'others of our most romantic schemes | Are something more than fiction', suggesting that Hood was aware of a symbolic purpose. The general effect of the poem resembles that of a story by Kafka or a poem by Walter de la Mare, with more of the precise smell of the grave than either has. Little, in fact, is said of the terror of the place—it is all conjured up by suggestion and impressionistic touches that evoke a mood of mystery and evil.

On one level the poem may be experienced as a capturing of the sense of ghostliness in physical corruption; on another it can be felt as a symbol of Hood himself—the house as the poet crumbling in his illnesses, and its haunting spirit the brooding subconscious from which he could conjure his poems of mystery, darkness, and death. The whole piece is dominated by his ever-present sense of mutability, decay and dissolution. Without a touch of his humour, but with plenty of his grotesque imagination, it evokes the very essence of man's mortality.

'The Haunted House' was by far the best of Hood's contributions to the new magazine. But his review of Dickens's *A Christmas Carol* in the same issue shows his continued admiration for the works of his friend. 'If Christmas, with its ancient and hospitable customs, its social and charitable observances, were in danger of decay, this is the book that would give them a new lease,' he said prophetically.

Certain difficulties attended the first number of *Hood's Magazine*. Tired of publishers' ways, Hood had decided to issue the journal from its own offices at 1 Adam Street, the Adelphi. The publishers tried to frustrate this gesture of independence by what Hood called a 'trade combination', presumably some way of blocking or limiting the ordinary means of distribution. But his name, now a household word, and the intrinsic quality of the first number, carried the issue through the obstacles.

It looked as if, at last, Hood was to enjoy a lucrative return from a periodical of his own. But the fate that had dogged his footsteps for years had allowed him only a temporary respite.

Trouble struck again in February. It turned out that his proprietor, Flight, was a man of straw, who had, to quote Jane's words, 'engaged in the speculation without sufficient means to carry it on—having been tempted by the goodness of the speculation, and hoping to scramble through it.' Flight was unable or unwilling to pay the printers of the first issue, Bradbury and Evans, and to discharge his debts of some £100 to Hood. Two other printers were tried for the February issue, the second being unable to get it out before February 16. Under such unsatisfactory conditions, Hood managed to get the February issue launched, although rather late; but this fresh anxiety took a heavy toll of his health. Wranglings and negotiations with Flight, and his brother, a silent partner in the proprietorship, resulted in some kind of final settlement, and Flight was replaced as backer, by Andrew Spottiswoode, the Queen's Printer, whom Dickens knew and respected. 'I am certainly a lucky man,' Hood told Dickens on April 1, 'and an unlucky one, too, for Spottiswoode is far better than the first promise of Flight. By the bye, I have heard one or two persons doubt the reality of Pecksniff—or the possibility—but I have lately met two samples of the breed. Flight is most decidedly Pecksniffian. . . . Conscience—said Flight—Sir, I have lived too long in the world to be a *slave to my conscience*! Was not this capital?'

Harassed by a new multitude of woes, Hood struggled along until May, astonishingly managing to turn out several more poems in his new social vein, including 'The Lady's Dream', a variant on the 'Song of the Shirt' theme, 'The Workhouse Clock', an allegory of the torrent of the poor, and 'The Lay of the Labourer', a forceful plea for the chance for all to work, with its refrain:

> A spade! a rake! a hoe!
> A pickaxe or a bill!

Recognizing Hood's extremity, his literary friends rallied round nobly. Monckton Milnes, assiduous in his kindly interest in deserving writers, was tireless in rounding up prominent writers to contribute to the magazine, often without payment. He himself wrote an article on *Coningsby* for the June, 1844, number and one on railways for the March, 1845, one. Dickens, in the midst of his usual hectic activities, promised 'a bit of writing'. 'It has been a cruel business,' Hood told him, 'and I really wanted help in it or I should not have announced it—knowing how much you have to do.' The contribution, duly delivered, was 'Threatening Letter to Thomas Hood from an Ancient Gentleman', in part a satire on the current craze for such midgets as Tom Thumb, which appeared in the *Magazine* for May, 1844. In Hood's need, Frederick Oldfield Ward undertook to conduct the magazine as editor without pay. He it was who, with Milnes, aroused the sympathy of various writers for one who, all now recognized, had only a brief time to live.

The May issue, compiled in the depths of pain and worry, contained, however, astonishingly, Hood's next most celebrated poem, 'The Bridge of Sighs'. Like 'The Song of the Shirt', this was an inspired improvisation, suggested, perhaps, as Alvin Whitley has argued,[1] by *The Times's* report and the subsequent agitation in March–April, 1844, on the case of Mary Furley, sentenced to be deported for the murder of her infant son and her own attempted suicide. Public clamour brought about a remission of her sentence to seven years' imprisonment. The title seems a fairly obvious one, but it is interesting to note that a popular song of the same name, written by E. Green, about a love triangle in Venice, appeared in the *London Singer's Magazine* for 1838 side by side with several of Hood's own comic poems.

The fame of 'The Bridge of Sighs' was almost to equal that of 'The Song of the Shirt'. This, wrote Thackeray, was 'his Corunna, his Heights of Abraham—sickly, weak, wounded, he fell in full blaze and fame of that great victory'. Like the earlier poem, this passionately felt interpretation of the popular heart belongs essentially to the ballad form—Richard Garnett grouped the two poems as 'genuine *Volkslieder* of the nineteenth century'—and in expressing the complete genuineness of Hood's compassion for the lonely, weary and suffering, caught perfectly the instinctive sympathy of the common man. It differs from the willed compassion or ideological logic of the intellectual, and equally from the fabricated sentimentalism of professional viewers-with-alarm; nobody reading the poem could

---

[1] 'Thomas Hood and "The Times" ', *Times Literary Supplement*, May 17, 1957, p. 309.

imagine that he was being got at. Above all, it is the pervasive note of genuine Christian charity that ensures the authenticity of the feeling:

> Take her up instantly,
> Loving, not loathing.
> Touch her not scornfully;
> Think of her mournfully,
> Gently and humanly;
> Not of the stains of her,
> All that remains of her
> Now is pure womanly. . . .
>
> Owning her weakness,
> Her evil behaviour,
> And leaving with meekness,
> Her sins to her Saviour!

Few will quarrel with the poem's sentiment, despite a rather pointless attempt to expose the piece as a vulgarization of bits from Goethe's *Faust*.[1] What of its form? Here opinions differ sharply. Oliver Elton described it as 'jarring tuneless dactyls', while W. H. Hudson found that its 'wild effect is marvellously enhanced by the headlong pace and mad jingle of the verses'. Although, to a modern ear, the chime of Hood's feminine rhymes carries an unfortunate echo of Gilbert's patter songs, it seems to me that Hood has instinctively chosen a remarkably apt form for this poem. The metre combines relentlessness with emphasis—as if to say, 'Look at her! Look at her! *You* are to blame!', that element of repetition that underlies nursery rhymes and popular jingles, and, most important of all, the shape and mood of the Litany. Certainly in reading the poem, I cannot myself escape memories of the Litanies of the Virgin and the Sacred Heart. It is highly improbable that anything of this kind was in the mind of the wholly unliturgical and asquiescingly Protestant Hood, but I feel certain that the poem's appeal has been due at least in part to the half-submerged memory of liturgical rhythms, and that the acknowledged religious tone of the poem proceeds largely from this.

It is true that the expression is sometimes clumsy and naïve;

---

[1] John Hennig: 'The Literary Relations Between Goethe and Thomas Hood', *Modern Language Quarterly*, Vol. XII, No. 1, March, 1951.

and that there are specific lapses, such as

> Wipe those poor lips of hers
> Oozing so clammily. . . .

> Lave in it, drink of it,
> Then, if you can . . .

and the rhymes like 'pitiful—city full', 'basement—amaze-ment' which teeter on the edge of absurdity. Taken together with the moving character of the whole poem, these can be accepted as a kind of guarantee of the thing's spontaneous sincerity, as the irregular rhythms of a folk-song are often a guarantee of its authenticity. Yet such an argument, if pressed far enough, would mean that 'The Bridge of Sighs' is not to be judged by the standards we normally apply to poetry at all.

The danger in this view is that of under-valuing Hood's art and literary tact. He had not only generous human sympathies, an awareness of man's inhumanity to man that enabled him to concentrate in this poem much of what Dickens said of such matters in a whole novel, and that personal experience of suffering that gives especial poignancy to

> Even God's Providence
> Seeming estranged,

but he had, too, a real flair for the handling of such tricky metres as that of 'The Bridge of Sighs' and an instinct for the memorable phrase that has made much of the poem part of the familiar currency of the language.

The answer may well lie in recognizing the fact that not only was Hood, inevitably, when we consider the circumstances in which he worked, a very uneven poet, writing good poems, bad poems and poems that are both good and bad, but also that he is one of that rare species, to which Kipling, for instance, be-longs, who have the drive, the emotional power, of a popular singer, of a Bessie Smith or a Leadbelly, but at the same time is anything but devoid of art. 'The Bridge of Sighs' is probably best described by that currently fashionable designation, 'a good-bad poem'; it has glaring faults, even absurdities, it is strained, it is sometimes only a short step away from self-burlesque—yet it compels, it lingers, it moves, it commands attention, it goes deeper into our instinctive responses than the cerebral lines of a poet who has assiduously read his Empson.

XI

The Rose above the Mould

BY the time the May issue of *Hood's Magazine* appeared, Hood
had collapsed. Jane wrote to Dr. Elliot on May 22, 'Hood could
not give up the hope of getting the magazine out till last night,
for it is quite a sin to let what might be so good, fall to the
ground. . . . Last night he fretted dreadfully, and, at one this
morning, was seized so suddenly with short breathing, and fullness of the chest, I thought he could not live.' Yet the next
morning, with his constantly surprising resilience, the poet
wrote a lively letter to Dr. Robert Elliot apologizing for being
unable to attend a party to which the Hoods were invited.
The postscript went: 'A pleasant party to you. To-day is my
birth-day—forty-five—but I can't tell you how old I *feel*;
enough to be your grandfather at least, and give *you* advice! viz.
don't over-polka yourself.

> Epigram on Dr. Robert Elliot of Camberwell.
>
> Whatever Doctor Robert's skill be worth,
>   One hope within me still is stout and hearty,
> He would not *kill* me till the 24th,
>   For fear of my *appearing* at his party!'

The faithful Ward continued to get the magazine out for
him, but at the end of the June number, a serious announcement appeared, beginning: 'It is with feelings of the deepest
concern that we acquaint our subscribers, and the public, with
the circumstances that have, during the past month, deprived
this Magazine of the invaluable services of its Editor. A severe

attack of the disorder to which he has long been subject, haemorrhage from the lungs, occasioned by enlargement of the heart (itself brought on by the wearing excitement of ceaseless and excessive literary toil) has, in the course of a few weeks, reduced Mr. Hood to such a state of extreme debility and exhaustion that, during several days, fears were entertained for his life. Nevertheless, up to Thursday the 23rd he did not relinquish the hope that he should have the strength to continue, in the present number, the novel which he began in the last.'

Even in this extremity, Hood struggled on gallantly, propped up in bed and compulsively trying to sketch a few comic designs. The pencil dropped from his tired hand, but Ward printed two of these 'sickroom fancies', one an arrangement of blisters, leeches and medicine bottles symbolizing 'The Editor's Apologies', saying that he hoped that 'the contrast of their sprightly humour with the pain and prostration in the midst of which they were produced, might give them a peculiar interest, independent of any merit of their own'.

But Hood was not done yet. By July he had recovered sufficiently to visit Blackheath, where he stayed convalescing for a couple of months. Before he left, his friends, knowing that he was killing himself with his labours, set to work to try to obtain a pension on the civil list for him. Lord Francis Egerton, well known for his interest in struggling authors, Monckton Milnes and Sir Edward Bulwer Lytton, on behalf of the others, asked Ward for a list of Hood's works to accompany the submission. Ward applied to Hood who sent the required details, together with a letter that more clearly perhaps than anything else he wrote, sets out proudly and defiantly his literary credo:

My dear Ward,

I send you the best list I can of my writings. They make no great show in the catalogue. Small fruits and few, towards what you will call my literary *dessert*. You must trust, I fear, to my negative merits. For example:—That I have not given up to party even a *party*ciple of what was meant for mankind, womankind and children. It is true that I may be said to have favoured liberal principles, but then, they were so liberal as to be Catholic—common to old, young, or new England. The worse chance of any reward from powers political, who do not patronize motley, but would have their very Harlequins all of one colour—blue, green, or orange; anything but neutral tint.

I have not devoted any comic power I may possess to lays of indelicacy or ribaldry. 'I stooped for truth,' as Pope *stooped*ly says, 'and moralized my song.'

I have never written against religion, anything against pseudo Saints and Pharisees notwithstanding; some of my serious views were expressed in an Ode to Rae Wilson in the *Athenaeum*.

I have never been indicted for libel.

I have never been called out for personality.

I have not sought pleasure or profit in satirizing or running down my literary contemporaries.

I have never stolen from them.

I have never written anonymously what I should object to own.

I have never countenanced, by my practice, the puffery, quackery and trickery of modern literature, even when publishing for years on my own account.

In short, though I may not have reflected any very great honour on our national literature, I have not disgraced it, all which has been an infinite comfort to me to remember when lately a *critical* illness induced a retrospective review of my literary career. . . .

My debts and difficulties indeed cost me trouble and concern but much less than if they had been the results of stark extravagance or vicious dissipation. At the very worst, like Timon, 'unwillingly, not ignobly, have I spent', and even that to a small amount. But, like Dogberry, I have had losses and been weighed down by drawbacks I should long ago have surmounted, but for the continued misconduct and treacheries of others called friends and relations. Only it provokes and vexes me that my position countenances the old traditional twaddle about the improvidence of authors, their want of business habits, ignorance of the world, &c, &c. Men can hardly be ignorant of what they professedly study; and as to business, authors *know their own*, as well as your mercantiles or traders, and perhaps something of accounts besides. They do not thrive like those who seek for money and nothing else, as a matter of course; nor can they be expected to prove a match for those whose life-long study has been how to over-reach or swindle. Their Flights have been in another direction; their contemplations turned towards the beautiful, the just and the good. They are not simply spooney victims, but martyrs to their own code. To cope with the Bailys and Flights one must be not merely literary men, but literary scamps, rogues, sharks, sharpers. Authors are supposed too often to be mere ninnies, and therefore plucked especially, in wit men, but in simplicity, mere children. A vulgar error. The first fellow who took me in, victimized also no few friends in trade, bankers and bill-brokers. To my next mishaps I was no party, being abroad, and the tricks played without my knowledge. Baily, a book-seller, had necessarily long odds in his favour against an author, by the force of position, and with the law to help him, which, whatever may be said, protects the wrongdoer—witness my barren verdict and yet costly. Flight you know—a practised pettifogger and money-lender to boot. And yet after all, much as I have suffered from it, I do not repent my good opinion of my fellows. There is a faith in human goodness, to renounce which altogether is, in its kind, an impiety. It is a total loss when a man writes up over his heart 'No trust'; one had better lose a thousand more, than keep such a pike. For my part, I would rather be done brown a little than go black for fear of it. . . .

I am almost spectre enough for the Phantom Ship, but too weak to work my passage. However, I will not strike; my colours (Yellow and white) must be hauled down for me. Meanwhile, I fight on as well as I can—at the very worst, when all is lost, I can *blow up the Magazine*—God bless you.

Yours affectionately,
Thos. Hood.

When Ward sent this letter to Bulwer Lytton, he wrote, 'Do not be deceived by his jocose style. He made jokes on the Friday night, when he said "I shall scramble on to my birthday [the next day] and no more." I was putting a mustard plaster round him, and he said, "Very little meat to so much mustard!" '

Accompanied by a medical certificate concerning Hood's state of health from Dr. W. Elliot, and a statement of Hood's services to literature, the appeal was lodged at the end of July, through Lord Francis Egerton.[1] But the Government machinery worked very slowly and on August 22, Egerton, writing to Peel to ask about the progress of the petition, stressed the poet's desperate need. Peel has been criticized by several critics for his lack of generosity to the poet; for instance, Douglas Jerrold in the Preface to Volume IX of *Punch* (July–December, 1845) wrote, 'Hood dies in penury, and it is a fine thing—a generous act—for the English Prime Minister to bestow fifty pounds upon those a man of genius leaves behind! English Ministers can only play the Maecenas over a man's coffin!'

That Jerrold and the others have been less than just to Peel is disclosed by a series of letters, hitherto unpublished, among the Peel papers in the British Museum. To Egerton's August letter, Peel replied on the following day: 'Mr. Hood's works, at least the humorous ones—are very familiar to me. If I can secure for him out of the general scramble one hundred per annum for life I will do so. In the mean while I enclose the sum of £150, which may be applied to the relief of his immediate necessities of which I sincerely lament to hear. He may receive this sum without the slightest scruple. It comes from a very limited fund called the Royal Bounty and the acceptance of it would not impose any personal obligation—or any such restraint as a sensitive and independent mind might discover in private bounty.'

Again, in October, Lord Egerton wrote to tell Peel that it was certain that Hood had not long to live, and asking if the proposed pension were any nearer. Peel replied on November 4, that he hoped to obtain the £100 a year, adding 'I wish it were more—but small as it is it has this recommendation—It is a public acknowledgement of Literary Eminence—and the acceptance of it imposes no obligations of a personal nature—no fetters on the perfect freedom and independence of him on whom it is conferred.'

The proposal for a pension came a few days later, with an official note to Hood asking him to name a 'very near female relative' on whom Her Majesty might be recommended to confer a pension. Through Egerton, Hood gave Jane's name as beneficiary, and also wrote a personal letter of appreciation

---

[1] The relevant letters and documents are among the Peel papers in the British Museum Manuscript Room.

to Peel on November 9, in the course of which he said: 'As an Author, I cannot but think it a good omen for the cause, that this mark of your favour has fallen on a writer so totally unconnected with party politics as myself, whose favourite theory of government is "An angel from Heaven, and a despotism". As a Man, I am deeply sensible of a consideration and kindness, which have made this "work-a-day" world more park-like to me, as well as to the people of Manchester, and will render the poor remnant of my life much happier, and easier, than it could be with the prospect that was before me. My humble name has sufficiently occupied your thoughts already, yet may it, with its pleasanter associations, recur to you, whenever you meet with a disinterested partisan, or a political ingrate!'

Hood was telling the truth when he disavowed political affiliations, but this did not mean an indifference to social conditions. The issue for the same month of *Hood's Magazine* contained his 'Lay of the Labourer', prompted by the case of Gifford White, a Huntington labourer of eighteen sentenced to transportation for life for sending a letter to the local farmers threatening arson if he could not get work. Hood added to his 'Lay' a moving prose appeal on behalf of the unemployed, that also asked the Home Secretary to inquire into the Huntingdon case, and sent a copy of the magazine with the article and poem marked, together with a covering letter to the Home Secretary himself. The only reply was a terse impersonal acknowledgment of Hood's communication. Graham, Hood told Mrs. Elliot, was 'a cold, hard man, bigoted to the New Poor Law'.

Nevertheless, Peel's reply to Hood's letter of thanks shows such a lively appreciation of Hood's independence of mind and outlook that it must be quoted in full:

Brighton, November 10th, 1844

Sir,—I am more than repaid by the personal satisfaction which I have had in doing that, for which you return me warm and characteristic acknowledgments.

You perhaps think that you are known to one, with such multifarious occupations as myself, merely by general reputation as an author; but I assure you that there can be little, which you have written and acknowledged, which I have not read: and that there are few, who can appreciate and admire

more than myself, the good sense and good feeling, which have
taught you to infuse so much fun and merriment into writings
correcting folly, and exposing absurdities, and yet never trespassing beyond those limits, within which wit and facetiousness
are not very often confined. You may write on with the consciousness of independence, as free and unfettered, as if no
communication had ever passed between us. I am not conferring a private obligation upon you, but am fulfilling the intentions of the Legislature, which has placed at the disposal of the
Crown a certain sum (miserable, indeed, in amount) to be
applied to the recognition of public claims on the Bounty of
the Crown. If you will review the names of those, whose claims
have been admitted on account of their literary or scientific
eminence, you will find an ample confirmation of the truth of
my statement.

One return, indeed, I shall ask of you—that you will give
me the opportunity of making your personal acquaintance.

Believe me to be, faithfully yours,

Robert Peel.

Hood's illness was to prevent him from ever meeting the
Prime Minister, although in his reply he expressed his delight
at the honour and his willingness to do so. On November 16,
both he and Egerton received official notifications from Peel
himself that the Queen had approved his proposal that £100
a year be granted to Mrs. Hood for life, to take effect from the
preceding June. Hood had returned from Blackheath to London in September, and with Ward's help had immersed himself once more in the affairs of *Hood's Magazine*, despite the fact
that he was going downhill fast and was forced to do most
of his work from bed. In the same month, he was able to tell
Dr. Elliot, 'The "Labourer" has made a great hit, and gone
through most of the papers like the "Song of the Shirt".'

Thanks to his unremitting application, the Christmas number of the magazine appeared on time. His son wrote later
about this period, 'His own family never enjoyed his quaint
and humorous fancies, for they were all associated with memories of illness and anxiety. Although Hood's "Comic Annual"
as he himself used to remark with pleasure, was in every house
seized upon, and almost worn out by the frequent handling of

little fingers, his own children did not enjoy it till the lapse of many years had mercifully softened down some of the sad recollections connected with it. The only article I can remember we ever thoroughly enjoyed was "Mrs. Gardiner, a Horticultural Romance", and even this was composed in bed. But the illness he was then suffering from was only rheumatic fever, and not one of his dangerous attacks, and he was unusually cheerful. He sat up in bed, dictating it to my mother, interrupted by our bursts of irrepressible laughter, as joke after joke came from his lips, he all the while laughing and relishing it as much as we did. But this was a rare—indeed almost solitary—instance, for he could not usually write so well at any time as at night, when all the house was quiet. Our family rejoicings were generally when the work was over, and we were too thankful to be rid of the harass and the worry, to care much for the results of such labour.'

Despite the fortitude with which Hood struggled on, he now knew in his heart that the end was very near. On about November 15, he took to his bed again, and, save for a brief hour or two, remained there until his death. 'On Christmas Day,' report his children, 'he crawled out, for our sakes more than for his own, into a little dressing-room next to his bed-room for a few hours; but it was a pitiful mockery of enjoyment.' So ill was he on this occasion that he scarcely even attempted to appear cheerful. Yet still, with heroic, although almost compulsive, determination, he continued writing. He carried on with 'Our Family', the last chapters of this unfinished story appearing in February, 1845, and for the January issue he wrote a review of Dickens's *The Chimes*. He found, as he thought, a flaw in the story, in that Toby Veck has 'a propensity, not very porter-like, to think small-beer of himself and the whole order of poor people in general—and small beer of the worst sort, too, sour and good for nothing', which Hood found incongruous with his character, as 'a practical philanthropist'. But in general his appraisal is a warm one, and ends, 'May they [the chimes] be widely and wisely heard, inculcating their wholesome lessons of charity and forbearance—reminding wealth of the claims of Want—the feasting of the fasting, and inducing them to spare something for an aching void from their comfortable repletion.'

Early in the year, he began writing brief notes of farewell to his friends, to Procter, for instance, asking him to come and say a last good-bye; and this typical note to Dr. D. W. Moir:

Dear Moir,

God bless you and yours, and good-bye! I drop these few lines, as in a bottle from a ship water-logged, and on the brink of foundering, being in the last stage of dropsical debility; but though suffering in body, serene in mind. So without reversing my union-jack, I await my last lurch. Till which, believe me, dear Moir,

Yours most truly,
Thomas Hood.

Ward, who had resumed virtual control of the magazine, wrote to Milnes at this time: 'My mind is overwhelmed with horrors about Hood and his family (who are weeping around him) and the magazine, the position of which is, of course, most precarious; but I feel bound to *try* to do myself what I ask others to do.' With Milnes's help, he rounded up various distinguished contributors; the March number contained pieces by himself and Milnes, as well as Landor's 'Dante and Beatrice' and 'The Bishop Orders his Tomb at St. Praxed's' by Browning, who had contributed four poems to earlier numbers. The April issue included Browning's 'Flight of the Duchess', Landor's 'To Major-General W. Napier', and 'Prayer of the Bees', 'A Word to Young Writers' by G. H. Lewes, and the song 'Old Meg', and a sonnet, by Keats.

Even at this time, under the shadow of death and with the relief of the Government pension in sight, the Hood household was not free from the anxieties of debt and persistent creditors. So desperate, indeed, was Jane's plight that she was forced, from sheer necessity, to turn again to Peel, who had already shown his practical sympathy, for urgent aid. The letter she wrote to him on January 14, 1845, pathetically shows the sad circumstances that had turned her into a beggar:

Sir,

It is with shame and timidity I venture to address you but I trust in your goodness to pardon me when I have stated the urgency of my distress. I am the Wife of Thomas Hood, on whom you have recently conferred such great benefits that I have scarcely courage to apply for further assistance. But my Husband's present dangerous state of health and my earnest wish to preserve him on his sick bed from the intrusion and painful annoyances of law proceedings induce a boldness in me quite foreign to my nature. The assistance you afforded my poor husband from the Government funds, Sir, rendered so grateful to his feelings by your handsome letter, enabled him to pay off a great part of his liabilities but there still remain a few creditors whose demands amount to about a hundred and twenty pounds and who finding the others have been paid threaten to proceed immediately. I have a hope that if I were enabled to pay each a part they would for a time desist—and if you, Sir, through me would avert these disasters from my dear Husband I cannot express the blessing you would confer upon me. He does not know of this application nor have I consulted any friend about it—as I fear his displeasure should I have the comfort of seeing him recover—but of this comfort my hopes are sad and faint—He has kept his bed for 2 months suffering most distressingly from cough, spasms in the breath and hemmorrhege from the lungs. Still with a power quite astonishing, he wrote and drew at intervals last month for his Magazine. A strong desire to afford us a subsistence urging him to extertion almost incredible. I fear he is too ill and weak to do the same for the present month.

I will not intrude further, Sir, upon your valuable time except to entreat you to pardon me if I am too intrusive and to then continue your kind opinion of my Husband as if I had never taken so great a liberty—for he is unconscious of it—and dwells with continued pleasure on your handsome letter to him,

I am, sir,

With the greatest respect and gratitude,

Your most humble servant,

Jane Hood.

The Prime Minister, far from taking umbrage at yet another appeal from this quarter, replied, three days later,

Madam,

Enclosed is the sum of one hundred pounds which I beg you to apply to the payment of those demands which are the most pressing.

I cannot hold out to you I fear the prospect of any additional aid.

I trust this will relieve your anxiety and prevent any immediate obstacle from the impatience of creditors to the recovery of your husband.

I am,

&c.

Robert Peel.

Ignorant of this further mark of Peel's interest and favour, Hood soon afterwards dictated to Jane his last letter to the Prime Minister regretting that they were not destined to meet in the flesh. 'Thank God my mind is composed,' he said, 'but my race as an author is run.' Almost certainly the last letter he penned was addressed on March 12 to his relatives in Dundee, Captain and Mrs. Keay:

My dear Uncle and Aunt—

With this you will receive a Magazine with the Portrait of me which I promised.

I little thought to have been alive at this date—but some strong point in my constitution has made a desperate struggle to recover, though in vain. I am now helpless in bed, dreadfully swollen by dropsy from weakness, and have suffered very much:—but only bodily, for my mind has been calm and resigned, as Mr. Nicholson would inform you. I am glad he came, on that account, for I have been a good deal pestered by Betsy, who, as you know, has some peculiar religious notions of her own, and would very likely describe me to you, as dying a pagan, or infidel, because I do not conform to her views.

God bless you both—we shall soon meet I hope in a better world.

Let it comfort you to know that I die beloved and respected and have met with unexpected kindness and distinction from very many strangers as well as friends. These are probably the last lines I shall write,

Your affectionate nephew,

Thomas Hood.

24th. Still alive—but cannot last long. God bless you and again a last farewell.

T. H.

228

The picture to which he refers was that of a bust of himself made by Edward Davis towards the end of 1844, shortly before the poet took to his bed for good. An engraving of the bust was used as a frontispiece for *Hood's Magazine* of February, 1845. As a farewell gift, Hood sent out some hundred signed copies of the engraving to his friends. Few people can have faced death with more complete acceptance nor with such a systematic attempt to round off his affairs, say a dignified farewell to friends, comfort his grieving family, and manifest his certainty of the resurrection.

On his death-bed, he wrote the following brief poem, which shows that, while Hood's knowledge of Christianity could hardly have been less doctrinal, he retained an unshaken belief in the great fundamental truths of orthodoxy; his confidence in a future life carries him through the thickening shadows of death:

> Farewell Life! my senses swim
> And the world is growing dim;
> Thronging shadows cloud the light,
> Like the advent of the night,—
> Colder, colder, colder still,—
> Upward steals a vapour chill—
> Strong the earthy odour grows—
> I smell the Mould above the Rose!
>
> Welcome Life! The Spirit strives!
> Strength returns, and hope revives;
> Cloudy fears and shapes forlorn
> Fly like shadows at the morn,—
> O'er the earth there comes a bloom—
> Sunny light for sudden gloom,
> Warm perfume for vapours cold—
> I smell the Rose above the Mould!

Hood's Magazine for March prepared its public for the editor's end—'Almost as much through incapacity of his hand to hold the pen, as of his brain for any length of time to guide it, he has at last been compelled to desist from composition . . . We have thought it due to our readers and the public, thus briefly to make known that Mr. Hood is more seriously ill than even *he* has ever been before; avoiding to express any hopes or forebodings of our own, or to prejudge the uncertain issues of life or death.' Dickens, who was at that time in Italy, wrote to Angela Burdett-Coutts on March 18, 'I also hear privately that Hood, the author, is past all chance of recovery. He was (I have a presentiment that even now I may speak of him as something past) a man of great power—of prodigious force and genius as a poet—and not generally known, perhaps, by his best credentials. Personally he had a most noble and generous spirit. When he was under the pressure of severe misfortune and illness, and I had never seen him, he went far out of his way to praise me; and wrote in the Athenaeum a paper on The Curiosity Shop; so full of enthusiasm and high appreciation, and so free from any taint of envy or reluctance to acknowledge me as a young man far more fortunate than himself, that I can hardly bear to think of it.'

The long-drawn-out agony of Hood's dying, inch by inch, found him more solicitous for the suffering it was causing Jane and the children than for his own comfort. Jane left his side only when worn out with fatigue. Young Tom took her place and his father, being unable to speak, wrote his directions on a slip of paper when a severe haemorrhage from the lungs demanded attention from the doctor. When the spasms ceased, and he could speak, he talked with complete composure to his family of their future plans and what he hoped would lie in store for them.

Although Hood was essentially an urban man, he retained a simple, unaffected love for the countryside. It gave him great joy that the spring that year was a fine one, and he savoured the fresh air and sunshine from his bed, drinking in the radiance of the season. On one occasion, he said to his family, 'It is a beautiful world, and since I have been lying here, I have thought of it more and more; it is not so bad, even humanly speaking, as people would make it out. I have had some very happy days while I have lived in it, and I could have wished to stay a little longer. But it is all for the best, and we shall all meet in a better world!' At other times he became delirious, and was heard to mutter fragments of verses.

Ward's announcement in the April *Magazine* left no doubt as to Hood's condition. It gave 'the sad tidings of his approaching death; a death long feared by his friends, long even distinctly foreseen, but not till now so rapidly approaching as to pre-

clude *all* hope'. The news of his extremity provoked an immediate response, not only from among his friends and acquaintances in the world of literature and art, but from ordinary
anonymous lovers of his work. Fruit, wine and delicacies, notes
of good wishes, gifts of money (alas, too late!) and flowers,
verses of cheer and solace, visits from neighbours and admirers
all helped to moderate the manner of his passing.

Even if we make every allowance for filial piety in the
lengthy account of his dying in the *Memorials* and for the conventional phraseology of late Victorian biography with which
Walter Jerrold describes his death-bed, there remains enough
evidence that Hood met his end with unruffled fortitude, that
of a man long familiar with death. According to his children,
on Thursday evening, May 1, he knew that he was at his last
gasp, and called Jane and the youngsters around him. 'He gave
us his last blessing, tenderly and fondly and then quietly
clasping my mother's hand, he said, "Remember, Jane, I
forgive all, *all*, as I hope to be forgiven!" He lay for some time
calmly and peacefully, but breathing slowly and with difficulty.
My mother bending over him heard him say faintly, "O Lord!
say, Arise, take up thy cross, and follow me!" His last words
were, "Dying! dying!" as if glad to realize the rest implied in
them.' Hood never spoke again, but sank into a deep coma
that lasted until the afternoon of Saturday, May 3, when he
slipped quietly away.

According to the *Memorials*, it was at first suggested that he
be buried in the Poets' Corner in Westminster Abbey. But all
Jane inherited was a few pounds, her pension, and a bundle of
debts—and it cost £200 to be buried among the vulgar tombs
in the Abbey. 'Is it not a grand thought,' mused young Tom,
ironically, 'surpassing Addison's solemn meditations, that any
humble, nameless, titleless, unknown man, may elbow Chaucer,
Spenser, Dryden, Jonson, and Prior in Poets' Corner—always
provided he have £200 or so to pay his way with!' It was finally
decided, at the suggestion of Richard Monckton Milnes, that
Hood be laid to rest in the new cemetery at Kensal Green.
There he was buried at mid-day on May 10, in the presence of
a small band of mourners, including the Elliots, Milnes and
Ward. It was a beautiful, clear spring day, and just as the
melancholy service ended, a lark mounted up singing over the

mourners' heads, as if it were the gay, untamable spirit of Hood himself rebuking the sorrow of the company.

A few days later, the indefatigable Milnes, with F. O. Ward, Samuel Phillips and other friends launched an appeal on behalf of Jane and the children. Carlyle, Charles Cowden Clarke, William Harvey, Robert Peel and others lent their support, and Thomas Reseigh, a solicitor's secretary and one of the poet's later friends, looked after the business side. A local committee in Manchester collected some £100 in two days, and by August, £1,311 15s. 6d. had been subscribed in sums ranging from a few shillings from humble readers to substantial donations from Lord Francis Egerton, Sir E. Bulwer Lytton, Lord Ashley, the Marquis of Northampton, Monckton Milnes, G. P. R. James and £50 from Sir Robert Peel. The promoters felt that this was not quite enough, and Ward wrote to Dickens for his advice. Dickens replied on August 14 that he felt that the public appeal was weakened by the existence of the pension, and that no more money was to be got. He recalled that, in respect of the Elton fund, in which Hood had assisted, where there were six young children without mother or father, £2,300 had been raised, but that this appeal had had support from the theatrical profession as a whole.

He had come, said Dickens, to the 'conclusion that it is not advisable to press Mrs. Hood's appeal to any greater extent. I think it would be useless to her, and would be tortured into an unpleasant association with the memory of our deceased friend. . . . My estimate of the great genius of poor Hood is as high as it is possible for man to form, and always has been, consequently I set her case on very lofty grounds indeed. But in turning the question in my mind I separate myself, or you, from the crowd who are addressed.'

The committee took Dickens's advice and the fund was closed. But Jane did not survive long to enjoy the fruits of the appeal. The long invalidism of her husband, as well as the anxieties and deprivations of their constant struggles against near-poverty, had taken a heavy toll of her meagre physical resources.[1] Towards the end of 1845, her mother, old Mrs.

---

[1] Jane, in fact, continued to be hard pressed to the end. In September, 1845, shortly before her death, she wrote again in appeal to the Prime Minister, asking if he could arrange a scholarship at Charter House for

The Rose above the Mould

Reynolds, fell seriously ill, and was believed to be at death's door. But the old woman recovered and outlived her daughter, who died in December, 1846, about twenty months after her beloved Thomas. She was buried beside him at Kensal Green.

Three years later, Eliza Cook, the popular poetess, lamented that 'poor Hood' had no stone to mark his grave; a short while afterwards, Mark Lemon added his incentive:

> Give Hood a tombstone, 'tis not much to give
> To one who stirred so oft our smiles and tears.

Largely as a result of Miss Cook's agitation, a committee was formed at the end of 1852 to solicit public subscriptions for a memorial over the poet's grave. Macaulay, Procter, De Quincey, Miss Mitford, and the Duke of Devonshire were among the contributors, and Longfellow sent a donation from America, with a letter in which he said, 'Poor Mrs. Hood and the children, who have lost him! They will have forgotten the stranger, who called, one October morning, with Dickens, and was hospitably entertained by them. But I remember the visit, and the pale face of the poet, and the house in St. John's Wood.' The fund was swelled by the proceeds from 'An Evening with Hood', an entertainment suggested by George Grossmith. Dickens opted out of the project on the grounds of principle, saying to the organizing secretary that he had 'the greatest tenderness for the memory of Hood', but was not 'very favourable to posthumous memorials in the monument way'. 'I shall have a melancholy gratification', he wrote, 'in privately assisting to place a simple and plain record over the remains of a great writer that should be as modest as he was himself, but I regard any other amount in connection with his mortal resting-place as a mistake.'

Matthew Noble, the sculptor, was commissioned to design the monument, which was unveiled at Kensal Green on July 18, 1854, when Monckton Milnes spoke a eulogy of Hood. While the motives behind the project were worthy ones, the memorial itself is a typically mediocre example of Victorian funerary taste, for which even Mr. John Betjeman would be

---

young Tom. Peel had to reply that the single presentation he had was already committed. (British Museum.)

233

hard put to find an excuse. The inscription reads, 'He sang the Song of the Shirt'.

Hood's children preserved the most affectionate memories of their father, and their *Memorials*, however imperfect they may be in detail, not only enshrine this tender regard, but remain the sole authority for many of the facts of Hood's life. In 1849, Fanny married the Rev. John Somerville Broderip, rector of Cussington, Somersetshire, who was some fifteen years her senior. Three daughters were born of the marriage; Broderip died in 1866. Fanny, who had inherited a little of her father's talent, not only collaborated with Tom in writing the *Memorials* and in editing her father's works, but also produced some thirteen books for children, some of which Tom illustrated, and among which perhaps the most charming are *Wild Rose* and *Tale of the Toys*. She died on November 3, 1878, at the age of forty-eight, and was buried in St. Mary's churchyard, Walton Bay, Walton-By-Clevedon.

After studying at University College, London, and Pembroke College, Oxford, Tom Hood went down without taking his degree and abandoned his original intention of entering the Church. He wrote for several journals and, in 1857, published his first book, *Pen and Pencil Pictures*, which he had written while at Oxford. Three years later he found employment in the War Office, but resigned in 1865 to edit *Fun*, a successful rival to *Punch*. His other works include several books for children and three-decker novels. His *Rules of Rhyme* (1869), a book on English versification, was several times reprinted. Although he was twice married, he left no children, and died in 1874, at the early age of thirty-nine.

Nothing Tom Hood wrote reached the level of his father's best work; yet he had inherited something of Thomas's metrical facility, sense of humour, and verbal agility, and in his better pieces, he produced work not unworthy of his father's average. Without doubt, Tom Hood suffered something through being the son of a famous father. It was the work of Thomas Hood the elder which was to endure throughout the Victorian age and give pleasure to many thousands for over half a century after his death, and a handful of whose poems were to remain alive wherever the English language is spoken, and beyond.

XII

The Man and the Poet

THE standard Victorian opinion of Hood's personality was that expressed in Thackeray's encomium: 'Oh, sad, marvellous picture of courage, of honesty, of patient endurance, of duty struggling against pain! . . . Here is one at least without guile, without pretension, without scheming, of a pure life, to his family and little modest circle of friends tenderly devoted.' While a more realistic appraisal of the facts of Hood's life would certainly modify the sentimental rhetoric of Thackeray's verdict, few would question the gallantry and dogged determination of Hood or deny the fine qualities of that spirit which, in the face of circumstances which could have plunged lesser men into despair, maintained its optimism and sense of joy.

One of the most attractive things about Hood is his continual ability to jest at his misfortunes, to turn the most dismal of occasions into a matter for whimsical philosophizing, to use, like Falstaff, the infirmities of his flesh as a subject for mirth. It is true that the many references in his letters to his health and the large part it plays in his everyday considerations may suggest morbid self-involvement, and that there were times when mental and physical exhaustion wrung from him lines like these:

> I'm sick of gruel, and the dietetics,
> I'm sick of pills, and sicker of emetics,
> I'm sick of pulses' tardiness or quickness,
> I'm sick of blood, its thinness or its thickness,—
> In short, within a word, I'm sick of sickness.

235

Yet these occasions are few by comparison with those in which cheerfulness breaks triumphantly through:

> My temples throb, my pulses boil,
>   I'm sick of Song, and Ode, and Ballad—
> So, Thrysis, take the Midnight Oil
>   And pour it on a lobster salad.
>
> My brain is dull, my sight is foul,
>   I cannot write a verse, or read—
> Then, Pallas, take away thine Owl,
>   And let us have a lark instead.

Some may be tempted to see in this kind of jesting merely a surface optimism beneath which lurks a terror of mortality, and in its very frequency an unhealthy fascination with sickness and even a trace of hypochondria. Yet it is clear that Thomas Hood was a very sick man, indeed. He was a fragile child; the sicknesses of his youth left him weak, and, as he grew to manhood, he became increasingly subject to chills and colds, and to disorders of the chest, liver and stomach. He was himself inclined to attribute many of his ills, especially when on the Continent, to the climate and the unfamiliar diet. Some earlier writers, possibly because of the blood-spitting so often referred to in the letters, have assumed that he was suffering from tuberculosis. In fact, the various diagnoses of the English and Continental doctors which Thomas or Jane retail are usually vague and sometimes contradictory. A much clearer picture is given by the medical certificate prepared by Dr. William Elliot to accompany Hood's application for a pension, which is among the Peel papers in the British Museum.[1] The certificate reads:

Mr. Hood's diseases are of a most complicated and serious nature; for the most part organic and incurable. He labours under enlargement of the heart, with contraction and hardening of the mitral valve, and, I fear, aneurismal dilatation of the aorta or its first branches. This renders him liable to sudden

---

[1] A confirmatory note is added to Elliot's certificate by Dr. Archibald Billing, of Grosvenor Gate, Park Lane, who attended Hood in May, 1844. This concurs in Elliot's diagnosis, and ends, 'in my opinion, he is a case likely to terminate in sudden death'.

paroxysms of violent palpitation, spasmodic difficulty of breathing, and profuse bleeding from the lungs. He has for ten years had a state of blood resembling that in scurvy in its old virulent form; with frequent accesses of slow fever, and an aguish susceptibility to the atmospheric changes, occasioned by exposure to malaria in Holland.

His body is wasted almost to a skeleton by continual loss of blood; and he has several hernial protrusions of the bowels, occasioned by general relaxation of his frame.

During last May, now six weeks ago, he had a series of frightful paroxysms, struggling for breath for ten or twelve hours together and coughing up large quantities of blood; he became delirious from exhaustion, and, for several days, I considered his life in danger. He is now out of immediate danger, but exceedingly emaciated, and so weak that a relapse at present would probably prove fatal. Repose and freedom from excitement and anxiety have been strictly enjoined.

In my opinion, he will never recover to the enjoyment of even his former indifferent strength; recent illness has thoroughly undermined his constitution, already impaired by organic and structural disease. I do not anticipate that his life, under the most favourable circumstances, is likely to be prolonged beyond a few years, and I consider the excitement of literary composition, in his present state, eminently dangerous to him.

W. Elliot, M.D.

Stratford, Essex.
23 July, 1844.

This certificate, taken together with the various symptoms shown over the years by Hood, leads to the conclusion that Hood was suffering from rheumatic heart disease; his case exhibits all the typical characteristics of this malady. The fever of 1823 was almost certainly rheumatic fever; the 1827 fever and probably later ones were repeated attacks of the same disease, each of which increased the burden on his heart. The rheumatism and lung disorders to which he was subject were most likely manifestations of sub-acute rheumatic fever. The stomach and liver complaints seem to have been expressions of venous engorgement of the organs that goes with chronic cardiac failure, but may also have been in part effects of a high intake of calomel (viz. mercury poisoning), which, with blood-letting, was almost all the therapy employed in those days.

A modern medical opinion supports the general soundness of Dr. Elliot's certificate in the light of medical knowledge at the time, and describes Hood as suffering from mitral and aortic valve incompetence. The dilation and progressive loss of efficiency of his heart led to a rise in pressure in the small arteries of the lung, resulting in breathlessness, bronchial spasms and blood spitting, becoming progressively worse as segments of the lung became occluded.

Had Hood not had to engage in his life-long struggle for a livelihood, he might well have lived longer. His incessant anxieties and his over-work unquestionably aggravated the disorders that plagued him. But he was no psychomatic case. He was genuinely ill, and he had that kind of temperament that forces a man to work or die. He worked hard, as some people do, under a form of inner compulsion, a driving creative energy, as much from the need to earn money, and, even had he been more comfortably situated, I doubt whether he would have driven himself less energetically. 'My mind,' he told Bulwer Lytton, 'refuses to be passive, and seems the more restless from my inability to exert much bodily activity.'

Illness, then, is the dominant fact of Hood's life—he is, almost from the beginning, an invalid poet. And while there were times when he wearily rebelled against the tyranny of his diseases, his most typical attitude is one of acceptance. A lively expression of this is found in 'An Inaugural Discourse on a Certain System of Practical Philosophy', written as a preface to the first collected edition of *Hood's Own* in 1839. 'It was far from a practical joke,' he writes, 'to be laid up in ordinary in a foreign land, under the care of Physicians quite as much abroad as myself with the case; indeed, the shades of the gloaming were stealing over my prospect; but I resolved that, like the sun, so long as my day lasted, I would look on the bright side of everything. The raven croaked, but I persuaded myself that it was the nightingale: there was the smell of the mould, but I remembered that it nourished the violets. However my body might cry craven, my mind luckily had no mind to give in.' And later, in the same essay, he adds, 'As to Health, it's the weather of the body—it hails, it rains, it blows, it snows, at present, but it may clear up by-and-by.'

Here is none of Carlyle's dyspeptic moroseness. However much we may seek in such proclamations for manifestations of a defence against reality, the fact remains that, with a rare fortitude and detachment, Hood was able to flog Brother Ass along and to accept his burdens with spirited jest. His way of describing his recovery from a severe illness is neither self-pitying nor pompous, but jocose: 'The joyous cheers you have just heard, come from a crazy vessel that has clawed, by miracle, off a lee-shore, and I, the skipper, am sitting down to grog, and recounting to you the tale of the past danger, with the manœuvres that were used to escape the perilous Point.'

To be sure, these are public utterances; yet his private ones, though naturally more directly aware of strain, are scarcely less matter of fact. 'I must "die in harness", like a Hero—or a horse,' is his comment to Bulwer Lytton not long before he died.

The invalidism must, of course, have had its influence upon his personality, as well as on his poetry. As all his intimates agree, he was kind, gentle, fun-loving and generous, although shy and retiring in company. Thackeray's response to him is typical. Recalling a dinner of the Literary Fund at which both were present, Thackeray said, 'I quite remember his pale face; he was thin and deaf, and very silent; he scarcely opened his mouth during the dinner, and he made one pun,' —a poor one, too, apparently, for Thackeray elaborately forbears to tell us what it was.

It is sadness more than fun that observers noted in his countenance; this quiet man, with the grave, lean face and tall thin figure always clothed in clerical black, suggested anyone but the jester of *Hood's Own*. 'His was, indeed,' writes S. C. Hall, 'a countenance rather of melancholy than of mirth; there was something calm, even to solemnity, in the upper portion of the face, seldom relieved, in society, by the eloquent play of the mouth, or the sparkle of the observant eye.' Yet his friendships, inevitably limited though they were, were, in the main, constant and enduring—with the Elliots, J. H. Reynolds, Wright, Ward, the Dilkes, De Franck, and others, and he earned the deep respect of such men as Dickens, Monckton

Milnes, 'Barry Cornwall', Allan Cunningham and Robert
Peel. The misunderstandings with Lamb, C. W. Dilke and
one or two more, none of them serious, were such as might
happen to anybody. He was a loving husband and father. His
whole happiness was rooted in his family, as witness the touching lines he wrote in Coblenz in 1835, 'On seeing my Wife and
Two Children Sleeping in the Same Chamber':

> And has the earth lost its so spacious round,
> The sky its blue circumference above,
> That in this little chamber there is found
> Both earth and heaven—my universe of love! . . .

Since these aspects of his character are so widely attested,
one is tempted to attribute to others all the blame for his
frequent disagreements with publishers, editors and booksellers.
As has been remarked earlier, the publishing business in Hood's
time was pretty much of a jungle, and men like Taylor, for
instance, whose irritating personality was notorious, quarrelled
not only with Hood, but also with Lamb, Hazlitt, Landor, De
Quincey, and John Clare. We must remember, too, that Hood's
law-suit against Baily was eventually settled in his favour.
Leslie A. Marchand suggests that Hood 'was probably im-
practical and an easy prey to sharp practices of the business
world, and his fault may have been nothing more than lack
of business sense in choosing his publishers, and lack of care
in making arrangements with them',[1] to which we may add
the consideration that often it was not a matter of choice so
much as one of desperation that led him to certain publishers.
There is much truth here; but some of Hood's difficulties may
well have been sparked by a touch of petulance induced by his
illnesses, by the sheer impossibility of his fulfilling certain commitments through unexpected collapses, by that living on the
knife-edge of poverty that made him feel that publishers were
his natural enemies, and by a sense that, in the entertainment
field, he had to work furiously merely to hold his own. That he
was at times testy, that he procrastinated out of sheer weariness,
that he was less than prudent with money when he had it—
these things may be held against him; but, given his state of
health, we can only marvel that he kept his temper so well, that

[1] Marchand, op. cit.

he did not hold grudges, and that he should have got so much happiness out of life. Whatever disagreements he had were very human ones, and have to be weighed against the placidity of his relations with others, and the warmth of his compassion for those still less fortunate than he. The balance is heavily in Hood's favour.

We look in vain in his work for any ideas or philosophy which may be said to form a coherent, conscious whole. For one thing, there is nothing whatever in his letters or his works to indicate that he thought of himself as an artist, that he had any ideas, as Keats had, on the nature of poetry, or that he felt any need to derive an aesthetic from his practice. If, after his youthful excursions into Keats's territory, he thought of his writings as anything other than the exercise of God-given talents and as a way of earning a living, it was as a craft and as a vehicle for the expression of emotion. It may be that had he continued in the line of *The Plea of the Midsummer Fairies*, he would have developed into a conscious analyst of his own work.

Yet, skilful though these poems were, they were basically faint carbons of the works of earlier poets. Had he pursued this style, he is hardly likely to have produced anything more than fainter and fainter carbons, as perhaps he came to realize. As it was, he found himself, like many of his contemporaries, a poet without an audience. He moved farther and farther away from the false world of literature—in Baudelaire's sense of the word —towards more popular forms of expression, towards poetry as journalism. With Hood, poetry enters the world of Mayhew. All of his humanitarian poems could have been poeticizations of incidents recorded in the pages of the great Victorian sociologist. But equally in his prose sketches, his 'character' pieces and his comic verses, the world of Mayhew is to be found—in the people who crowd London, the chimney-sweeps, the roadmenders, the greengrocers, the pub-keepers, the zoo-keepers, the coachmen, the washerwoman, the Cockney family in the parks or on holiday. These are Hood's characters, not the countrymen of Wordsworth or the Renaissance figures of Keats.

This world and these characters are those of Dickens as well. Just as Dickens was an artist without a conscious aesthetic, so in his way was Hood. They shared much the same kind of background—that of the shabby genteel lower middle-class—

and the same kind of outlook. Both had had bitter experience of poverty; both hated cant, sanctimoniousness, hypocrisy and cruelty; both were zealous in the expression of humanitarian sentiment. Both had a similar vision; Dickens constantly saw relationships between incongruous things, as well as between people and objects; Hood saw similar analogies between incongruous words and ideas. Both, too, held a sentimental and undoctrinal Christianity, which they tended to reduce to the Golden Rule of secular humanism; for both, the major virtues were those of the English bourgeoisie—decency, industry, domesticity, although it was Hood, rather than Dickens, who fulfilled the latter more completely in his own life.

In such ways, Hood shared in, and gave impetus to, the move away from the frigid reason and fashionable toughness of the previous century towards an exaltation of 'the heart', which dominated so much mid-nineteenth-century literature and conventional mores. For him, as for the Victorians, the norm of conduct and of morality was the instinctive good feeling of the decent man.

> Spontaneous is pure devotion's fire;
> And in a green wood many a soul has built
> A new Church, with a fir-tree for its spire,

as he wrote, fairly well expresses Dickens's negative attitude towards institutional Christianity. For them both, the chief element in Christianity was the second of the Great Precepts. Ingenuous and incomplete as this may be for professing Christians, it was a fairly common outlook for men of good will at a time of stagnation in the Anglican Church, and it did in its way represent a reaction against abstract formulas and universals and towards the validity of individual subjective responses, not dissimilar to the modern existentialist mood.

In no sense of the word was Hood a cerebral poet. He lacked neither art nor craftsmanship, but they were more matters of instinct with him than of calculation; his poetry is to a great extent the spontaneous outflow of feeling. What he wrote, in fact, depended largely on quite simply 'how he was feeling' at the time; hence the wide range of themes and moods, the varying expressions of pathos, humanitarian sentiment, irony, indignation, sarcasm, slapstick, jocosity. He was without the concentration of purpose necessary to transform these feelings into universal emotions as frequently as a great poet does, but often the happy combination of an apt form and powerful personal feeling did the trick, and because Hood spoke eloquently from the heart of a man, he spoke to the hearts of all men.

It was because he was so open to instinctive feelings that he reflected, without being aware of it, the major inner realities of his age—the new emotionalism, the sentimental religiosity, the code of middle-class ethics, and also the sense of exhaustion and malaise that accompanied the breakdown of ideals in a period when the ideas of the French Revolution had petered out in frustration and the young Romantics had died out like combusted meteors. Hood's invalidism made him a sounding-board for the sense of death and decay in his day. Of course, this sense is not confined to Hood, nor did it come in with the Romantics. Yet there are not many poets in whom death is more constant a theme—nine-tenths of Hood's comic poetry concerns death, usually in unpleasant forms, men being bitten in half by sharks, skewered, eaten by cannibals, blown apart by shells, run over by coaches, and so forth. 'The Bridge of Sighs' is about a suicide, 'Miss Kilmansegg' ends in a brutal murder, 'Eugene Aram' and 'The Haunted House' have a murder at their heart. 'The Elm Tree' confronts his own death, 'The Last Man' that of the whole human race—to name but a few examples. To be sure, Hood's vitality of presentation, his brisk humour in the comic poems and his imaginative strength in the serious ones, and his avoidance of gloating detail in both kinds, prevent it all from being morbid, yet the themes, especially when they receive treatment as vivid as in 'The Haunted House', and, in other moods, the gentle, bloodless melancholy, indicate that Hood's poetry reflects not only his own tenuous hold on life, but the inner disturbance of his age, that he shares in the Romantic Agony and was perhaps half-conscious of the transitional character of his times.

One thing is clear. Although Hood's art or control over his material developed little, he did significantly change his poetic direction. Beginning as a Romantic imitator of 'literature', he came closer to reality in his verse as he gained more bitter experience of life. It has been suggested more than once that Hood suffered continually from a sense of frustration in his ambition to be a serious poet and that this interfered with his later work. I can see no evidence for this either in the letters or in the poetry itself. It is my opinion that, after the failure of the *Midsummer Fairies* volume, Hood moved steadily towards a kind of near folk-poetry and a highly individual blend of the pathetic and the grotesque elements from popular songs and ballads. If we may say, as I think we might, that Hood is a poet of real genius who just misses greatness, and ask why this is so, I think we shall find the answer in his versatility. He could do so many things so very well, and found the opportunity to do these things so often that he lacked the time and the impulse to develop any one type to the fullest. It is range that surprises us most in Hood; few poets have written so skilfully in so many fields.

His range is wide, indeed, from the delicate fancy of 'Midsummer Fairies', the soft melancholy of songs like 'Fair Ines' and 'Sing on, sad heart', the sensitive pathos of 'We watch'd her breathing', the whimsicality of 'Remonstratory Ode from the Elephant at Exeter Change', the gravity of the sonnets, some of which have the precise ordering of a Dutch painting, the meditative gentleness of 'Ode: Autumn' and his sonnet on Silence, the impassioned indignation of 'The Song of the Shirt' and 'The Lay of the Labourer', the warm nostalgia of 'I remember', and 'A Retrospective Review', the passion of 'The Bridge of Sighs', the exuberant fun of 'The Epping Hunt', the joyous rush of the comic ballads, the impressionistic terror of 'The Haunted House', the dignity of 'Farewell, Life', the dark horror of 'Eugene Aram', the satirical broadside of 'Ode to Rae Wilson', the savage grotesquerie of 'Miss Kilmansegg', the spirited comic narrative of 'The Knight and the Dragon', the pointed shrewdness of his topical comments in 'Odes and Addresses'. Even this by no means exhausts the variety of moods and tones in Hood. In none of them did he reach the highest rank, for he was not an obsessed, dedicated poet, nor the kind of writer who goes deep because his range is narrow. Nor were the times and the public propitious for great poetry. But if Hood did not write one really great poem, he wrote many good poems in different genres, for he had a share of almost every poetic gift, and sufficient poetic tact, not, even in the most cruel conditions, to spoil what he wrote.

What daunts most readers today is the sheer bulk of his work.

The Man and the Poet

There is a temptation to flit through the formidably fat green volumes of the Collected Edition prepared by his children, and, inevitably, to be repelled by the inequality of the writing, the outdated jokes and frequent horse-play, the mechanical regularity of the puns and the broad obviousness of much of the humour, while to a modern eye the drawings seem both unsophisticated in subject and often crude in technique. Yet, taken in small doses, preferably in the volumes in which they were first published, it is surprising how amusing Hood's poems can be, how many pleasing discoveries await the reader and how the admiration grows for the adeptness of his technique, his resourcefulness, and prodigality of ideas. There is a genuine poetic personality here, one that is closer to the real human being than most poetic personalities are, for there was nothing disingenuous about Hood's work; it was the unconditioned projection of his moods. Quite often one can see clear traces of the pressure of having to be a 'funny man', comic matter forced out against the mood of the moment, but this is much rarer than one would suppose after reading the laments of those critics who are convinced that in Hood there was a major poet frustrated by the exigencies of earning a living.

What kind of poetry is his serious work? Given the conditions of the time and his own debilitation and temperament, it is not surprising that even his best lyrics have a touch of drabness and greyness. They are all in the minor key; there is no Elizabethan energy or Romantic verve; they have none of the freshness of Tom Moore's songs, nor the exquisite art of Tennyson's. His poems of this type, in fact, remind us rather of the poems of the Georgians in the kind of restraint that prompted Roy Campbell's 'But where's the bloody horse?' And yet, they have a true delicacy of feeling, which is something more than absence of passion, an insinuating melancholy and a brooding tenderness which cannot be lightly disdained. Their positive virtues are an economy and directness of statement. A characteristic and, within its limits, successful poem of this restrained kind is 'Ruth':

> She stood breast high amid the corn,
> Clasp'd by the golden light of morn,
> Like the sweetheart of the sun,
> Who many a glowing kiss has won.

On her cheek an autumn flush
Deeply ripened;—such a blush
In the midst of brown was born
Like red poppies sown with corn.

Round her eyes her tresses fell,
Which were blackest none could tell,
But long lashes veil'd a light,
That had else been all too bright.

And her hat, with shady brim,
Made her tressy forehead dim;—
Thus she stood amid the stooks,
Praising God with sweetest looks:—

Sure, I said, heav'n did not mean,
Where I reap thou shouldst but glean,
Lay thy sheaf adown and come,
Share my harvest and my home.

Although the absence of imagery makes some of Hood's
poems unexciting, again and again one's attention is elsewhere
caught by touches of poetic magic, as in the final lines of 'The
Sea of Death':

and with them Time
Slept, as he sleeps upon the silent face
Of a dark dial in a sunless place.

Or we are jolted by a cry of personal pain in the midst of a
generalized poetic statement, as in the lines from 'To Hope':

Another life-spring there adorns
Another youth—without the dread
Of cruel care, whose crown of thorns
Is here for manhood's aching head—

Still, this is not the centre of Hood. Most of the poems of the
essential Hood have in common a lack of obvious literary
ancestry; they are either poems close to popular forms or poems
with his own particular blend of the comic, the grotesque, the
fearful and the serious. As he moved away from the world of

earlier poets to the world of popular forms, of street-songs, of popular ballads, hymns, broadsheet stories, comic jingles and music-hall songs, he found the medium that most suited his particular talents. The broadsheet ballads formed the springboard for his delightful comic ballads. 'Faithless Nelly Gray', 'Faithless Sally Brown', 'The Poacher', 'John Jones', 'John Trot', 'Pompey's Ghost', and the rest, and for grim poems like 'Eugene Aram'. From the hymn and the nursery rhyme, he took the devices of repetition that give extra power to 'The Song of the Shirt' and 'The Bridge of Sighs'. The popular form of parody, as used in the music-halls, he turned to good use in parodying Coleridge in 'The Sea-Spell', Gray in 'Ode on a Distant Prospect of Clapham Academy', Moore in 'The Stag-Eyed Lady', Shenstone in 'The Irish Schoolmaster', Cowper in 'The Epping Hunt', Dryden in 'Ode for St. Cecilia's Eve' and so on. His skilful use of topicalities, too, is a popular form of expression. It is significant that Jonathan Blewitt's musical versions of his comic ballads became successful music-hall songs.

Just as typical is his brilliant exploitation of the macabre and the hauntingly horrible, as in 'The Haunted House', which seems to have no literary ancestry, save a vague relationship to the Gothic tradition, and in 'The Last Man'. When this mood is fused with his sense of the oddly comic, as in 'Miss Kilmansegg', the result is a flavour in poetry hard to match, a blend of the ghastly and grimly comic that is kept from gloomy indulgence by the sheer dexterity with which the subject is handled. This is a strange form of artistic distancing, indeed, wherein the poet finds that the humorous form is the most suitable one in which to express his fears and torments, in which his criticism of life reaches its finest expression. In these grotesque poems, with a savage raillery that sometimes reminds us of medieval depictions of the Dance of Death, a compound is created from disparate elements. Poe found Hood's 'marked originality' to lie in a '*glowing* grotesquerie, uttered with a rushing *abandon* vastly heightening its effect'. And he added: 'The field in which Hood is *distinctive* is a borderland between Fancy and Fantasy. In this region he reigns supreme. Nevertheless, he has made successful and frequent excursions, although vacillatingly, into the domain of the true Imagination. I mean to say that he is never truly or purely imaginative for more than a paragraph at a time. In a word his peculiar genius was the result of vivid *Fancy* impelled by Hypochondriasis.' This is much more accurate as a description of Poe's own poetry than of Hood's, but it has a measure of truth in it.

It is when Hood uses his jauntily comic technique on a serious subject that he is most individual and often through his seeming flippancy succeeds in conveying serious truth. 'Miss Kilmansegg' is the supreme example of this type, but the 'Ode to Rae Wilson', 'The Open Question', the 'Ode to Sir Andrew Agnew, Bart.', 'Death in the Kitchen', 'Jack Hall' (a typical Hood pun on 'jackal'), 'A Friendly Address to Mrs. Fry', 'Moral Reflections on the Cross of St. Paul's', 'A Charity Sermon', and 'A Tale of a Trumpet', in varying degrees mingle the ironical, the comic and the satirical with a serious purpose, which may be a comment on contemporary social conditions or more searching assessments of the moral character of the times. The very freakishness of the anecdote, the wit of the comment, and the resourcefulness of the detail make these poems as telling in their way as the humanitarian pieces and certainly more potent than most of the serious social verse produced later in the century.

One persistent theme in Hood's poetry is the contrast between appearance and reality. This is a familiar subject for poetry, but with Hood it bulks exceptionally large. For one thing, so much humour is based upon incongruity; for another, Hood's own death-in-life makes him particularly aware of the decay that lurks just beneath the beauty of efflorescence and of the death's head behind the fairest face. Many of his comic effects proceed from this sort of contrast, for instance, in well-known pieces like 'Domestic Asides' and 'A parental Ode to My Son':

> Thou happy, happy elf!
> (But stop—first let me kiss away that tear)—
> Thou tiny image of myself!
> (My love, he's poking peas into his ear!)
> Thou merry, laughing sprite!
> With spirits feather-light,
> Untouch'd by sorrow and unsoil'd by sin—
> (Good heavens! the child is swallowing a pin!)

or in those anti-climactic poems like 'The Demon-Ship' and

'The Desert-Born', which, in the final line, destroy the illusion built up in the poem itself. There is, too, that other type of contrast, in 'Our Village—by a Villager', with its disenchanted picture of a 'loveliest village of the plain', and, since Hood used most subjects at least twice—'Rural Felicity', in which a townsman finds how unlike the idyllic scenes of popular imagination the country really is, and the calculated incongruities of poems like 'The Stag-Eyed Lady', with its Arabian Nights conventions mocked by puns and topicalities.

The place of dreams in Hood's poetry is relevant here, also, as it is relevant to his essential duality as a person and to the whole twilight world of Victorian sensibility. The confusion in the dream between what is and what seems, and the ambiguity of the dream world were special poetic concerns of Hood, and another of his ways of pin-pointing the difference between illusion and reality. Not only in 'The Dream of Eugene Aram' and 'The Haunted House' does the dream serve to blur the frontiers between life and nightmare, but in different ways in 'Bianca's Dream', 'The Desert-Born', 'Napoleon's Midnight Review', 'The Lady's Dream', 'The Elm Tree' (subtitled 'a Dream in the Woods') and other poems, the ambivalence of the dream is exploited. Sometimes the whole thing is a sleep-induced vision from which the sleeper wakes with new knowledge:

> She clasp'd her fervent hands,
>   And the tears began to stream;
> Large, and bitter, and fast they fell,
>   Remorse was so extreme.

But sometimes there is no difference between the nightmare and the reality:

> Seam, and gusset, and band,
>   Band, and gusset, and seam;
> Till over the buttons I fall asleep,
>   And sew them on in a dream.

Hood uses this duality in various ways. He is not a great ironist, but he can employ irony rewardingly at times, as in 'The Pauper's Christmas Carol', with its sardonic treatment of the popular saying, 'Christmas comes but once a year', as a refrain; in

> It was a childish ignorance,
> But now 'tis little joy
> To know I'm farther off from Heav'n
> Than when I was a boy . . . ;

in 'The Workhouse Clock'

> Hungry—passing the Street of Bread;
> Thirsty—the street of Milk;
> Ragged—beside the Ludgart Mart;

in 'A woman sate in unwomanly rags'; in 'But what is your opinion, Mrs. Grundy?'; in the whole argument of 'Miss Kilmansegg'. In the recurrence of the notion of doubleness in his verse, the 'double thread' that runs through it and is illustrated most fully by the remarkable passage on 'doubles' in 'Miss Kilmansegg', we can see another representation of his sense of bifurcation.

Hood's life and his practice show a consistent pattern. A jester who was always ill, a public comedian loaded with debts and anxieties, a man of poetic talent living in an age that scarcely valued poetry, a writer almost evenly divided between melancholy, pathos, farce and fun, and who was both true poet and versifying journalist, a practical-joking, pensive, laughing, worrying man, filled with Jacques's 'most humorous sadness', at the heart of his personality lies duality. And this is expressed not only in the ways we have mentioned, but in his puns as well.

I have left the discussion of his puns to this stage largely because the pun is the first thing many people think of in connection with him. He is regarded not only as the supreme punster, but also as the writer who used the pun so often and so daringly as to spoil the form for almost everyone else. Hood's gifts as a punster have been illustrated often enough in these pages. Some readers of his poems, while admitting the ingenuity of his verbal play, complain that his punning quickly tires, as pun after pun explodes like a string of fire-crackers, and the joy in the unexpected gives place to satiety. In a sense this is true, especially in his more mechanically turned poems; yet, in pieces like 'Spring', 'The Epping Hunt', and 'The Angler's

Farewell' and many others, the initial delight at the suddenness of the pun is followed by admiration at the brilliance of the infallibly recurring play upon words. Nor is it puns alone that make Hood's work entertaining; he is a genuinely funny writer, full of bizarre jokes, comic situations and themes, amusing ideas and characters and happy energy. The puns enhance the fun, they do not create it.

However, Hood's adeptness at punning has deeper implications. For one thing, it shows in his use of language a doubleness which is part of his outlook on life. For another, it reveals an awareness of the flexibility and ambiguities of language considerably beyond that of most serious poets of his time, and closer to the operations of the metaphorical process than they were able to come. Hood's sensitivity to semantic possibilities, his ability to see bizarre verbal connections, his command over the playful innuendo, the curious fancy and the grotesque quibble—these are all attributes of a poet. Nobody who could pun so often and as ingeniously as Hood can be denied the name of poet.

Yet it is true that, while the poetic image fuses disparate experiences to create a new one, and that poetic sensibility operates on several levels at once, Hood's word play is often sub-poetic, since it draws attention to its own cleverness and hence thrusts its meanings into the background. It is seldom that Hood's puns do not reveal some old, unexpected relationship between ideas; yet the very nature of his punning in his particular kind of context means that the response produced is more like the effect of the wise-crack than of the image, and seems a feat of legerdemain designed to distract our attention from the implications of words. It is almost as if Hood is exploiting one aspect of language, verbal resemblance, in a kind of game to prevent himself exploring the emotional and intellectual significances of words. Sometimes, in fact, this is what he did. I have no doubt, either, that a predominance of 'not quite imagery' in his verse is what makes many under-rate his achievement.

Yet punning, as Hood most often practised it, was an aspect, if a minor aspect, of poetry. Unlike most punsters, who see nothing more in the pun than verbal coincidence, he used word-play as a vehicle for his pathos, his fancy, his social conscience.

The Man and the Poet

On many occasions, when he was dealing with something that moved him deeply, he used the pun as naturally as other poets use an image, as naturally and unself-consciously, in fact, as Shakespeare did in the tragedies. When he does this, with confidence in its illuminating power, the pun does not focus attention on itself; it is so manifestly a vehicle for feeling imaginatively realized that it moves into the realm of genuine poetic expression, as with his use of 'twit' in 'The Song of the Shirt'. Not surprisingly with Hood, such transformations and use of double meanings often happen when he is writing of death:

> Like the sweet blossoms of the May
> Whose fragrance ends in must.
>> ('Ode to Melancholy')

> Then what is Man's Estate? Alas!
> Six feet by two of mould and grass
> > When I am dust and bone.
> > > ('Stanzas on Coming of Age')

> Cook, butler, Susan, Jonathan,
> The girl that scours the pot and pan,
> > And those that tend the steeds—
> All, all shall have another sort
> Of service after this—in short—
> > The one the parson reads!
> > > ('Death in the Kitchen')

Again and again, the unemphasized, unitalicized pun or verbal quibble lights up his verses with delicate touches of intellectual alertness:

> While half the young—ay, more than half—
> Bow'd down and worshipp'd the Golden Calf,
> > Like the Jews when their hearts were harden'd.
> > > ('Miss Kilmansegg and her Precious Leg')

> A hoop was an eternal round
> Of pleasure. In those days I found
> > A top a joyous thing:—
> But now those past delights I drop,
> My head, alas! is all my top,
> > And careful thoughts the string.
> > > ('A Retrospective Review')

252

The broad distinction in a line to draw,
As means to lead us to the skies above,
You say—Sir Andrew and his love of law,
And I—the Saviour with his law of love.
('Ode to Rae Wilson, Esq.')

What could be more apt, for cleverness and intellectual force, than the lines from his 'Ode to Sir Andrew Agnew, Bart.', sponsor of a narrow Sabbatarian Bill:

Go down to Margate, wisest of law-makers,
And say unto the sea, as Canute did,
(Of course, the sea will do as it is bid)
'This is the Sabbath—let there be no Breakers!'?

The pun illuminates, too, with its own whimsicality such poems as 'The Assistant Drapers' Petition', in which he treats with a not unserious lightness of touch the petition of the overworked assistants for a few weekly hours of leisure:

O come then, gentle ladies, come in time,
O'erwhelm our counters, and unload our shelves;
Torment us all until the seventh chime,
But let us have the remnant to ourselves.

Though we may lament that Hood was forced to use this gift too often in trivial ways and was prevented from pressing his verbal sensibility up to the stage of full metaphorical realization, at least we can acknowledge the existence of this power in him and its successful operation in his best poems.

One other aspect of his genius calls for comment—his metrical skill, which was hardly inferior to his punning ability. In his serious poems, especially, Hood's metres are mainly conventional ones; he works almost always in orthodox textures. And yet, within these limits, he employs a wide range of metres and forms, all with an easy mastery, a tremendous capacity for rhyming and a lively interest in light-hearted experiment. There seems to have been no stanza-form that Hood favoured above another; the ballad quatrain occurs several times in his comic ballads, but the forms he used range from the Skeltonics of 'A Public Dinner' and 'She is Far from the Land', to the sprawling lines of 'Lycus the Centaur' and 'The Desert-Born' and the comically interminable measure of 'Our Village' and 'The Sweep's Complaint', with, in between, almost every form one could imagine, including that of the irregular ode, the sonnet and the Elizabethan song. With an almost insolent assurance, he seems at home with every form, and always able to find one fitted to his subject.

To some extent he was forced into this diversity by the need to provide his public with plenty of variety in periodicals crammed with his own work. But there was a gleeful exercise of his powers and an exuberant outflowing of his metrical ingenuity in such experiments as these, usually prefaced by a burlesque apologia—his 'Nocturnal Sketch', a method of 'writing blank verse in rhyme':

> Even is come; and from the dark Park, hark,
> The signal of the setting sun—one gun!
> And six is sounding from the chime, prime time
> To go and see the Drury-Lane Dane slain—
> Or hear Othello's jealous doubt spout out—
> Or Macbeth raving at that shade-made blade . . .

his 'Double Knock', with the rhymes at the beginning instead of the end of the line:

> Rat-tat it went upon the lion's chin.
> 'That hat, I know it!' cried the joyful girl:
> 'Summer's it is. I know him by his knock,
> Comers like him are welcome as the day! . . .'

and his 'First Attempts in Rhyme', in which each couplet has the identical word for rhyme:

> If I were used to writing verse
> And had a Muse not so perverse,
> But prompt at Fancy's call to spring
> And carol like a bird in Spring;
> Or like a Bee, in summer time,
> That hums about a bed of thyme. . . .

No other author of his generation brought to poetry a better technical equipment, more resource and more dash. If the results were often trivial, sometimes flat, sometimes ephemeral, more often than not Hood made full and happy use of his considerable skills.

It is not surprising that an author as popular should have had a considerable influence on the literature of the age after his death. His reputation at the time he died and immediately afterwards stood very high. The opinions of Dickens, 'Barry Cornwall', Allan Cunningham, Poe and others have been quoted already. Browning wrote to Alfred Domett on February 23, 1845, 'I occasionally do something for poor Hood who is dying fast, and shall have some poetry in his next magazine. Do you ever see it? His own contributions are admirable—I mean his verses. One, Waterloo Bridge ["The Bridge of Sighs"] is alone in its generation, I think; and the "Haunted House" of Number 1 was of admirable power.' Ruskin admired Hood's use of his gifts for moral improvement, and especially liked 'Miss Kilmansegg'. Miss Mitford, we learn from a letter of Elizabeth Barrett's, thought Hood 'the greatest poet of the age'.

With the public at large, his posthumous popularity was even greater than in his lifetime, and continued at a high pitch for over half a century. Edition after edition of his poems appeared, the first being his friend Moxon's *Poems by Thomas Hood* (1846) 'made in fulfilment of his own desire', as the preface says, and *Poems of Wit and Humour* (1847). These, and the two volumes of his verse edited by William Michael Rossetti, other editions and innumerable 'Selections', books of his 'Humorous Verse' and 'Serious Verse' continued to be issued up to the beginning of this century, culminating in Walter Jerrold's excellent Complete Poetical Works for the Oxford University Press in 1906. Editions, too, of the *Whims and Oddities*, of the *Whimsicalities*, and other works, kept pace with these, while Hood's children set the seal on his reputation with their full edition of his *Works* in eleven volumes between 1882 and 1884. In this way, Hood remained one of the most widely read of writers during the age of Victoria. And that he continued to be held in high critical esteem can be seen from W. E. Henley's comment in his essay on Hood, printed in his *Views and Reviews* (1890), 'Hood was a true poet . . . it is not too much to say of them ["The Song of the Shirt" and "The Bridge of Sighs"] that they will only pass with the language', and Saintsbury's saying in the same year: 'Hood had the advantage of Praed in purely serious poetry; for Araminta's bard never did anything approaching "The Plea of the Midsummer Fairies", "The Haunted House" and a score of other things. He had also the advantage in pure broad humour.'

During this half century and more, Hood was one of the most influential of popular poets. Much of his appeal came, obviously, from the fact that, like Dickens, his particular brand of sentiment accorded with that of the age. The pathos of his domestic poems, the humanitarian feeling of his social ones, the upholding in his serious poems of the gentler middle-class virtues, the absence from his poetry of tumultuous passion or harsh political sentiments, the sense of humour that prevented his poems from toppling over into maudlin sentimentality—all of these help to explain his status with Victorian readers. His life, too, fitted in so well with the ideals of the Victorian middle-class. Here was no wild promiscuous Romantic, no popular novelist publicly explaining his separation from his wife, but a respectable husband and father, a man of social conscience with a Christian sensibility not too tied to dogma, and a hard-working writer. To many Victorians, Hood seemed to offer, both in his life and his writings, a kind of ideal writer, whom it was only too easy to sentimentalize, and whose poems, with a little strain, could be made to provide a moral structure satisfying for the ordinary man.

The ability he had to poeticize the average emotions of the ordinary man called, of course, for a skill beyond the reach of the ordinary man. This is where Hood's emotional quality stood him in good stead. Spontaneously reacting to circumstance, at times with something like automatic writing, he projected personal feelings and instincts typical of those of his middle-class audience. It was his accomplishment to maintain a nice balance between this high averageness of feeling and his grotesque fancy, between the commonplace and the poetic; he had the knack of maintaining the decencies while at the same time bringing a witty liberalism to bear on cant and Phariseeism; and his ability to extract a gently satirical fun from the matter-of-fact was a particularly endearing quality. In addition, his propriety in sexual matters made him approved family reading, and his obviously genuine humanitarian sympathies were endorsed by the strong reformist instincts of the age.

These qualities and others left clear impressions on not only popular literature, but also on writers at a higher level. Hood was the first poet to recognize the high originality of Keats by imitating him. We have seen that, in most of the pieces written under Keats's influence, the tone and treatment express Hood's more ordinary temperament, for he neither possessed nor probably fully appreciated the sensuous intensity of his master. But he did respond generously to Keats's special vision, and helped to create a climate in which this could be appreciated. In Hood's early serious poems, Keats's passion is muted to a gentle aestheticism. At its best, in 'Ode: Autumn' and 'The Two Swans', the tone strongly resembles that of Tennyson, especially in such passages as these, from the latter poem:

> And bright and silvery the willows sleep
> Over the shady verge—no mad winds tease
> Their hoary heads; but quietly they weep
> Their sprinkling leaves—half fountains and half trees;
> There lilies be—and fairer than all these
> A solitary Swan her breast of snow
> Launches against the wave that seems to freeze
> Into a chaste reflection, still below,
> Twin-shadow of herself wherever she may go.

Such poems, indeed, may have influenced Tennyson to some degree, for he knew Hood's work. In any case, Hood's adaptation of Keats's style at a time when the Romantic was little recognized outside of a small circle, was not only the first, giving a lead to other poets, but also indicated the particular type of adaptation of Keats the Victorians were to favour.

Hood, too, was an important channel by which several of the Gothic elements in the later eighteenth century passed over into Victorian writing. The sense of lurking horror is one of his pervasive qualities. His talent for the macabre is seen in such poems as 'The Haunted House' and 'Lycus the Centaur'; others, like 'The Last Man' and 'The Dream of Eugene Aram', show a puzzled awareness of evil and the brooding menace of a hallucination or a drugged dream. It is not surprising that Poe admired Hood so much, that he closely imitated Hood's sonnet 'Silence' in his own poem of the same name, and that he wrote 'The Haunted Palace' to match Hood's 'The Haunted House', of which, however, it falls short. Such elements, a recognized part of Victorian writing, together with others in

Hood, affected some of the Pre-Raphaelites later in the century. The Rossetti family were all admirers of Hood. W. M. Rossetti, in his introduction to his edition of the poems, calls Hood 'the finest English poet between the generation of Shelley and the generation of Tennyson'. D. G. Rossetti had a deep affection for Hood's work, recognized his pioneering work in adapting Keats, and also borrowed from him on occasion. The resemblance between Rossetti's 'My Sister's Sleep' and Hood's 'The Death Bed' has been pointed out more than once, and some of Rossetti's lighter pieces are not very happy attempts to imitate another manner of Hood's. Christina Rossetti, too, was as fond of Hood as she was of Maturin; and in poems like 'My Dream' (of which her brother William Michael said that it illustrated 'the odd freakishness which flecked the extreme and almost excessive seriousness of her thought') shows something of his sensibility. It is also possible that, in her favourite devices of iteration and refrain, she was strongly influenced by Hood's example.

It was as much Hood's subtle use of detail in poems like 'The Haunted House' as his sense of dream and his Keatsian imagination that drew the Rossettis to him. And later in the century, we find Francis Thompson's 'To a Snowflake', echoing, rather incongruously, 'The Bridge of Sighs', while Oscar Wilde's 'The Ballad of Reading Gaol', as Lord Alfred Douglas has pointed out, owes much to 'The Dream of Eugene Aram' in its form and in certain verbal reminiscences.

No poems of Hood's had more influence than 'The Song of the Shirt' and 'The Bridge of Sighs'. With these and such others as 'The Lay of the Labourer', 'A Drop of Gin' and 'The Workhouse Clock' he virtually created the humanitarian poem of social protest, outdoing Ebenezer Elliott and others who preceded him. The oppressed classes and various bodies agitating for reform saw in the poems a stirring statement of their aspirations. Sir John Bowring, in his *Autobiographical Recollections*, makes the interesting claim, which I am unable to find confirmed elsewhere, that 'the anti-Corn Law League was desirous of making him their poet-laureate by engaging him in their service, and I invited Cobden, John Bright and some others of the leaders of that formidable body to meet Hood at my table, but his death put an end to any such arrangement'. Whether or not Bowring, in his recollections in dimmed old age, mistook an aspiration for the deed, the fact that he could make such an assertion indicates the stir Hood's humanitarian verses aroused.

Certainly his poems of this kind became symbols of nineteenth-century humanitarianism and inspired a whole flock o writers on similar subjects—Ernest Jones, J. C. Prince, Ebenezer Jones, Gerald Massey, Capell Loft and the Chartist poets— and Elizabeth Barrett Browning's 'The Cry of the Children'. Poems like Ernest Jones's 'The Factory Town' of 1855 clearly derive from 'The Song of the Shirt':

> Women, children, men were toiling
> Locked in dungeons close and dark,
> Life's fast-failing thread uncoiling
> Round the wheel, the modern rack . . .

and Gerald Massey summed up the debt he and his fellows owed to Hood in his long poem to the author of 'The Song of the Shirt' which begins:

> O! blessings on him for the songs he sang—
> Which yearned about the world till then for birth!

If for nothing else, this capturing and making articulate early in the century of the spirit of humanitarian compassion would make Hood a significant influence in his age.

He left, too, an immense comic legacy. Much of his light verse and prose has faded with the passing of ephemeral fashions in humour, but his nimble inventiveness, his sense of the absurd, his delight in deflating the pompous and the immediate intelligibility of his humour were of great importance in establishing the typical mode of Victorian middle-class humour, a type neither as elegant as Praed's nor as knockabout as Hook's. Whatever Hood owed to the broadsheet ballads and to the light verse of Southey, he created a distinctive comic verse of his own—light-footed, whimsical and funny. The success of the comic ballads did more than anything else to make the pun so distinctive a form of Victorian humour, although few of his successors could match his agility. Even today, poems like William Plomer's ballads and Louis MacNeice's 'Bagpipe Music' recognizably belong to the tradition that Hood began.

We have seen that, unlike most Victorian melancholy, Hood's

was personal and not endemic, and that hardly one of his comic poems does not use a fundamentally painful subject, or deal with death, decay, mutilation, ghosts, deserted maidens, drownings and so on. These were to become almost the stock themes of Victorian humour—in Gilbert, Barham, à Beckett, Thackeray, Aytoun and Martin and others. These subjects, while not originating with Hood, were popularized by him. His combination of the macabre and the outrageously comic—an early form, surely, of 'comédie noire'—helped to set the tone for such later collections as the *Ingoldsby Legends* (1844), the *Bon Gaultier Ballads* (1844) and the *Bab Ballads* (1869).

In Hood, also, we find the origin of many still vigorous comic metres, of which he was a prolific inventor. In this respect and others, W. S. Gilbert owes him a handsome debt. The *Bab Ballads* and his early burlettas show Gilbert using metres invented or perfected by Hood, and puns quite as daring as Hood's own, as in his 1866 burlesque of *Ruy Blas*, *The Blasé Roué*:

> Unhappy Queen, unhappy maiden I,
> In vain to get a wink of sleep I try,
> But wander, dressing-gowny and night-cappy;
> I seldom get a nap—I'm so unnappy.

The sprawling metre Hood used in 'Our Village' and 'The Sweep's Complaint' reappears in the *Bab Ballads* in 'Lost Mr. Blake', for instance, and has formed the staple metre in our own day for Mr. Ogden Nash. I feel sure, too, that the inspiration for Gilbert's well-known lines in *The Mikado*:

> To sit in solemn silence in a dull, dark dock,
> In a pestilential prison with a life-long lock . . .

can be found in Hood's 'A Nocturnal Sketch', quoted above, just as 'It were profanity' from *Princess Ida* is most oddly reminiscent of 'The Bridge of Sighs'. A whole army of humorists from James Russell Lowell in *The Biglow Papers* to those of modern times are indebted to Hood, and it is interesting to find how much of his writing anticipates that of modern comic journals—(the comic correspondence familiar from *Punch*, for instance, has forerunners in Hood's 'The Corresponding Club', 'The Earth-Quakers' and others), to discover that James Thurber's *The Pet Department* is anticipated by Hood's 'Queries in Natural History' giving dead-pan replies to such questions as 'Are Fish Deaf as Well as Dumb?', while such drawings as Thurber's 'Touché!', showing a duellist slicing off his opponent's head, have the same quality as many of Hood's.

In his enterprise, the *Comic Annual*, we have the earliest of the many comic journals of the century. The Annual and its successor, *Hood's Own*, inspired such publications as Louisa Sheridan's *Comic Offering*, W. Harrison's *The Humourist*, Gilbert à Beckett's *Comic Magazine*, George Cruikshank's *Comic Annual*, to name a few. Out of these emerged *Punch*, the sole modern survivor, and *Fun*, which Tom Hood edited. As we pass from the wit of the eighteenth century, and the farce, knockabout and laboured topicalities of the turn of the century to the comic writings of Hood with their ebullient fancy, rich abundance of jests, warm whimsicality and domestic fun, we recognize that, despite the dull patches, we have arrived at something distinct and individual, which is, in fact, the prototype of the bulk of Victorian humour.

In a fundamental way, Hood made his contribution to modernizing English poetry. His use of popular material from the music-hall, from the comic papers, broadsheets and spoken anecdotes drew him closer and closer to a non-literary vocabulary and, perhaps more importantly, to the rhythms of contemporary speech. In this respect, Hood continues, in his own way, the revolution begun by Wordsworth and directed towards freeing poetry from the earlier conventions of formal vocabulary and rhythms. In poems like 'A Singular Exhibition at Somerset House' and 'The Sweep's Complaint', we catch the exact cadences of Cockney speech rendered as nobody had done so before in verse, and the plain, unrhetorical language of the people, while, of course, in other poems, the Comic Odes, for instance, he could exploit elaborate mock-metaphysical metaphors for humorous effect. There was, too, as an influence on Victorian poetic vocabulary, Hood's careful simplicity, akin to that of Wordsworth, in his pathetic poems.

It is possible that, had he lived, Hood might have pushed his style considerably further in these directions. As it is, his original work acted as a solvent on the lingering remains of eighteenth-century modes, while his parodies of Romantic solemnities carried the process on in another direction. I believe that Mr. J. M. Cohen[1] is right in suggesting that Browning took over from Hood and incidentally passed on to Ezra Pound and so to our own day rhythms half-way between the spoken and the dramatic, as well as the inspiration and the form for such poems as 'The Pied Piper of Hamelin', and that his practice did much to free Browning from conventional forms. Mr. Cohen's comparison between Hood's effect on some major poets of Victorian times and that of Jules Laforgue on those of our own time is especially apt. Long before Hopkins, Auden and MacNeice responded to the lively rhythms of the nursery-rhyme, the popular song and the music-hall comedian's patter, Hood pointed the direction. Yet he still waits to receive credit for his substantial contribution towards changing the emphasis in the English poetry of the past century.

His influence was not limited to his own country. The American writers who created the native poetry of placid sentiment, domestic tranquillity and whimsical fun—Longfellow, Whittier, Lowell and Holmes—knew Hood's work and studied it at formative stages in their own career. The Germans, too, found Hood to their liking; as we have seen, 'The Dream of Eugene Aram' and *Up the Rhine* became well known in Germany during his lifetime. Ferdinand Freiligrath translated several of the poems into German, including 'The Song of the Shirt', 'The Bridge of Sighs', and, unexpectedly, 'A Paternal Ode', and included no fewer than fifteen of Hood's poems in *The Rose, Thistle and Shamrock*, his collection of English poetry issued in Germany in 1853. Two aspects of Hood appealed especially to the ordinary German reader—his domestic sentiment and his humour. But more serious ones were stirred by the humanitarian ardour of 'The Song of the Shirt' and its companion pieces, and these played no small part in the development of the German school of social protest poetry in the nineteenth century. Even Goethe himself did not disdain Hood; in a discussion of *Whims and Oddities* in 1827, he warmly praised Hood's fantastic imagination, his human warmth and his descriptions of the sea.

Hood's popularity in Russia and the Soviet Union has been even greater than in Germany—chiefly, as one might expect, by virtue of the humanitarian poems, which incarnated the nineteenth-century Russian's sense of exploitation and wish for

[1] *Robert Browning*, Longmans, Green and Co., 1952.

262

a better life, but not exclusively. The first biographical sketch of Hood in Russian was published soon after his death—in the *Literaturnaya Gazetta* in 1848. The first of his poems to be translated was 'The Song of the Shirt', rendered by the revolutionist and poet, Mikhail Mikhaylov (1829–65) and published in the well-known democratic journal *Sovremennik* in 1860; this is still regarded in Russia as the best of the many translations of this poem. Mikhaylov, in fact, did much to make Hood known to his fellow-countrymen; he translated several other poems, including 'The Death Bed'; his essay, 'Humour and Poetry in England: Thomas Hood', in *Sovremennik* in 1861 was one of the first critical appraisals to appear in the country; and, when he came to London to have some revolutionary pamphlets printed there, he met Tom Hood, who later wrote to Mikhaylov to thank him for 'making me acquainted with a still further spread of my father's fame'.[1]

At least eight different translations of 'The Song of the Shirt' have been made into Russian, from Mikhaylov's to that of the Soviet poet, E. Bagritsky, in 1923; it remains his most popular poem in Russia, still learnt in school by many children. Well over twenty poems of Hood have been translated, some several times, including 'The Bridge of Sighs' (four different versions); 'The Lay of the Labourer' (three); 'The Death Bed' (three); 'The Dream of Eugene Aram' (two); 'The Lady's Dream' (two); and 'The Workhouse Clock'. His poems were so popular with broad democratic Russian circles in the nineteenth century that N. G. Chernyshevsky used the second part of 'Farewell, Life', in Mikhaylov's translation, at the end of his famous novel, *What is to Be Done?* (1863), and Moussorgsky composed his 'Seamstress', a work for piano, on the basis of 'The Song of the Shirt' in Mikhaylov's version.

Russian interest in Hood has continued into this century; in 1901, a volume of Russian translations of his poems with a biographical essay was published in Moscow. There have been several subsequent essays on Hood's work, notably the section devoted to it in F. P. Schiller's *Essays on Chartist Poetry* (1933)

[1] In a Soviet collection, *Unpublished Letters of the Foreign Writers of the 18th–19th Centuries From Leningrad State Archives*, edited by M. P. Alexeyev (1960), two letters from Tom Hood to Mikhaylov were published for the first time, in English and Russian translation.

and the *History of English Literature* edited by the Soviet Institute of World Literature in 1955. While Hood has not become a kind of folk-poet with the Russian people in general, he has become one of the most familiar of English poets to Russian readers and has played his part as one of the inspirers of democratic intellectuals in the nineteenth century.

In England, Hood's influence lasted until at least the first decade of this century; his work helped to shape the characteristic music-hall song of the last century and the comic and sentimental recitations of those popular entertainers who flourished up to the threshold of the First World War. Kipling was probably the last major poet in the line of Hood. The new poetry of the last forty years or so has outmoded Hood's styles, at least in academic circles. Yet he remains an anthology poet; some half-dozen of his pieces are known to almost every English-speaking person; on the popular level, his brand of sentiment and humour is far from dead, and more sophisticated types have not extinguished its appeal. But what of his status as a writer?

Granted, if anything, two or three lines in recent histories of English literature, Hood no longer enjoys that reputation he held in his own day as a sturdy moralist, poet of the heart and humorist. Yet it is hard to understand why, unless it be a temporary result of fashion, his highly original vision is overlooked, why poems of such fine originality as 'Miss Kilmansegg and her Precious Leg', 'The Haunted House' and 'Death in the Kitchen', for instance, are so little known, and why he should be so stubbornly regarded as primarily a punster. By comparison with Tennyson and Browning, for instance, he is obviously an inferior poet, much of whose work exists merely on the sub-literary level. His faults are plain enough—much laboured work produced under the pressure of financial need, much pleasant enough verse with little pressure behind it, faults of taste that mar even some of the better poems, mechanical punning, a rather commonplace mind, and so on.

Yet his positive merits as a singer of the people, an entertainer and a poet of minor, but real, capacity, seem to have been largely forgotten. I am making no large claims for Hood as a neglected genius; but I feel that he has much still to offer to this age, and later ones. His versatility, his deep feeling and his intriguingly freakish vision can hardly be denied; and, in the somewhat feverish and febrile character of his poetic outlook, in his anxieties, in his revelation of the haunted corners of the mind, in his ultimate optimism and good sense, in his combination of commonplace detail and bizarre innerness, he is especially fitted to appeal to readers of the mid-twentieth century. A poet who found his own voice in an age indifferent to original expression, a transition poet who both mirrored the transitional values of his age and transcended them, and a writer who, by the mysterious intuition of genius, sensed the values of the age to come, Hood merits our serious regard and a somewhat higher place in the literary hierarchy than he occupies today, almost 120 years after his death.

If we cannot accord him that higher place, if we refuse to recognize the shaping force of his talent, if we are reluctant to sift his work for the surprises and excitements it can give, at least we can pay tribute to his dignifying of the mundane burdens of existence by his unfailingly optimistic and valorous struggle against the hosts of disease, debt and misfortune. Hood may more appropriately have said than Oscar Wilde: 'I have put my genius into my life: I have put only my talent into my works.' His common sense, industry and faith afford us a rare example of moral courage, earning our high respect, if not our love.

A Note on Sources

THE *Memorials of Thomas Hood* by his children, first published in two volumes in 1860 and in a revised form as Volume X of the *Collected Works* (1869–73), are inaccurate in detail, full of gaps and with letters condensed or imperfectly transcribed. Yet they remain the only authority for many facts of Hood's life and for the text of letters since lost. Alexander Elliot's *Hood in Scotland* adds new facts about the Scottish periods and prints valuable new letters. Walter Jerrold's admirably systematic and exhaustive biography, *Thomas Hood: His Life and Times*, also gives the text of other letters, frequently in full. The two most important recent gatherings of Hood letters are found in Leslie A. Marchand's *Letters of Thomas Hood from the Dilke Papers in the British Museum* (16 new letters) and Alvin Whitley's 'Hood and Dickens: Some New Letters' (*Huntingdon University Quarterly*), giving the complete text for the first time of 20 interesting letters from Hood to Dickens. Other letters to and from Hood are to be found in the biographies and memoirs of his contemporaries. I have drawn upon all these sources for the facts and the quotations from letters in this book; I have, too, made considered use of Hood's own 'Literary Reminiscences', which, although calculatedly distorted and often factually inaccurate, give colourful accounts of several real happenings.

A considerable number of Hood's letters, many of them in the United States, remain unpublished. The chief collections in Britain which I have seen, among which are several unpublished or published in part only, are in the Bodleian Library, Oxford, the British Museum Library, the Bristol University Library, the Bristol Public Library, and the Scottish National Library, Edinburgh. Of special interest among these are the letters from John Wright, in the Bristol Public Library, and from De Franck in the Bristol University Library.

In addition, I have found among the Peel papers in the

British Museum, several important letters between Lord Francis Egerton and others and Peel concerning the application for a pension for Hood, as well as the application itself and Dr. Elliot's medical certificate, and letters exchanged between Jane Hood and Peel which throw fresh light upon Hood's financial position at the end of his life. Three unpublished letters from Dickens to the Hoods, in the possession of the editors of the forthcoming Pilgrim Edition of Dickens's letters, have also been drawn upon.

In the notes, I have given references only to those letters which are unpublished or those from which I have quoted an unpublished part. All other letters quoted from will be found in one or other of the sources mentioned above.

Select Bibliography

(Throughout, unless otherwise stated, the place of publication is London)

I. WORKS BY THOMAS HOOD

This is a list of Hood's major publications, with a representative selection of posthumous editions. In each case, the date of the first edition only is given.

Odes and Addresses to Great People (with J. H. Reynolds) (Baldwin, Cradock and Joy), 1825.
Whims and Oddities (Relfe), 1826.
National Tales (2 vols.) (Ainsworth), 1827.
The Plea of the Midsummer Fairies, Hero and Leander, Lycus the Centaur, and Other Poems (Longman, Rees, Orme, Brown and Green), 1827.
Whims and Oddities (Second Series) (Tilt), 1827.
The Gem (ed.) (Tilt), 1829.
The Epping Hunt (Tilt), 1829.
Comic Annual, 1830 (Hurst and Chance).
Comic Melodies (Clementi), 1830.
The Dream of Eugene Aram (Tilt), 1831.
Comic Annual, 1831–1834 (Tilt).
Tylney Hall (3 vols.) (Baily), 1834.
Comic Annual, 1835–1839 (Baily).
Hood's Own, 1839 (Baily).
Up the Rhine (Baily), 1840.
Comic Annual, 1842 (Colburn).
Whimsicalities (2 vols.) (Colburn), 1844.
Hood's Monthly Magazine (ed.), 1844–5.
Poems (Moxon), 1846.
The Headlong Career and Woeful Ending of Precocious Piggy. Edited by Mrs. F. F. Broderip and illustrated by Tom Hood, 1859.
Serious Poems, with a preface by Tom Hood (E. Moxon, Son and Co.), 1870.
Complete Works (11 vols.). Edited by Mrs. F. F. Broderip and Tom Hood (E. Moxon, Son and Co.), 1882–4.
Poetical Works (2 vols.), with a critical memoir by W. M. Rossetti (Ward, Lock and Co.), n.d.
Serious Poems (George Routledge and Sons), 1886.
Poetical Works, with Memoir and Notes by John Ashton (Griffith, Farron, Okedin and Welsh), 1891.

Select Bibliography

Humorous Poems, with a preface by Alfred Ainger (Macmillan and Co.), 1903.
Complete Poetical Works. Edited, with notes, by Walter Jerrold (Henry Froude: Oxford University Press), 1906.
Poems. Selected and Introduced by Clifford Dyment (Grey Walls Press), 1948.

II. BOOKS ON HOOD

BRODERIP, F. F., and HOOD, TOM: *Memorials of Thomas Hood* (2 vols.) (E. Moxon, Son and Co.), 1860. 2nd edition, revised, included as Vol. X of *Collected Works*.

ELLIOT, ALEXANDER: *Hood in Scotland* (Dundee: James P. Mathew and Co.), 1885.

JERROLD, WALTER: *Thomas Hood: His Life and Times* (Alston Rivers Ltd.), 1907.

—— *Thomas Hood and Charles Lamb: The Story of a Friendship* (the 'Literary Reminiscences' of Hood, edited with certain additions) (Ernest Benn Ltd.), 1930.

M'ILRATH, J. M.: *Thomas Hood* (A Paper read to the Belfast Literary Society) (Belfast: Dorman and Co.), 1935.

MARCHAND, LESLIE A. (ed.): *Letters of Thomas Hood, from the Dilke Papers in the British Museum* (New Brunswick: Rutgers University Press), 1945.

III. BOOKS CONTAINING ARTICLES ON, OR EXTENDED REFERENCES TO, HOOD

ASHTON, JOHN: *Eighteenth Century Waifs* (Hurst and Blackett), 1887.

BALMANNO, MRS.: *Pen and Pencil* (New York: D. Appleton and Co.), 1858.

BATHO, EDITH C., and DOBRÉE, BONAMY: *The Victorians and After, 1830–1914* (The Cresset Press), 1950.

BAUGH, ALBERT C. (ed.): *A Literary History of England* ('The Nineteenth Century and After' by Samuel C. Chew) (New York: Appleton-Century Crofts Inc.), 1948.

BLUNDEN, EDMUND: 'Hood's Literary Reminiscences', *Votive Tablets* (Cobden-Sanderson), 1931.

COLLINS, JOHN CHURTON: *Studies in Poetry and Criticism* (George Bell and Sons), 1905.

CUNNINGHAM, ALLAN: *Biographical and Critical History of the British Literature of the past Fifty Years* (Paris: Baudry's Foreign Library), 1834.

ELTON, OLIVER: *A Survey of English Literature, 1780–1830* (2 vols.) (Edward Arnold), 1912.

EMPSON, WILLIAM: *Seven Types of Ambiguity* (Chatto and Windus), 1947.

FIELD, JAMES T.: *Princes, Authors and Statesmen of Our Time* (New York: Thomas Y. Crowell and Co.), 1885.

HALL, S. C.: *A Book of Memoirs of Great Men and Women of the Age* (Virtue and Co.), 1871.

HEATH-STUBBS, JOHN: *The Darkling Plain* (Eyre and Spottiswoode), 1950.

HENLEY, W. E.: *Views and Reviews; Essays in Appreciation* (David Nutt), 1890.

HORNE, RICHARD HENGIST: *A New Spirit of the Age* (Oxford University Press), 1907. (First published, 1844.)

HUDSON, WILLIAM HENRY: *A Quiet Corner in a Library* (George Harrap and Co.), 1915.

MORE, PAUL ELMER: *Shelburne Essays: Seventh Series* (New York and London: G. P. Putnam's Sons), 1910.

PATMORE, P. G.: *My Friends and Acquaintance* (3 vols.) (Saunders and Otley), 1854.

POE, EDGAR ALLAN: *Poems and Essays* (J. M. Dent), 1927.

—— *Representative Selections* (American Book Co.), 1935.

PRITCHETT, V. S.: 'Our Half-Hogarth', *The Living Novel* (Chatto and Windus), 1946, pp. 59–65.

REPPLIER, AGNES: *In Pursuit of Laughter* (Boston and New York: Houghton Mifflin Co.), 1936.

ROSSETTI, WILLIAM MICHAEL: *Lives of Famous Poets* (E. Moxon, Son and Co.), 1878.

SAINTSBURY, GEORGE: *Essays in English Literature, 1780–1860* (Percival and Co.), 1890.

SHELLEY, HENRY C.: *Literary by-Paths in Old England* (Grant Richards), 1909.

STEDMAN, EDMUND CLARENCE: *Victorian Poets* (Chatto and Windus), 1887.

THACKERAY, WILLIAM MAKEPEACE: *Roundabout Papers* (Vol. XII of *Works*) (Smith, Elder and Co.).

VINES, SHERARD: *100 Years of English Literature* (Gerald Duckworth and Co.), 1950.

WALKER, HUGH: *The Literature of the Victorian Era* (Cambridge: at the University Press), 1910.

WALLIS, N. HARDY: 'Thomas Hood, 1799–1845', in *Essays by Divers Hands* (Oxford University Press), 1947, pp. 103–15.

WHIPPLE, EDWIN P.: *Essays and Reviews* (2 vols.) (Boston: Ticknor, Reed, and Fields), 1853. (3rd edition.)

IV. PERIODICAL ARTICLES ON HOOD AND HIS WORK

A.E.D.: 'Thomas Hood, the Poet', *Notes and Queries*, August 29, 1942, p. 143.

ALTICK, RICHARD D.: Review of *Letters of Thomas Hood*, ed. by Leslie Marchand, *Modern Language Quarterly*, Vol. VII, No. 3, September, 1946, pp. 366–7.

ANON.: 'Biography—Thomas Hood', *Literary Gazette*, No. 1477, May 10, 1845, p. 300.

—— Review of *Letters of Thomas Hood*, ed. by Leslie Marchand, *Notes and Queries*, July 28, 1945, p. 44.

—— 'Thomas Hood: The Poet behind the Jester's Mask', *Times Literary Supplement*, No. 2257, May 5, 1945, p. 210.

BENSLY, EDWARD: 'Letter of Hood to Mark Lemon', *Notes and Queries*, No. 2, 13th Series, July 14, 1923, p. 35.

BLUNDEN, EDMUND: 'The Poet Hood', *A Review of English Literature*, Leeds. Vol. I, No. 1, January, 1960, pp. 25–34.

Select Bibliography

COHEN, J. M.: 'Thomas Hood: The Language of Poetry', *Times Literary Supplement*, September 19, 1952, pp. 605–6.

DENT, ALAN: 'What Porridge had Tom Hood?', *John O'London's Weekly*, No. 1258, May 4, 1945, pp. 41–2.

DUDLEY, RT. REV. T. U.: 'Thomas Hood: Punster, Poet, Preacher', *Harper's New Monthly Magazine*, April, 1891, pp. 719–24.

EDEN, HELEN PARRY: 'Thomas Hood', *The Catholic World*, Vol. CXXIII, 1926, pp. 731–8.

FIELDING, K. J.: 'The Misfortunes of Hood', *Notes and Queries*, December, 1953, pp. 534–6.

GILMAN, MARGARET: 'Baudelaire and Thomas Hood', *The Romanic Review*, Vol. XXVI, No. 2, April–June, 1935, pp. 240–4.

HALL, ANNA MARIA: 'Francis Freeling Broderip', *Social Notes*, No. 42, December 21, 1878.

HENNIG, JOHN: 'The Literary Relations between Goethe and Thomas Hood', *Modern Language Quarterly*, Vol. XII, No. 1, March, 1951, pp. 57–66.

HUDSON, DEREK: 'Hood and Praed', *Times Literary Supplement*, May 19, 1945, p. 235.

JENNINGS, AUDREY: 'Hood's "Autumn"', Letter to *TLS*, June 26, 1953, p. 413.

JERROLD, WALTER: 'Charles Lamb and "The Laughing Philosopher"', *Cornhill Magazine*, November, 1924, pp. 541–52.

L. B.: 'Thomas Hood: A Centenary Note', *Notes and Queries*, May 19, 1945, pp. 211–12.

LUCY, HENRY W.: 'Tom Hood: A Biographical Sketch', *Gentleman's Magazine*, Vol. XIV, January–June, 1875, pp. 77–88.

MABBOTT, THOMAS O.: 'Letters of Leigh Hunt, Thomas Hood and Allan Cunningham', *Notes and Queries*, May 23, 1931, p. 367.

MARCHAND, LESLIE A.: 'Thomas Hood, the Poet', *Notes and Queries*, July 18, 1942, p. 49.

MASSON, DAVID: 'Thomas Hood', *Macmillan's Magazine*, Vol. II, August, 1860, pp. 315–24.

OLIVERO, FEDERICO: 'Hood and Keats', *Modern Language Notes*, December, 1913, pp. 233–5.

'QUINTUS QUIZ': 'Tom Hood', *The Christian Century*, August 23, 1944, p. 968.

SCOTT, NOEL: 'Thomas Hood?', *Notes and Queries*, August 6, 1949, p. 348.

THORNTON, RICHARD H.: 'Letter of Hood to Mark Lemon', *Notes and Queries*, Series 12, No. XII, June 30, 1923, p. 509.

TURNBULL, J. M.: 'Reynolds, the Hoods and Mary Lamb', *Times Literary Supplement*, November 5, 1931.

VOSS, ARTHUR: 'Lowell, Hood and the Pun', *Modern Language Notes*, Vol. LXIII, No. 5, May, 1948, pp. 346–7.

WHITLEY, ALVIN: 'Hood and Dickens: Some New Letters', *Huntingdon Library Quarterly*, Vol. XIV, No. 4, August, 1951, pp. 385–413.

—— 'Thomas Hood as a Dramatist', *University of Texas Studies in English*, Vol. XXX, 1951, pp. 184–201.

—— 'Two Hints for *Bleak House*', *The Dickensian*, Vol. LII, pt. 4, No. 320, September, 1956, pp. 183–4.

Select Bibliography

WHITLEY, ALVIN: 'Thomas Hood and "The Times" ', *Times Literary Supplement*, May 17, 1957, p. 309.

WILLY, MARGARET: 'Thomas Hood: The Man and the Poet', *English*, Vol. VI, No. 31, Spring, 1946, pp. 9–13.

V. HOOD'S CONTEMPORARIES

ADAMI, MARIE: *Fanny Keats* (John Murray), 1937.

AINGER, ALFRED: *Charles Lamb* (Macmillan and Co.), 1893.

ALTICK, RICHARD D.: *The Cowden Clarkes* (Oxford University Press), 1948.

BARHAM, REV. R. H. D.: *Life and Remains of Theodore Edmund Hook* (Richard Bentley and Son), 1877.

BEAVAN, ARTHUR HENRY: *James and Horace Smith: A Family Narrative* (Hurst and Blackett), 1899.

BLUNDEN, EDMUND: 'New Sidelights on Keats, Lamb and Others', *London Mercury*, June, 1921, pp. 141–9.

—— *Charles Lamb and his Contemporaries* (Cambridge University Press), 1934.

—— *Keats's Publisher: A Memoir of John Taylor* (Jonathan Cape), 1936.

BOWRING, SIR JOHN: *Autobiographical Recollections* (Henry S. King and Co.), 1877.

CHEW, SAMUEL C.: *Byron in England* (John Murray), 1924.

COHEN, JOHN M.: *Robert Browning* (Longmans, Green and Co.), 1952.

COLVIN, SIDNEY: *Keats* (EML. Series) (Macmillan and Co.), 1887.

DICKENS, CHARLES: *The Nonesuch Dickens*. Edited by Arthur Waugh, Hugh Walpole, Walter Dexter and Thomas Hatton (16 vols. with 3 vols. of letters), 1933.

DILKE, SIR CHARLES WENTWORTH: *The Papers of a Critic, from the writings of Charles Wentworth Dilke, with a Memoir* (2 vols.) (John Murray), 1875.

ELLIS, S. M.: *William Harrison Ainsworth and His Friends* (2 vols.) (John Lane: The Bodley Head), 1911.

ELWIN, MALCOLM: *Landor: A Replevin* (Macdonald), 1958.

FORD, GEORGE H.: *Keats and the Victorians* (Yale University Press), 1944.

FORMAN, MAURICE BUXTON: *The Letters of John Keats* (Oxford University Press), 1952 (4th edition).

FORSTER, JOHN: *Life of Charles Dickens* (Chapman and Hall).

GRIGGS, GRACE E., and EARL, LESLIE: *Letters of Hartley Coleridge* (Oxford University Press), 1937.

HARTMANN, HERBERT: *Hartley Coleridge: Poet's Son and Poet* (Oxford University Press), 1931.

HAZLITT, W. CAREW: *Four Generations of a Literary Family* (2 vols.) (London and New York: George Redway), 1897.

HEWLETT, HENRY G.: *Henry Fothergill Chorley; Autobiography, Memoir and Letters* (2 vols.) (Richard Bentley and Sons), 1873.

HOGG, DAVID: *Life of Allan Cunningham* (Dumfries, Edinburgh and London: Hodder and Stoughton), 1875.

HUGHES, T. ROWLAND: 'John Scott: Editor, Author and Critic', *London Mercury*, Vol. XXI, No. 126, April, 1930, pp. 518–28.

JENKINS, ROY: *Sir Charles Dilke: A Victorian Tragedy* (Collins), 1960.

Select Bibliography

JERROLD, WALTER: *Douglas Jerrold and 'Punch'* (Macmillan), 1910.
JERROLD, WILLIAM BLANCHARD: *Life of George Cruikshank* (2 vols.) (Chatto and Windus), 1882.
JOHNSON, EDGAR: *Charles Dickens: His Tragedy and Triumph* (2 vols.) (New York: Simon and Schuster), 1952.
KEATS, JOHN: *Letters of John Keats.* Edited by M. Buxton Forman (Oxford University Press), 1952 (4th edition).
KENYON, FREDERICK G.: *Robert Browning and Alfred Domett* (Smith, Elder and Co.), 1906.
KING, R. W.: 'Charles Lamb, Cary and the "London Magazine" ', *Nineteenth Century and After*, Nos. DLIX and DLX, September and October, 1923.
—— *The translator of Dante: The Life, Work and Friendships of Henry Francis Cary* (Martin Secker), 1925.
LAMB, CHARLES and MARY: *Letters.* Edited by E. V. Lucas (3 vols.) (J. M. Dent and Methuen), 1935.
LEY, J. W. T.: *The Dickens Circle* (Chapman and Hall), 1918.
LOCKHART, JOHN GIBSON: *Life of Sir Walter Scott* (Edinburgh: A. and C. Black), 1853.
LUCAS, E. V.: *Bernard Barton and His Friends* (Edward Hicks), 1893.
—— *Life of Charles Lamb* (2 vols.) (Methuen and Co.), 1905.
LYTTON, V. A. R. G.: *Life of Edward Bulwer, First Lord Lytton* (2 vols.) (Macmillan and Co.), 1913.
MACFARLANE, CHARLES: *Reminiscences of a Literary Life 1799–1858* (John Murray), 1917.
MASSEY, GERALD: *The Ballad of Babe Christabel and Other Lyrical Poems* (David Bogue), 1855.
MATHEWS, MRS. ANNE: *Memoirs of Charles Mathews, Comedian* (4 vols.) (Richard Bentley), 1839.
MERRIAM, HAROLD G.: *Edward Moxon, Publisher of Poets* (New York: Columbia University Press), 1939.
MORLEY, EDITH J. (ed.): *Henry Crabb Robinson on Books and their Writers* (3 vols.) (J. M. Dent and Sons), 1938.
POPE-HENNESSY, JAMES: *Monckton Milnes: The Years of Promise, 1809–1851* (Constable), 1949.
POPE-HENNESSY, UNA: *Charles Dickens, 1812–1870* (Chatto and Windus), 1945.
PRAED, WINTHROP MACKWORTH: *Selected Poems.* Edited with an introduction by Kenneth Allott (Routledge and Kegan Paul), 1953.
PROCTOR, BRYAN WALLER ('Barry Cornwall'): *Literary Recollections.* Edited with an introduction and notes by R. W. Armour (Boston: Meador Publishing Co.), 1936.
REID, T. WEMYSS: *Life, Letters and Friendships of Richard Monckton Milnes, 1st Lord Houghton* (Cassell and Co.), 1890.
REYNOLDS, JOHN HAMILTON: *Poetry and Prose.* Edited with an introduction by George L. Marsh (Humphrey Milford), 1928.
RICHARDSON, JOANNA: *Fanny Brawne: A Biography* (Thames and Hudson), 1952.

ROLFE, FRANKLIN P.: 'The Dickens Letters in the Huntingdon Library', *Huntingdon Library Quarterly*, No. 3, April, 1938, pp. 335–63.

ROLLINS, HYDER EDWARD (ed.): *The Keats Circle: Letters and Papers, 1816–1878* (2 vols.) (Harvard University Press), 1948.

ROSSETTI, CHRISTINA GEORGINA: *Family Letters*. Edited by W. M. Rossetti (Brown, Langham and Co.), 1908.

ROSSETTI, DANTE GABRIELE: *His Family Letters*. With a memoir by W. M. Rossetti (Ellis and Elvey), 1895.

ROSSETTI, WILLIAM MICHAEL: *Preraphaelite Diaries and Letters* (Hurst and Blackett), 1900.

SADLEIR, MICHAEL: *Bulwer and his Wife: A Panorama, 1803–1836* (Constable), 1933.

SMYTH, ELEANOR C.: *Sir Rowland Hill: The Story of a Great Reform* (T. Fisher Unwin), 1907.

SPIELMANN, MARION HARRY: *The History of 'Punch'* (Cassell and Co.), 1895.

TALFOURD, T. N.: *Three Speeches Delivered in the House of Commons in Favour of a Measure for the Extension of Copyright* (Moxon), 1840.

TEGG, THOMAS: *Letter to Rt. Hon Lord John Russell on the Extension of Copyright Proposed by Serjeant Talfourd*. Published at Cheapside, Febuary 25, 1840.

THACKERAY, WILLIAM MAKEPEACE: *Letters and Private Papers*. Collected and edited by Gordon N. Ray (Oxford University Press), 1945–6.

TIBBLE, J. W. and ANNE: *The Letters of John Clare* (Routledge and Kegan Paul), 1951.

—— *John Clare: His Life and Poetry* (Heinemann), 1956.

WALLER, R. D.: *The Rossetti Family 1824–54* (Manchester University Press), 1932.

WATTS, ALARIC ALFRED: *Alaric Watts: A Narrative of his Life* (2 vols.) (Richard Bentley and Son), 1884.

WHITE, HENRY KIRKE: *Poetical and Prose Works*. Edited with a life by Robert Southey (Gall and Inglis), n.d.

WILSON, JUNE: *Green Shadows, The Life of John Clare* (Hodder and Stoughton), 1931.

YATES, EDMUND HODGSON: *Edmund Yates: His Recollections and Experiences* (2 vols.) (Richard Bentley and Son), 1884.

VI. GENERAL

ANON.: *The London Singer's Magazine and Reciter's Album* (John Duncombe and Co.), 1838–9.

BERRY, FRANCIS: *Poet's Grammar* (Routledge and Kegan Paul), 1958.

BUSH, DOUGLAS: *Mythology and the Romantic Tradition in English Poetry* (New York: Pageant Book Co.), 1957.

CRUSE, AMY: *The Englishman and his Books in the Early 19th Century* (George G. Harrap and Co.), 1930.

—— *The Victorians and their Books* (George Allen and Unwin), 1935.

CUNDALL, JOSEPH: *A Brief History of Wood Engraving* (Sampson, Low, Marston and Co.), 1895.

Select Bibliography

DODDS, JOHN W.: *The Age of Paradox: A Biography of England, 1841–1851* (Gollancz), 1953.

GRAHAM, WALTER: *English Literary Periodicals* (New York: Nelson and Sons), 1930.

HEATH-STUBBS, JOHN: 'The Defeat of Romanticism', *Penguin New Writing*, No. 23, 1945, pp. 140–67.

JACKSON, JOHN, CHATTO, W. A., and BOHN, H. G.: *A Treatise on Wood Engraving* (Henry G. Bohn), 1861.

LEMON, MARK: *The Sempstress: A Drama in Two Acts* (Dick's Standard Plays), n.d.

LINTON, W. J.: *Wood-Engraving: A Manual of Instruction* (George Bell and Sons), 1884.

MARCHAND, LESLIE A.: *The Athenaeum: A Mirror of Victorian Culture* (University of North Carolina Press), 1941.

RICHARDSON, MRS. HERBERT: *Parody. English Association Pamphlet*, No. 92, 1935.

TAVE, STUART M.: *The Amiable Humorist* (University of Chicago Press), 1960.

WARBURG, JEREMY: *The Industrial Muse: An Anthology* (Oxford University Press), 1958.

WOODBERRY, GEORGE E.: *A History of Wood-Engraving* (New York: Harper and Bros.), 1883.

Index

Index

Broderip, Rev. J. S., 234
Bromberg, 154, 167, 168, 179
Browning, Robert, 1, 4, 211, 226, 255, 262, 264
Brunel, Sir Isambard, 116
Buckingham, James Silk, 106
Burdett-Coutts, Angela, 230
Burns, Robert, 165
Burton, Robert, 45
Bush, Douglas, 81-2
Butterworth, Mrs., 21-3, 26
Byron, Lord, 1, 13, 26, 52, 88, 93, 126, 165, 168, 189

Calverley, C. S., 63
Camberwell, 177, 191
Campbell, Roy, 245
Campbell, Thomas, 75
Carey, David, 10
Carlyle, Thomas, 232, 239
Carr, Sir John, 11, 12
Carrol, Sir Parker, 139
Carroll, Lewis, 56
Cary, Henry Francis, 40, 42, 126, 194
Castor Hof, 141
The Champion, 36, 52
Chapman, George, 81
Chartist Poets, 259
Chaucer, Geoffrey, 94, 231
Chernyshevsky, N. G., 263
Chesterton, G. K., 63
'Childe Roland to the Dark Tower Came', 211
The Chimes, 225
Christ's Hospital, 49
Christie, J. H., 36
A Christmas Carol, 213
Clare, John, 3, 5, 36, 39, 41, 42, 55, 94, 99, 240
Clark, Charles, 110
Clarke, Charles Cowden, 232
Clarke, Rev. Mr., 140
Cobden, Richard, 258
Coblenz, 121, 137, 139, 140-60, 163, 168, 169, 170, 172, 180, 240
Cohen, J. M., 262
Colburn, Henry, 193, 200-2, 203

Colebrooke Cottage, 46-7
Coleridge, Hartley, 99, 105-6, 113, 116
Coleridge, Samuel Taylor, 1, 3, 4, 27, 47-8, 62, 63, 65, 66, 78, 104, 126, 247
Colman, George, 45, 98
Cologne, 139, 142, 163, 172
Comic Magazine, 261
Comic Offering, 111-12, 261
'Complaint of the Decay of Beggars', 46
Coningsby, 214
Cook, Eliza, 233
Cousen, J., 211
Cowper, William, 247
Crabbe, George, 126
Creswick, Thomas, 211
Cruikshank, George, 75, 109, 114, 195, 261
Cruikshank's Comic Annual, 261
Cunningham, Allan, 36, 39, 42, 66, 71, 106, 179, 240, 255
Cunningham and Mortimer, 202

Dali, Salvador, 116
Dante, 40
The Darkling Plain, 86
Darley, George, 3, 4, 42, 94
Davis, Edward, 229
Defoe, Daniel, 13
De Franck, Lieutenant Philip, 19, 144-5, 146, 149, 150-2, 154-6, 157, 160, 161-2, 167-8, 170, 172, 181, 191, 194, 197, 239
De la Mare, Walter, 213
De Quincey, Thomas, 36, 40, 63, 233, 240
Devonshire, Duke of, 115-16, 210, 233
Devonshire Lodge, 210
Dibdin, Charles, 19
Dickens, Charles, 1-2, 75, 118, 123, 124, 125-6, 166, 179, 180-1, 182, 186-8, 193, 195-7, 199, 200, 201-2, 205, 208, 213, 214-15, 217, 225, 230, 232, 233, 239, 241-2, 255, 256

Index

Index

Index